Best of
Valley Quest

Treasure Hunts to Special Places

A project of:

VITAL COMMUNITIES
104 Railroad Row
White River Junction, VT 05001
Phone: 802.291.9100
www.vitalcommunities.org

Published by Vital Communities, White River Junction, VT 05001
©2008 by Vital Communities

ISBN: 0-9708460-1-0

Printed in Canada.

Art, maps, clues and stamps by Valley Quest children, parents, teachers & volunteers.
Photographs © by Jon Gilbert Fox, Ted Levin and the Valley News.
Used with permission of the photographers.
Valley Quest regional maps designed by Tele Atlas, Inc.
Book Design by Suzanne Church / Blue Door Communications

DISCLAIMER:
While students, teachers, partners, land owners, the editor, and the publisher have tried to make
the information presented in this book as accurate as possible, they accept no responsibility for
loss, injury, death or inconvenience sustained by any person using this book. All Questers should
exercise caution, and consider the current conditions—as well as their own abilities and limita-
tions—at all times. Valley Quest and Vital Communities will assume no responsibility for events
that may occur during a Quest. All Quest participants recognize and acknowledge that they
Quest at their own risk.

VALLEY QUEST is a protected trade name and trademark of Vital Communities. For permission
to utilize the names Valley Quest, Quest and Questing, contact the publisher at
www.vitalcommunities.org.

VITAL COMMUNITIES works to engage citizens in community life and to foster the long-term
balance of cultural, economic, environmental and social well being in our region. For more
information, please contact Vital Communities at (802) 291-9100, or on the web at
www.vitalcommunities.org.

The world is all clues, and there is no end
to their subtlety and delicacy.
The signs that reveal are always there.
One has only to learn the art of reading them.

— Paul Shepard, *Nature and Madness*

Dedicated to Lora Robins
and her family,
and to the families
of the Upper Valley.

Contents

Cornish, New Hampshire

Elkins, New Hampshire

Enfield, New Hampshire

Fairlee, Vermont

Grafton, Vermont

Hanover, New Hampshire

Hartford, Vermont

Haverhill, New Hampshire

Keene, New Hampshire

Lebanon, New Hampshire

Lyme, New Hampshire

Meriden, New Hampshire

New London, New Hampshire

Newbury, New Hampshire

Newbury, Vermont

Newport, New Hampshire

Norwich, Vermont

Orford, New Hampshire

Plainfield, New Hampshire

Introduction

Going on a Quest will take you to places that you have never been before.

Valley Quest

Think back to your childhood for a moment, to exploring the natural areas and structures surrounding your home. Like many, you perhaps had "secret places" where you would go: places where you could step out of ordinary life and into an extraordinary, vibrant world. Perhaps in your play you created treasure maps, too; maybe you even hid treasures for future, unknown children to find. These time-honored forms of play, these simple "Quests," formed the basis for many of the explorations and adventures that fill up our bank of childhood memories.

These small-scale expeditions took us on epic adventures; yet, we never left the neighborhood or community we lived in. While life has changed in so many ways for children growing up today, some things remain true: not every child wants to get to the top of a mountain; not every child is content to see the world through the lens of technology; and ALL children love treasure hunts! Who can resist the lure of a good clue?

> "Pass between two trees—white pines.
> To identify them is simple, so do not whine.
> Five letters there are in the word white ...
> And these bundles of 5 needles are in your sight!"

Capitalizing on the inherent fun of treasure hunts—rhyming clues and hand-drawn maps leading to hidden treasures—the award-winning Valley Quest program has created a series of recreational and education treasure hunts that map and share special places in the Connecticut River Valley of Vermont and New Hampshire.* The Quests explore villages, cemeteries, forests, wetlands, fields and more. They are the perfect way to spend an afternoon or weekend with family or friends. This book collects 70 Quests created over a twelve year period, from 1997 to 2008.

The Valley Quest idea was born out of a 150-year-old tradition in the region surrounding Dartmoor National Park in Southwest England. In Dartmoor, people—from toddlers to teens to pensioners—don their Wellington boots, and following maps and rhyming riddles, traipse the moors in search of hidden boxes. "Letterboxing," as the tradition is called, is a popular pastime,

---

* Valley Quest was awarded the prestigious "Environmental Program of the Year" award by the New England Environmental Education Alliance in 2005.

Keep your eyes open; clues are everywhere.

Valley Quest

with thousands of boxes hidden in natural and cultural locations. The tradition helps people connect with their heritage, each other, and have a great time out for a good walk.

Vital Communities built upon this tradition by developing the Valley Quest program. Our letterboxes—or Quests as we prefer to call them—are the outcomes of an educational program that has a goal of fostering place-based education and stewardship.

Each Quest is the result of a core group (perhaps a 4th grade class) and one or more community partners (e.g. the town historical society), who come together to explore, investigate and deepen their connection with a specific site in the community. Their project might last a month, a semester, or even an entire school year. Upon completing their work, the group submits its Quest, which summarizes their findings and shares them with others.

Our first small booklet of Quests was published in 1996, with eleven Quests in nine Upper Valley towns. During the next decade, more than 200 Quests were created by groups across the region: Brownies, Boy Scouts, elementary schools, high school students, historical societies, park rangers and museum staff. The partner and participant list grew and grew, and the good news spread.

Valley Quest: 89 Treasure Hunts in the Upper Valley was published in 2001 (with a 2nd printing in 2002), and went out of print in 2005. *Valley Quest II: 75 More Treasure Hunts in the Upper Valley* was published in 2004, and will soon be out of print. Valley Quest has inspired replication across the country, with Quest programs in Massachusetts to Oregon. There are now Quests in more than fifteen states and five countries!

This book collects 70 Quests that we believe are of enduring community value. A full third of the Quests are selected and updated from the first *Valley Quest* volume; a second third are adapted and revised from *Valley Quest II.* The final third are newer Quests, created between 2005 and 2008. Published as companions to these "best" Quests are wonderful Upper Valley images, taken by photographers Jon Gilbert Fox and Ted Levin, and the staff of the *Valley News.*

As a whole, the book invites you to come to a deeper relationship with the Connecticut River Valley: its history, habitats, inhabitants and stories. It shares our special places: places worth knowing, preserving, and conserving for future generations. Any one of the individual Quests, as well, can be a doorway for the kind of day that will linger in your memory for a lifetime: feeling fully embraced and alive, nestled in the magical web of a special place. More than 100 community partners and 1,000 children, adults, families, scouts, students and historical society members contributed to the creation of the Quests collected in this book. Out Questing, you will celebrate student achievement and our community's natural and cultural heritage. You will see

Questers explore Beaver Meadow — looking through the eyes of the Marion Cross School students who created the Quest.

Photograph by Jon Gilbert Fox

and learn through the eyes of others: from the dedicated work of children, adults and civic groups. You will deepen your sense of place—and love for this region—as you forge connections with our shared landscape and culture.

How to Quest

Search through the table of contents, flip through the book, or review the Quest directory. Find a Quest that excites you. Note that in many cases, there are several Quests clustered in the same general area—so you can spend an afternoon or day going on a few! Then use the regional map (located on the inside cover of the book) and the location directions (found on the individual Quest page) to determine your Quest's starting point. Once you are there, you will use the Quest map, the verse clues and your intuition to solve the Quest and discover two treasures: (a) the special place; and (b) the hidden treasure box.

Treasure Boxes

Each Quest ends with a treasure box, hidden just out of view somewhere at the Quest site. Treasure boxes are rarely buried, so you will not have to dig underground to find them. You may, however, have to look in a secluded cranny, or see through a clever disguise. Inside this treasure box, you will discover more information about the site, a rubber stamp, a sign-in journal and a pencil. Sign your name in the book, adding notes or sketches about your experience Questing; and collect an impression of the stamp as a memento of your journey. Then, carefully re-hide the box exactly where you found it.

Passport Book & Stamps

If you plan to go on more than one Quest, you may wish to create your own "passport book" or field journal into which you can collect your stamp impressions. Alternatively, you can record the stamps on individual Quest pages or in the "Stamp Here!" pages found at the back of the book. You may also wish to create (or buy) your own personal stamp— so that you can leave your mark in each Quest's logbook. Program enthusiasts like to invent a unique Questing persona, and create a stamp which carries that message. Are you a Coyote? Or a sunflower? It's fun to see the stamps of other participants, and read of their adventures. Likewise, it is fun to make books and stamps, and keep scrapbooks with memories of your explorations. More information about making books and stamps can be found on the Vital Communities website: www.vitalcommunities.org.

Valley Quest Patches & Hats

When you have solved twenty or more Quests, send a copy of the stamp impressions you've collected to Valley Quest at Vital Communities, 104 Railroad Row, White River Junction, VT 05001. We will send you a Valley Quest certificate and a beautiful Valley Quest patch, which shows our valleys and hills clothed in bright autumn foliage. When you have collected 50 stamps, send us your records and we will send you the coveted Valley Quest hat.

Valley Quest on the Web

Groups are continually creating and submitting new Quests. There are also older Quests not included in this book that are available in the Online Quests section of our website. Visit www.vitalcommunities.org to find, upload and download additional Quests. Also use the web site to check for any changes that are posted on the Quest Directory.

Box Monitors

Each Quest treasure box is checked on a regular basis during the Questing season by a volunteer box monitor. These generous, fun-loving people help keep the Valley Quest program alive and running smoothly. If you have a problem with a particular Quest or treasure box, please contact the Valley Quest office via the telephone or email. We'll pass the word along to the appropriate monitor. If you are interested in becoming a box monitor for a Quest in your town, please let us know!

Rovers

Some Questing enthusiasts choose to become Valley Quest "Rovers." Rovers carry along extras when they Quest, prepared to not only participate in the program but also maintain and improve it. Rovers carry ziplock bags, an extra stamp pad (to replace a dry or leaky one), stamp making material, a pencil sharpener, an extra pen, and an extra utility box to put out in case a box has gone missing. Please let us know if you'd like to become a rover.

Updates, Problems, or Questions

Updates regarding all Quests are posted on the Valley Quest website (www.valleyquest.org). If you have any trouble finding the site or the box, or have any other news to report to us, please do not hesitate to contact us.

What to Bring

Each Quest names any specific items required to complete that Quest (e.g. compass, boots, binoculars). These specifics are also cross referenced in the Quest directory. As is the case with any outdoor activity, be prepared for changes in the weather! It is also important to bring a good map to help locate the specific Quest site. The DeLorme Atlas and Gazetteers for Vermont and New Hampshire work well. Also, bring a compass, a water bottle, snacks, and comfortable shoes. It is always a good idea to carry a first aid kit if you will be out in the woods. And definitely consider bringing along a field guide to local plants and animals, binoculars, a hand lens for magnification—as well as your passport book/field journal and personal stamp. Some families find that putting together a special Quest Backpack—stocked and ready to go—helps them to get out of the house and out on the trail.

Making New Quests

If you wish to make a Quest, please refer to the information about making Quests located at the back of the book (pages 240–246). You may also wish to purchase our "how to" book: *Questing: A Guide to Creating Community Treasure Hunts.* This book is published by the University Press of New England. More information is available on our website: www.vitalcommunities.org.

Questing as an Education Tool

The Valley Quest program has developed standards-based curriculum to help you bring Questing to your school, community or region. To learn more about upcoming Valley Quest workshops, Valley Quest curriculum materials and Questing supplies, write us or visit us on the web:

Valley Quest Coordinator
Vital Communities
104 Railroad Row
White River Junction, VT 05001
(802) 291-9100
www.vitalcommunities.org

Crossing the Bridge in Woodstock
Photograph by Jon Gilbert Fox

How many bridges span the beautiful Ottauquechee River in downtown Woodstock? You could know.

How to Use This Book:
Advice for Parents, Teachers, & Group Leaders

With Very Small Children

When out Questing with very young children, preview the Quest's clues. Notice that there are two kinds of clues: movement clues, which guide you along your route; and teaching clues, which convey the storyline of the Quest. With younger children, you may wish to focus more on the movement clues: reading them aloud, and invite the children to search for (and find) the next destination.

With Early Readers

As the children get older, they can transition from hearing abridged clues, to hearing them read fully, and then to beginning to read them for themselves. A lot of Questing families have enjoyed the program simply as a shared literacy and recreational experience.

With School Groups

With elementary school children—and larger groups—you may wish to photocopy the Quest you are working with, and cut it into sections. By passing these sections out one at a time, each individual will have a set length of text to read. It will also be clear where one section ends and the next clue begins. In addition, this technique helps larger groups stick together, and the process is fun.

With Ambitious Groups

Does your group tend to run ahead? In addition to cutting the Quest into sections (so participants can't rush ahead to the end), you might decide to seal each clue in its own envelope. You can number these envelopes and pass them out ahead of time; or you can pass them out sequentially, upon the successful completion of the previous clue. With advance planning you can also pre-visit the Quest site and disperse the clues along the route. Place them in ziplock bags and weight them down with rocks. This takes time but can really play up the treasure hunt aspect of Questing.

With Large Groups

When working with larger classes, consider going to a location where there are several Quests with a central starting point (e.g. Woodstock); and break into smaller groups. Alternatively, break your group into small teams and stagger their start times using five minute (or out-of-sight) intervals.

Science Field Trips

For groups working with the sciences, consider making a field trip to a Quest site, and using it as an outdoor classroom for a half- or full-day field trip. Supplement the Quest with readings, journaling, and age-appropriate field science activities. Ten good Quests to utilize for science field trips include:

4. Wrights Mountain Quest, Bradford, VT: *Northern Forest ecosystem*
12. Esther Currier Quest, Elkins, NH: *Wetlands and beaver habitat*
18. The Cave Quest, Grafton, VT: *Combine with a visit to the Grafton Nature Museum*
20. Mink Brook Quest, Hanover, NH: *Several habitats: field, brook and forest*
25. Sally's Salamander Meander, Hartford, VT: *A large vernal pool.*
42. Montshire Quest, Norwich, VT: *Combine with a visit to the Montshire Museum*
47. VINS Quest, Quechee, VT: *Combine with a visit to the VINS Nature Center*
57. Lonesome Pine, Thetford, VT: *Field, forest and wetland habitats, plus swimming.*
62. Boston Lot, West Lebanon, NH: *Science content, and several habitats to explore*
67. Forest Quest, Woodstock, VT: *Do it on your own; or join one of the Quests led by Marsh Billings Rockefeller National Historic Park staff.*

Social Studies Field Trips

For groups focusing on social studies, consider making a field trip to a Quest, and folding it into a half- or full-day expedition. These are eight Quests located at important historical sites and museums:

2. Ben Thresher's Mill: *A well-preserved 19th century mill and blacksmith shop*
11. Saint-Gaudens Quest: *Learn about art, and one of America's great sculptors*
14. Shaker Feast Ground: *Combine with a tour of the Enfield Shaker Museum*
22. Center of Town: *Early settlement: 1st meeting house, school, inn, mustering ground.* (Visit www.vitalcommunities.org to see our Village Quest curriculum.)
23. Hartford Civil War: *A great outing before making a Civil War Quest in your town.* (Visit www.vitalcommunities.org to see our Civil War curriculum.)
45. Coolidge Homestead: *Visit the boyhood home of President Calvin Coolidge.*
53. Morrill Homestead: *A tremendous feat of architecture, botany and engineering.*
64. Precision Museum: *Discover Windsor's prominent place in industrial history.*

Quest Directory

Quest Number, Name, & Location	Estimated Duration	Special Features	Walking Conditions	Physical Difficulty	Optional Gear	Season	Year Created
Acworth, NH							
1 Acworth Bird Collection	:45	H	P	E	C	M–N	2007
Barnet, VT							
2 Ben Thresher's Mill	:45	H	I	E	FL, P	J–O	2005
Bellows Falls, VT							
3 Bellows Falls History	1:30	A, H	P	M	C	M–N	2000
Bradford, VT							
4 Wright's Mountain	2:30	N, V	T	D	Bi, C, F, P	M–N	2003
Charlestown, NH							
5 Fort # 4's Past & Present	1:30	A, H	P	E	C	M–N	2003
Chelsea, VT							
6 Shiretown	1:00	A, H	P	E	C, P	M–N	2002
Chester, VT							
7 Chester	:45	A, H	P	E	C, P	M–N	2002
Cornish, NH							
8 Blacksmith Bridge	:20	H, N	T	E	C	M–N	2000
9 Cornish Flat	1:00	H	P	E	C	M–N	2002
10 CREA	:45	N	T	E	Bt, F	M–N	2003
11 Saint-Gaudens	1:00	A, H, N	T	E	C, $	J–O	2008
Elkins, NH							
12 Esther Currier	1:15	N	T	M	Bt, Bi, C, F	M–N	2003
Enfield, NH							
13 Enfield Rail Trail	1:30	N, H, V	T	E	Bk, C	M–N	2000
14 Shaker Feast Ground	1:00	N, H	T	M	C	M–N	1998
Fairlee, VT							
15 Glens Falls	:30	N	T	M	F	M–N	2000
16 Miraculous Tree	1:00	N	P	M	F, MT, P	M–N	2000
17 Palisades	1:00	N	T	D	Bi, C, F	M–N	1998
Grafton, VT							
18 Grafton Cave	1:15	N, H	P, T	M	F	M–N	2007
Hanover, NH							
19 Balch Hill	1:15	N	T	M	F, Bt	M–N	1998
20 Mink Brook	:45	N	T	M	Bt, F, S	M–N	2002
21 Velvet Rocks	1:00	N	T	D	C, F	M–N	1999
Hartford, VT							
22 Center of Town	:40	H	P	E	Bi	M–N	2003
23 Civil War	:45	H	T	M	P	M–N	2007
24 Jericho District	1:00	H, V	P	M	Bk	M–N	2003
25 Salamander Meander	1:00	N	T	M	Bt, F	A–N	2004
Haverhill, NH							
26 Haverhill Corner	1:00	A, H	P	E	C, P	M–N	2002
27 Floodplain Quest	1:00	H, N, V	T	E	Bt, Bi, F, P	M–N	2003
Keene, NH							
28 Horatio Colony	:15	H	P	E	C	M–N	2002
29 Stonewall Farm	:45	N	T	E	C	M–N	2007
Lebanon, NH							
30 Old King's Highway	1:30	N, H	T	E	Bt, F	M–N	2007

Quest Number, Name, & Location	Estimated Duration	Special Features	Walking Conditions	Physical Difficulty	Optional Gear	Season	Year Created
Lyme, NH							
31 Chaffee Sanctuary	:45	N	T	E	Bt, Bi, F	M–N	2003
32 Pinnacle	2:00	N, V	T	M	F	M–N	2008
33 Porter Cemetery	:45	H	P, T	E	C	M–N	2003
Meriden, NH							
34 Bridge and Beyond	1:00	N	T	E	F	M–N	2007
New London, NH							
35 Sargent Hayes	1:30	N, H	T	M	Bt, F	M–N	2000
36 Wolf Tree	1:30	N, H	T	D	Bi, F	M–N	2000
Newbury, NH							
37 The Fells	1:00	N, H	T	M	P, $, F	M–N	1998
Newbury, VT							
38 Sleeper's Meadow	1:00	H, N, V	T	M	Bi, C, F, P	M–N	2002
Newport, NH							
39 Historical Newport	:45	A, H	P	E	C	M–N	2005
Norwich, VT							
40 Gile Mountain	1:00	N, V	T	D	Bi, F	M–N	2000
41 Grand Canyon	1:15	N	T	M	C, F	M–N	1998
42 Montshire	:30	N	T	E	F, $	M–N	2008
Orford, NH							
43 Flat Rock	:15	N	T	E	S	M–N	1998
Plainfield, NH							
44 French's Ledges	1:00	N, V	T	D	Bi, F	M–N	1997
Plymouth, VT							
45 Coolidge Homestead	1:00	A, H	P	M	P	J–O	2008
Quechee, VT							
46 Quechee Gorge	1:00	N, A	T	M	P, S	M–N	2007
47 VINS	:45	N	T	M	F, P, $	M–N	2008
Rockingham, VT							
48 Rockingham Carvers	:45	H, A	T	E	C, P	M–N	2007
Springfield, NH							
49 Kidder Brook	1:00	N, H	T	M	Bt, C, P	M–N	2000
Springfield, VT							
50 Black River History	1:00	N, H	T	E	Bt	M–N	2007
51 Springfield Mills	1:30	N, H, A	P	E	P	M–N	2003
52 Springweather	:45	N, V	T	M	Bi, C, F	M–N	1999
Strafford, VT							
53 Justin Morrill	:45	A, N, H	T	E	Bt, C	J–O	2001
54 Town House	:45	A, H	P	E		M–N	2005
Sunapee, NH							
55 Sunapee Harbor	1:00	N, H, V	P	E	Bi, C, S	M–N	2008
Thetford, VT							
56 Bill Hill	1:00	N, H, V	T	M	Bi, F	M–N	2004
57 Lonesome Pine	1:00	N	T	M	Bi, F, S	M–N	2000
Vershire, VT							
58 Copperfield	:45	N, H	P, T	E	C	M–N	2000
59 Quest for the Raven	1:30	N, V	T	D	Bi, C, F	M–N	2003
Weathersfield, VT							
60 Crystal Cascade	2:00	N	T	D	Bi	M–N	1999
West Fairlee, VT							
61 Linny's Loop	2:00	N, H	P	D	Bk, C, P, S	M–N	2000
West Lebanon, NH							
62 Boston Lot	:45	N	T	M	F, C	M–N	2004
White River Junction, VT							
63 The Junction	:45	A, H	P	E	C, P	M–N	1999
Windsor, VT							
64 Precision Museum	:45	A, H	P	E	P, C	M–N	2007
65 Kestrel	:30	N, V	T	E	Bi, F, C	M–N	2003
66 Windsor Architecture	:30	A, H	P	E	P	M–N	2002
Woodstock, VT							
67 Forest / MBRNHP	2:00	N	T	M	Bi, C, F, P	M–N	2002
68 History Mystery Barrel	:45	H	P	E		M–N	2003
69 Mt. Tom	1:30	N, V	T	D	C	M–N	1997
70 Room with a View	1:00	N, V	T	D	Bi, C, F	M–N	1999

Valley Quest Code

1. Allow yourself plenty of time.
2. Be prepared for weather.
3. Keep to established paths.
4. Avoid damaging fences and stone walls.
5. Do not disturb or remove cultural or historical artifacts.
6. There's no need to dig—none of our Quest boxes are buried underground.
7. Respect the "treasures," the places and boxes as the private property of others.
8. Keep the location of the treasure boxes a secret!
9. Carefully re-hide the treasure box precisely where you found it.
10. Keep pets under control.
11. Observe wildlife from a distance.
12. Please do not feed wild animals.
13. Don't litter—pack it in and out!
14. No fires.
15. Carry sufficient drinking water.
16. Respect wildlife, plants, and trees.
17. Be careful in wet areas, on steeper slopes, and in sensitive wildlife habitat.
18. Keep eyes, ears, and hearts wide open.
19. Look, listen and learn from the world.
20. Always follow the Valley Quest Code.

Don't risk getting lost. Have a good map and compass whenever you go into an unfamiliar area—as well as a field guide and first aid kit. Be respectful of other beings and the land, and have a wonderful time Questing!

1 The Acworth Bird Collection & History Mystery Quest

:45

easy

bring:
compass

historical

Going south on Route 12, turn left in Charlestown onto Sullivan Street. If you pass the Jiffy Mart, you missed the turn! At .6 of a mile, turn right at the Y intersection onto the Acworth Road. Travel 7.5 miles, steadily climbing uphill. At the top, you will finally enter the small village of Acworth with a large white church on the left. Immediately, you will be in an intersection of tar and dirt roads. The library is a small brick building almost straight ahead on the left side of the dirt road called Lynn Hill Road. Use this dirt road to enter the parking lot of the library. The phone at the library is 603-835-2150. The Library is open on Tuesdays, Thursdays and Sundays from 11:30–4:30pm.

Clues

Welcome! This library was built for you way back in 1892.
We invite you now to hike through some history,
  with clues.
To build our town library, the State gave 100 dollars,
But Acworth's Ithiel H. Silsby gave thousands!
When his will was read, the town got to work: they moved
  Thornton's blacksmith shop,
And where the elder Silsby's store used to be, the library
  was plopped on top.

Go look at the Bird Collection in the room by the door.
You will definitely want to learn a whole lot more!
We've looked at these shelves filled with fur and with feathers.
We've studied the times these were all put together.
We've learned about birds and some mammals too,
And of course, Gawin Gilmore Dickey, born in 1842.
Look up over the birds … his portrait smiles at you!

This bird collection was made by Dickey: we call him "our guy."
We also solved a mystery—and here we'll tell you why!
His family called him "Gilmore," which was news to us.
He was quite a fine woodworker and taxidermist.
Town records call him "crippled," "hunchback," "injured in childhood."
But as to <u>how</u> this might have happened, the records were no good.
So of course this made us wonder … as anybody would.

Then we found a Mr. Porter, who lives in Minnesota (r!).
And <u>his</u> great, great grandmother was Gilmore Dickey's aunt!

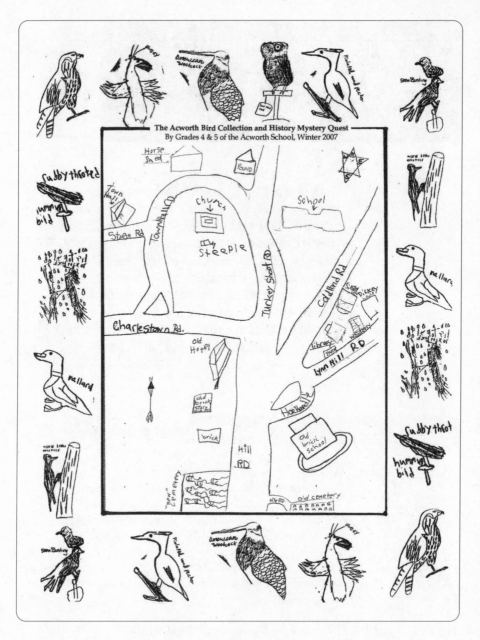

The Acworth Bird Collection and History Mystery Quest
By Grades 4 & 5 of the Acworth School, Winter 2007

Right there in Minnesota was an old note in a box.
The note answered THE QUESTION, which gave us a shock!
The note was simple. The note was sad.
Gawin Gilmore Dickey fell down long, steep stairs as a very young lad.
His spine was injured badly, and he grew up bent and frail.
He never did get married. He stayed on with his folks,
but lived a full life and people liked him without fail.
His only brother, Freeman, moved to Holyoke "M-A."
Sometimes Gilmore took the train to visit, following the river the whole way.
We're glad we got to know him and a bit about his art.
Gilmore used his head and hands and the smarts in his heart.

Yes, G. studied birds by stuffing them and modeling them as in real life.
This was a brand new art form that Gilmore took to new heights.
From 1880 through '87 his collection grew and grew;
People from all around brought birds in by the slew.

Some Ruddy Ducks from Alstead are here from '84;
A Cedar Waxwing, a Northern Shrike ... each time you'll see more.
The dangling tags—in perfect script—all tell important facts:
The year, the date, the sex or age, the town the bird was found in;
The Latin names, and now and then, the man who killed or found them.
Some sadness is behind the glass; a once-wild bird ... extinct.
From flocks of millions the Passenger Pigeon lives on with a tag of ink.

(If you want to read a full list of the 218 specimens
That are in the collection, you may ask our librarian.)

Before we move along, look out the left window ... quick.
See Ithiel Silsby's house that he built in 1806.
There's a hiding place inside the house ... behind the largest bookshelf.
Dr. Lyman Brooks lived in this home when the Civil War broke forth.

Behind glass: a once wild bird ... now extinct. This passenger pigeon lives on with a tag of ink.

Were slaves safely hidden here on their way traveling to the north?
Now move outside into Gilmore Dickey's Acworth.
From the library parking lot, please walk down Lynn Hill Road.
The Dickey house is second house on the left and has a long long story.
There were so many relatives it spins our heads in a hurry!
But Gilmore lived here his whole life and you can read about the family ...
When you finish this hunt and find our treasure box, by golly!

As you head up toward the Stop sign, pause just awhile:
On your left is a street called "Hoe Handle" though no sign exists today.
But a mill down the hill on a stream that's still there, made pile upon pile of
handles for tools ... and the neighbors built fences of those thrown away! The
lovely brick home here on Hoe Handle Street was once "Daniel Robinson's
store." Then in 1848, more school space was sought, so the Town bought the
store ... and twenty years here students were taught!
Perhaps Gilmore Dickey attended this school, going home 'cross the street for
  his lunch?
Did his mother come here? Or his father chop wood? We don't have a hunch.

Now up to Hill Road! Across the intersection, there is a large white house.
As Gilmore was starting his bird collection, summer guests came to
  Acworth to dwell,
and some of them may have stayed right here...since this used to be a hotel!
Left of the hotel were two big brick buildings, though leaves may block
  your view.
The middle one was the "Brick Store and Post Office," but burned long ago.
Now, please cross safely (look all ways) to get to the wide, green
  Town Common.
We don't want to lose you or write poems of those meeting cars fast down
  upon them!

The Common was cleared in Seventeen seventy-six.
It took 2 whole days for all the men in town to chop down the trees
   into sticks.

The church on the hill is a sight you can't miss
On this very high site was the town's first "Meetinghouse."
It was very rough and not good in the rain for dry people.
Taken apart in 1821, the meetinghouse was used to build our Town Hall
   that you see.
This large church before you was built the same year;
Up front were tall stairs that the pastor did climb.
As he spoke to the people below in the pews, the hours passed by and by ....

Then this church was remodeled in 1886,
and Gilmore Dickey was part of the mix.
He helped design the new upstairs plus handled the correspondence.
When all was said and done, three thousand bucks had been spent.
Through all that work, Gilmore was there to the end.
Our guy was a dedicated man, and a true friend.

Then came the Civil War. Abe Lincoln put out the call
And many men of Acworth answered and gave their all.
All hoped for the best and were cheered on by their
   loved ones,
but some were badly hurt and others never again saw
   their sons.
When the war was finally over, many farmers just kept
moving and settled their families "out west".
But for our town's *One Hundredth Birthday* in 1868
most all came home, saying Acworth was <u>the best</u>!

Now ... see if the Town Hall is open,
If so, please step right on in.
They will give you warm greetings and show you the
stage where <u>our</u> plays
   and our songs long have been.
The Horse Sheds, out back, were filled once a week,
when church and town groups held their meetings.
Imagine your horse eating hay ... June through May,
Thinking "Hooray for these plays and these greetings!"
Beyond the Horse Sheds is the old stone "Town Pound."
In earlier days, all pigs, cows, and horses here would stay
If they broke fences at home and then ran away!

Now, head down to the school that <u>we</u> use.
(We feed birds there each day but don't stuff them!)
A Baptist church was built right here the same year Ithiel Silsby built
   his house.
But in 1868 the church moved to South Acworth,
Where mills and families were growing fast.
Then the brick school on Hoe Handle was sold and a new school was built
   <u>right here</u>.
A big classroom below with big gathering room above ... it was proudly
   named "Eagle Hall."

But fire took it late at night in December 1929 … long after Gilmore
  was gone.

Bill Mitchell was only seven when he saw the flames that night.
His dad had cleared a view of school so his mother could see it right,
And thus they saw, so far away, the fire that burned so bright.
Bill lost his favorite pencil box plus his whole beloved school.
Classes did continue, but held at the Town Hall.
By fall, a brand new school, with no upstairs hall was ready for their studies.
You see it here, much longer now, with room for us and our buddies.

Imagine this: Acworth had twelve schools around town at one time.
All students had to walk to and from their nearest school back then.
Even in the winter!

Our Quest is almost over, so go to where you began it.
Don't worry if the library is locked up tight … unless your keys are in it!
To the south of the library there is a post, you'll see it's made of granite.
Please walk east down that nice lawn, though it'd be faster if you ran it!
Now turn north until you find a posted reservation.
Nearby there is a treasure in a place too small for us …
  … too small for you … though very nice for wrens or mice.

A treasure there is waiting and we hope that you will like it.
Find it! Find it! Find it! We made it for you not for them!

Created by Grades 4 & 5 of the Acworth School, Winter, 2007.

2 The Quest at Ben Thresher's Mill

:45

easy

historical

From I-91 get off at Exit 18. Head west on West Barnet Rd. Pass the Barnet School on Kid Row, pass Barnet Center Road, and keep going until you get to a yellow building that says "Ben Thresher's Mill" on it. You may park in the lot just beyond the mill. Ben's Mill is open weekends from 11 am until 3 pm from Memorial Day through Columbus Day Weekend.

Clues

1. Go down the stairs from the parking lot. Take a left to the mighty Stevens River. Look at the dam! Wood, metal, bars and chains flowing that once held back the water. See how much lower the water is now. It is fascinating but do not look too long or your adventure will be gone.

2. Take a 180-degree turn to your right with a wooden water tub in your sight. Ben used to make these tubs for horses and cows. Keep looking down and you will find a plaque. Read the history on the plaque and then turn back.

3. Straight ahead up a granite step into Ben Thresher's Mill. Just inside is a door that holds a sharp up and down rusty saw. Climb this staircase to the second floor to find something that was used to haul. Three boards attach this crane to the wall. The crane brought up through the door, wagons, wheels, sleighs and more.

4. In the same room can be found small and tall wagon wheels—all round!

5. Listen for the river. Follow the sound. Then take the stairs that lead you down. Take a sharp right up three steps to the apple chute. This is where families used to bring apples to press. The mill power made cider to drink … and created a sticky mess.

6. Go back down the steps and make a sharp left. Look up high to see a message from Ben that he may have carved with a hot iron. On this plaque Ben gives his opinion about marriage and a wife.

7. Turn 135 degrees to find a six-spoke black iron wheel with a red stripe and a lever under it. The water flows from the penstock to the turbine with a push or pull of the lever. This is the wheel which controlled the waterpower that would run the machines by the hour.

8. Heading downstream on a floor beam, pass through a door. Find an anvil in the blacksmith's shop. In here a smith would bend, mend and tend metal. The fire and hammer would forge the iron that shaped shovels, rakes and wheels.

9. Walk upstream on a floor beam. Think of the smithy of old with a gleam in your eye. Turn 90 degrees right under a stovepipe. Turn left and you

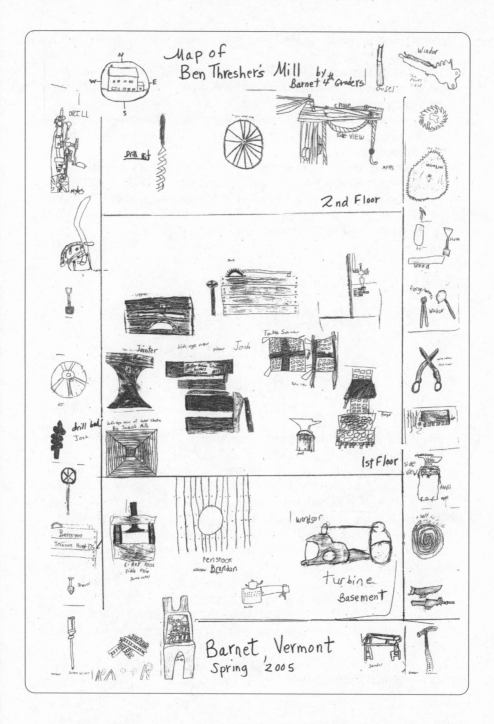

Map of Ben Thresher's Mill by Barnet 4th Graders

will see a machine with a wagon wheel on the bottom and top: this band saw has a long thin blade. Both ends of the saw are connected in a circle and the saw goes round and around to create a ring that will take you to town.

10. Continue on two paces. The planer is a helpful tool, it smoothes away the board's rough faces. Its power comes from the water as it falls over the river's ledges and steeper places. If you look out the window you can see the source of power.

11. Walk straight ahead three steps. On your left rhombuses, diamonds and triangles appear in an iron lattice pattern. This "cutting off" saw was used

to cut wood to length for very little pay. Clearly, math was used in this mill every single day.

12. Take 2 steps forward and turn left, study the ripper of Ben's time. The ripper rips boards into different widths. A single blade sticks out like the quill of a porcupine.

13. Move close to the chimney and view the jointer. The jointer has two semi circles and a wheel with five snake spokes. It angles the edge of the boards for folks.

14. Turn right toward the river. On your left pass the sander and the duplicating lathe and then you will find the stairs that lead you down to walls of stone. Watch your head and watch your step especially if you're tall! Turn right. Look for the penstock that looks like a huge silo lying on its side. The many bolts in the cement hold back water.

Listen for the river.
Follow the sound.
Take the stairs
that lead you down.

The water waits to bring power to the turbine. Hiram Allen has plans to build a new, working penstock.

15. Now look to your left and walk over to the cider press. The Northeast Kingdom was once rich with many thousands of apples trees. Folks had apples pressed at Ben Thresher's Mill with this very Hess Press.

16. Turn back to the stairs but don't go up; walk past to the fire breathing boiler. From there you will see a big pipe with two huge holes. The puzzle unfolds. The round fitting matches the fit of the penstock hole. Imagine the strength of the water ... that turns the turbine ... which turns the shaft ... which turns the wheel ... turning the belts that move the gears ... powering all of the machines upstairs.

17. Travel back to the steam making dragon from Oswego, NY and answer the following questions. See how much you've learned ... and try to find our treasure!

Here's where Ben pressed apples to make ___ ___ ___ ___ ___
1

Ben was a miller, wainwright, wheelwright & a

___ ___ ___ ___ ___ ___ ___ ___ ___
2

The river running behind this mill is called the ___ ___ ___ ___ ___ ___ ___
3

This boiler was made in ___ ___ ___ ___ ___ ___, NY
4

The two main materials Ben worked with were iron and ___ ___ ___ ___
5

This thing was a ___ ___ ___ ___ -breathing boiler
6

This place is called Ben Thresher's ___ ___ ___ ___
7

Ben's mill is powered by ___ ___ ___ ___ ___
8

The ___ ___ ___ ___ ___ lifted heavy items through the 2nd floor door
9

The ___ ___ ___ ___ ___ ___ rips boards into different widths
10

Families came here to make juice using the cider ___ ___ ___ ___ ___
11

The last letter of Ben's last name is ___
12

The blacksmith would hammer with a hammer on his big, black
___ ___ ___ ___ ___
13

So where is the treasure box? Look behind these words:

___ ___ ___ ___   ___ ___ ___ ___   ___ ___ ___ ___ ___
13 7 1 3   6 10 4 9   8 5 12 2 11

Sign in and tell us you solved our Quest ... and learned all about Ben Thresher's Mill!

Created by the Barnet School Fourth Graders, Spring, 2005.

3 Bellows Falls History Quest

1:30

moderate

bring: compass

historical architectural

Travel on I-91 and take exit 6, go south on Route 5 to downtown Bellows Falls. From the downtown square in Bellows Falls head south on Rt. 5 or Westminster St. and park in the parking lot at the corner of Hapgood and Westminster. To complete this Quest, you must finish within the hours of 9am until 5pm Monday through Thursday; 9am and 6pm on Friday; 9am and 4pm on Saturday and 10am and 3pm on Sunday.

Clues

Start at the Victorian house that is green, pink and white.
Built in 1892, the gargoyle on the roof is quite a sight.
The house is on the corner of Hapgood and Westminster
The gargoyle on top – do you think it looks sinister?
Step back and take in the details from where you stand.
A house with such style—isn't it grand?
Look for the asymmetrical porch and steeply pitched roof.
Find the delicate porch supports. You're a real sleuth!

Walk north on Westminster Street, and at the fork bear right.
Then at the curve, right again: Bellows Falls P.O. in sight!
The Post Office was built during the great depression,
In both Spanish Colonial and Georgian Revival style.
Look under the windows for a concrete tile.
After the Post Office, walk east to the Fish Ladder.
As you cross over the first chartered canal in the US,
Imagine how the fish climbing up the river felt.
Walk east for a while, until you pass the big yellow tanks.

Look over the south side of the second bridge where the balusters
  (supports) begin.
You will see carvings marked by yellow paint on the right side of the rock.
No one knows why these were made, who made them, or when!
They may have been made by the Abenaki people.
We know this spot was a place to fish and trade,
It's amazing that these markings did not fade.
Experts say they are between 300 and 2000 years old.
How imprecise! But that is what we've been told!

You might want to know on this bridge called Vilas
You stand in two states NH and VT, pretty cool, huh.
But be careful of the cars and trucks that drive too fast.

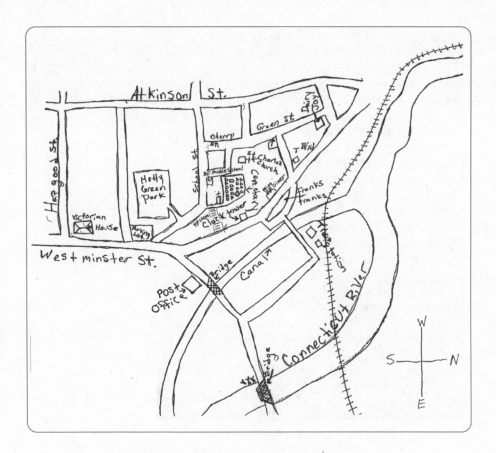

Turn around, walk west onto Island Street, and take the next right.
Go past the old waxed paper mill also built in 1892
Until a building named for the green mountains is in sight.
A very important part of Bellows Falls' history this railroad played
And this is where part of the movie "The Cider House Rules" was made.

Next, go across the railroads tracks and past Island Park.
Keep going over the bridge and turn left and then right at two arches.
Cross the street into the tunnel and up the steps.

Here lies Ms. Green who was once The richest woman in America.

You just passed through The Rockingham Canal House,
Which was once a theater and hotel.

Now, cross the street and walk north past the Miss Bellows Falls diner.
This 20's-style restaurant with barrel roof has food that couldn't be finer.

Take the next left onto Williams Street, note and see
On your left, a street named for Ms. Greens ex-husband's family.
Who is Ms. Green you may ask yourself now?
Continue the Quest to learn more about Ms. Green
And see a beautiful place where people take vows.

Go up the second flight of 48 steps.
Ahead of you is St. Charles Church.

In front of the church, turn right onto the footpath not too far away.
Walk east up Cherry Street and turn right at the top of the hill.
Keep walking until you see the last gate into the graveyard.
Go 30 paces to the tall granite gravestone.
(Remember: A pace is equal to two steps)
Here lies Ms. Green. She was once the richest woman in America.
She brought great wealth to Bellows Falls.

Continue on through the graveyard and out the gate,
Turn south down the road and then go straight.
Ahead, you will see Ms. Green's Park.
Its granite statue is your next landmark.

In 1806, the house Ms. Green lived in was built
It was later torn down and is now a city park.

Turn north once more and find the 49 steps
That will take you down into town
Now find your way back to the place
Where lots of letters can be found.
As you face the building
Take note of the five blue windows
Designed in 1930 by James Wetmore, Architect

Now if you'd like more information about your town
We know a fine place to plop yourself down.
Walk north to the clock tower in the middle of town.
In 1753 it started its fate. In 1925 it burned down.
And then was rebuilt in colonial revival style.

Cross the street and carefully look
for a place filled with many books.
Inside you'll find there is much to see:
Stories, information, even mysteries!
Ask inside and you will find they have your treasure.
Sign your name. Tell us where you're from,
And do it all at your leisure.

Created by the 7th and 8th grade class of the Compass School in 2000.

4 Wright's Mountain Quest

2:30

difficult

Get off I-91 at Exit 16 (the Bradford / Piermont exit). Go northwest up the Waits River on Route 25. Continue for 4.8 miles. Turn right onto Wright's Mountain Road and then head up hill for 2.5 miles (staying to the right as it forks). You will park in the Wright's Mountain parking lot on your right. The Quest begins here.

natural vista

Overview

Wright's Mountain—Bradford, Vermont's highest peak—is protected by a conservation easement held by the Upper Valley Land Trust. In response to local conservation priorities, UVLT works with individuals and communities to permanently protect land and water resources in 40 Vermont and New Hampshire towns in the Upper Valley region, www.uvlt.org. The Wright's Mountain trail system and Quest are maintained by the Bradford Conservation Commission, believing that protection of Bradford's natural resources is vital to the security of its economic future and cultural heritage. This forest is being managed as wildlife habitat, and is also utilized by Bradford Elementary School and Oxbow High School as an "outdoor classroom." The Quest leads to a fine view of the Waits River Watershed.

Clues

Note: *This Quest counts **water bars**—logs, stones, or soil mounds crossing the trail to divert water and prevent trail erosion. As you head up the trail, **remember to notice and count all the water bars.***

1. Heading up the trail notice tall, straight red pine.
    With needle leaves found in clumps of two
    This plantation (planted) tree is now in view.

2. As we hike, we want to discover
    What plants grow here—and why.
    Nutrient poor soil you will learn
    Is good habitat for the 3-branched bracken fern.

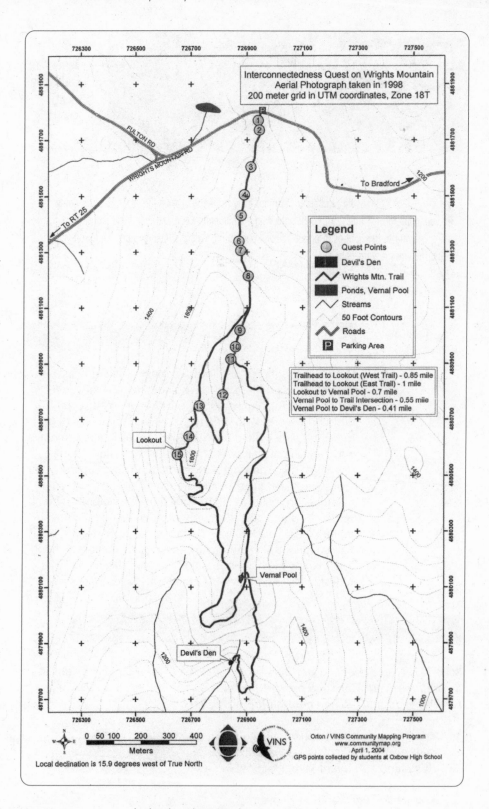

Interconnectedness Quest on Wrights Mountain
Aerial Photograph taken in 1998
200 meter grid in UTM coordinates, Zone 18T

Legend

- Quest Points
- Devil's Den
- Wrights Mtn. Trail
- Ponds, Vernal Pool
- Streams
- 50 Foot Contours
- Roads
- P Parking Area

Trailhead to Lookout (West Trail) - 0.85 mile
Trailhead to Lookout (East Trail) - 1 mile
Lookout to Vernal Pool - 0.7 mile
Vernal Pool to Trail Intersection - 0.55 mile
Vernal Pool to Devil's Den - 0.41 mile

FULTON RD
WRIGHTS MOUNTAIN RD
To Bradford
To RT 25
Lookout
Vernal Pool
Devil's Den

0 50 100 200 300 400
Meters

Local declination is 15.9 degrees west of True North

Orton / VINS Community Mapping Program
www.communitymap.org
April 1, 2004
GPS points collected by students at Oxbow High School

3. As you approach the fourth water bar—
    A simple device to divert the flow of water—
    Notice the large root system of a tipped-up tree.
    This opening in the canopy lets in the sun for raspberry.
    This forest has been logged carefully
    To make the land better for animals and plant life.

Indian Pipes
Photograph by Ted Levin

Indian Pipes are found on the forest floor. They feed on the decaying roots of plants and trees. Can you find any on this Quest?

This forest is being managed for animals:
Turkey, white tailed deer, black bear, moose, bobcats.
Take note of the beautiful sign
Made lovingly by students to mark this special place.

4. Continue on, through the softwood forest,
Looking for tracks in the mud.
Animals and plants change over time and adapt,
Some of these adaptations have been mapped.*

5. At water bar 8, the forest changes to deciduous hardwoods:
Sugar maples, American beech and yellow birch.
On the left is an old stone fence
Telling us this was pasture in days long hence.

6. This trail, as well, was once a "maple sugaring" road
Heading up to the Appleton's sugar stand.
Over the many years of rain and snow
Erosion has exposed the bedrock below.
Water bar #10 is made of soil.

---

* Oxbow High School Biology Students used GPS units to map vernal pools with the Community Mapping Project and Bradford Conservation Commission. Amphibians adapt to living in water and on land.

7. Water bars 11, 12 and 13 are also made of stone and soil,
   Even strong water bars can be damaged by ATV's or trucks.
   Be careful as you travel along any woodland trail.
   Good ethics "leave no trace," while bad choices leave quite a tale.

8. Managing plants for animal habitat is a big task.
   Students, citizens, the county forester, the conservation commission all
      lend a hand.
   As you hike over water bars 15, 16 and 17,
   Look for jack-in-the-pulpit, black bear food that might be seen.

Good ethics "leave no trace," while bad choices leave quite a tale.

9. At the fork in the trail, keep left with Sylvia and meander.
   Uphill on the right look for cavity trees with holes in their trunks.
   Hairy woodpeckers and barred owls (sometimes) make homes in the
   holes, barred owls are nocturnal, hunting at night for mice and voles.

10. Do you know what animals like to eat?
    Bears and turkey enjoy acorns, seeds of the oak.
    Deer and especially porcupines will nibble and browse
    On tender, evergreen eastern hemlock boughs.

11. Look down on the left to see the remains of the sugar arch (sap
       boiling pan)
    Where Appletons boiled sap into syrup.
    Trees give us lumber, nuts, shelves and swings.
    We can age trees with a borer and count up the rings!

12. As you go along, a second fork you will find.
    Bear right uphill; ahead on the left,
    Can you find evidence of rich fertile soil?
    Look for the maiden hair fern on the left
    with purple stems that coil.

    In the spring, frogs and salamanders lay eggs
    In temporary basins of rain and snowmelt called vernal pools.
    The eggs have hatched and tadpoles grown by fall,
    But up the mountain "in season" you might hear them call.
    The wood frogs "croak,"
    Spring peepers, of course, "peep."
    The American toads "trill" so long and sweet.
    Enjoy this meander in the flat where the soil collects.
    A carpet of emerald green including knot weed for you to inspect.

13. At the third fork bear left,
    And listen for the soft puh-puh-puh drumming of ruffed grouse.
    How does the tread way feel underfoot?
    Is it the difference of soil, rock or root?

14. Along the rocky ridge,
    Find the mosses and lichens forming soil.
    Not far along you'll come to a view,
    You've reached the end, & are among the lucky few!

15. A treasure box awaits you now,
    From the dead pine snag, look down in the crevasse of the rocks
    And you will find your treasure box.
    Please remember those before you,
    And respect those yet to come.
    When you've finished with the box,
    Do not hide it cleverly like a red fox.
    But be as accurate as a bat,
    And put the box back exactly where it was at!
    On your way down, a shorter steeper option exists.
    Simply heading straight (or bearing left) at each junction
    Will return you to the parking lot.
    Thanks to Bradford and to the Appletons—for sharing this sweet spot!

Wright's Mountain Quest Species Check List

What did YOU see?

- ☐ Red Pine
- ☐ Blackberry
- ☐ White-tailed Deer
- ☐ Moose
- ☐ Red Maple
- ☐ American Beech
- ☐ Red Eft
- ☐ Redback Salamander
- ☐ Jack-in-the-pulpit
- ☐ Barred Owl
- ☐ Ruffed Grouse
- ☐ Hermit Thrush
- ☐ _____

- ☐ Bracken Fern
- ☐ Turkey
- ☐ Black Bear
- ☐ Sugar Maple
- ☐ Red Oak
- ☐ Yellow Birch
- ☐ Spotted Salamander
- ☐ Wood Frog
- ☐ Hairy Woodpecker
- ☐ Maiden Hair Fern
- ☐ Red Squirrel
- ☐ Rose-breasted Grosbeak
- ☐ _____

Created by Nancy Jones of the Bradford Conservation Commission and Heather Trillium Toulmin from Hulbert Outdoor Center. The map was created by Oxbow High School students with support from the VINS/Orton Community Mapping Program in 2003. This Quest and the Wellborn Ecology Fund Natural Communities Quest Series as a whole were made possible by generous support from the Wellborn Ecology Fund of the New Hampshire Charitable Foundation/Upper Valley region: www.nhcf.org.

5 Fort #4's Past & Present Quest

1:30

bring: compass

easy

historical
architectural

Take I-91 to Exit 7; and then travel east on Route 11. At the intersection of Routes 11 & 12, take Route 12 south towards Charlestown Village. Upon entering the village, look for the fire station — it's the first building on the left. Enter the driveway beyond the station building as this is a one-way driveway. Please park in back of the fire station, well out of the way.

Clues

Start at the Fire Station and head south toward town.
The very first house on the left is where you are bound.
This is the site of the Johnson's cabin.
They were captured by Indians in 1754.
They returned to Charlestown after a ransom was paid.
The original cabin is hidden underneath the modern exterior.

Keep heading south. Do you hear the sound of a bell?
Is it the church or the brick house next to it that would ring so well?
It is the brick house that in 1772 was built as a one- room schoolhouse.
This is the oldest schoolhouse in Charlestown and it held 40 students,
The youngest learning their ABC's and the oldest algebra.

Continue down the sidewalk quite a ways,
Until a pizza parlor comes into your gaze.
You could stop in to have a bite to eat,
But when you're done go back outside and cross the street.
The place you should find yourself to be
Is in front of the Silsby Public Library.
The library holds a lot of interesting things, including a carved wooden eagle
And some of Charles Hoyt's plays (one of only five in existence).

Travel south once again, to the site of what was the Walker Tavern
A place where (once-upon-a-time) you were able to walk right in.
This stone house was the home of Mary Walker,
The great granddaughter of an original grantee of #4.
The "stone cottage" as it is commonly called, used to be the Walker Tavern.
It had a sign with bees and a beehive on it,
Just like the Beehive Tavern of Philadelphia, PA.
I'll mention here as a last note,
They say this place is haunted by two ghosts!

(Oh I almost forgot to say,
So was the first house along the way!)
The next house south that is on your right, is Fort #4's original site!
At your back is a stone with a plaque. Go over and read a little history.
Now travel south to house #304.
Stop here and of history you'll learn more.
Hidden in the back of this house is a well that is thought
to have been originally used by the fort.

Now look for a brick house as you journey along
And I will tell you of a poltergeist's song.
This house underwent re-construction to return it to its original state.
It was then that the owners heard the ghost!
It banged boards together and slammed doors.
When the re-construction was done, the noises disappeared.

At the next crosswalk you will do just that …
Come to some grand trees upon a large lawn.
Can you identify these large evergreens?
Let's hope they never have to be sawn.
South you roamed the first part of this Quest,

It was then that the owners heard the ghost! It banged boards together and slammed doors.

Now traveling north I think would be best.
Onward to a place where you can sleep
And eat while resting your very weary feet.
Now a bed & breakfast this house
was built by Phineas Stevens in 1752.
He was very careful while building this house,
For Indians captured him as a youth.
Keep traveling north along Main.
Go to place you would visit if your tooth had a pain.
Moses Willard, an occupant of the fort, called this "mine."
Later, two brothers bought it (that was in 1839).
They married two sisters and split the house in two, each living in half.

Keep going toward a brick building called Dan's,
you can buy everything here from cards to pans.
The street next to this is Perry Ave.,
Travel up it if the treasure you want to have.
On the side of this building you will see
A mural dedicated to Charlestown's past history.
Continue to the end of this street.

You will come to a street named
After the direction you were just heading.

Now head north along the street named East.
You will come to a cemetery I am betting.
Turn right through the first gate.
Hurry now, let's not be late.
Now inside, bear right at the 1st fork; then left at the 2nd fork
Onto a dirt roadway to some stone steps.
Go up the steps and walk straight and narrow
Until adjacent to the 2nd oak tree off to your left.

You are looking for the gravestone of Moses and Susannah Willard,
Who were killed by Indians June 16th of 1756.
Pay your respects to these fort settlers buried here.
Now look straight ahead, slightly to your left,
For a chalice standing high in the sky.
It is the Johnson's burial spot, also settlers of the fort.

The people from the fort have been here a long time ...
But so has something that is living.
Can you guess what it may be?
Look ahead at the edge of the woods.
My goodness it's a huge sycamore tree!
How many times do your arms go around?
18 feet the diameter was found.
Just imagine how long this tree has been standing here.

History we have discovered and trees of many year.
It's almost time to find our treasure, which is very near.
Facing the tree turn right and head down the road.
Be careful not to step on a camouflaged toad!

Along the way, go to a white pillar on your right (a memorial) just this
  one more.
Placed in memory to those taken captive by the Indians in 1754.
Now facing west go down the stone steps you came up.
The treasure is where the pine tree leaves the earth.

Created by Maeghan Paulhus in 2003.

"12/4/06 - Asked my beautiful to marry me. She said YES!"

— Quest sign-in book

historical
architectural

You can reach Chelsea via Vermont Route 110 (heading north from South Royalton) or Vermont Route 113 (traveling northwest from Thetford). The Quest begins on Chelsea's South Green, in front of the Court House. To complete this Quest, you must finish up sometime between 7am and 9pm Sunday through Thursday, and 9am until 10 pm on Friday and Saturday.

Clues

Chelsea Shiretown has secrets to share with you.
To start our Quest on this fine day
Travel to the south green I say
And arrive at the court to solve your first clue.

On the South Common look up and you will see
A golden dome shining like the sun
Making us the Shiretown, a special one.
Judicial sessions keep us so safe and free.

Look for the letter that appears in each word. Write it here: ___
                                                              1

Turn southwest to a house once famed for its gardens.
It was built by Hall in Eighteen Thirty.
See what's left of the old elm tree.
Hall rounded Cape Horn, farmed here, and raised hens.

What is left of the old elm tree? ___ ___ ___ ___ ___
                                    2

Proceed to the fanciest porch on Main Street.
How many acorns are found in each arch?
Sitting here you could see the school band march.
Built in Eighteen thirty-two this home is so sweet.

The covered sitting place is called a ___ ___ ___ ___ ___
                                        3

Walk south, some "fans" to cool you down? Not this kind in Chelsea town!
Look for this "fan" over a brick house's doorway.

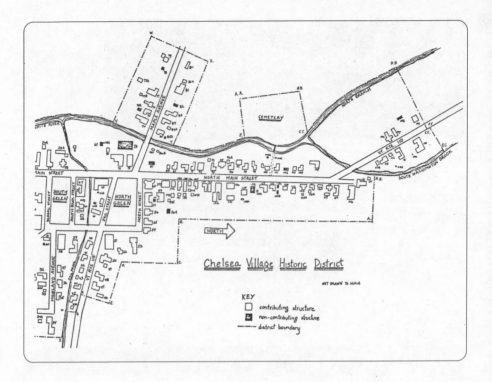

This fine homestead was built in 1832 they say.
Two beautiful elm trees that sat in the front yard were cut down.

The place you are at is called the ___ ___ ___ ___ ___   ___ ___ ___ ___ ___
                                                    4

"Turn and walk north," the Chelsea fifth graders sung.
On your right still can be seen
This Shiretown's South Green
And where Rebecca Peake was never hung.

Hammers, nails, buckets, screws—so many things that you could use.
This building, built way back in Eighteen Eighty-five
Was called "Tracy's," & sold things people used in their lives.
Now, Chelsea folks go here to wash clothes of many different hues.

To wash clothes they walk up the ___ ___ ___ ___ ___ ___
                                            5

In 1927 the flood blew through—
It took the mill works with it, too.

In front of Bacon and Hall you should now be.
Once burned by flames, but again like new.
It was rebuilt in eighteen ninety-two.
Bacon financed this building. Look up to see!

The machine that flows with dough is called a ___. ___. ___.
                                                    6

Will's Store
Photograph courtesy of
Valley News

There has been a store
on this corner since
1870.

Now cross over Route One Thirteen to the north green.
Don't take the sidewalk—meander toward the clock
To where the fancy arrow is, continue to walk.
On top of Eighteen twelve this "pointer" can be seen.

A pointer like this is called a ___ ___ ___ ___ ___ ___ ___ ___ ___ ___
7

On the corner's a place where we check out books.
Round on two corners, it's plain to see.
When you are here you must whisper quietly.
A sign above the front door is where you should look.

The 1st letter of the 5th word: ___ ___ ___ ___ ___ ___
8

Next door, the second floor is the Masonic Lodge.
It was build in Nineteen Nineteen.
Dixie's next door is a great scene.
Beautiful red bricks with inlaid arches ... quite odd.
Letters on the lodge are the color of ___ ___ ___ ___
9

Two houses beyond, there I am with white waves.
Behind me is where we go to get grain.
I once sold gas, but no more, it's a shame.
Across the road, do you see the house for the aged?

Keep pacing north to the mills where grist was ground.
In 1927 the flood blew through—
It took the mill works with it too.
Collect the letter that repeats thrice, it's easily found: ___
$$\overline{}\ 10$$

Turn around and skip down to Will's store.
This was the place to go when you were sick!
Will's was built out of old schoolhouse brick,
And we hope this Quest wasn't a big bore.

Go in to the store and then say …
"I'm feeling quite ill …

I need some

$$\overline{}\ \overline{}\ \overline{}\ \overline{}\ '\ \overline{}$$
$$7 \quad 1 \quad 1 \quad 9 \qquad 2$$

$$\overline{}\ \overline{}\ \overline{}\ \overline{}\ \overline{}\ \overline{}\ \overline{}\ \overline{}\ \overline{}\ \overline{}\ \overline{}\ \overline{}$$
$$2 \quad 6 \quad 3 \quad 2 \quad 5 \quad 8 \quad 6 \quad 3 \quad 4 \quad 10 \quad 10 \quad 5$$

And your Quest is done for the day!

Created by Patty Collins and the Chelsea Elementary 5th grade in 2002.

"June 22, 2007 Windy! Hiked with my beautiful children
(bribed them with M&Ms)! Brought our dogs—actually, they
dragged us up! What a glorious way to spend the day with my
kids—nothing is better than this."

—Quest sign-in book

7

The Chester Quest

:45

bring:
pencil
compass

easy

Take Exit 7 from I-91. Go west on Rt. 11 to the Green in Chester (about 11 miles). Park on Main Street, near the cemetery and Historical Society.

historical
architectural

Overview

In 1850 a unique Italian Colonnade home was built across from the village green in Chester, Vermont. It saw many years, many seasons and went through many changes. It had different owners, was a schoolhouse for a period and went through the Victorian era, which transformed it into a beautiful Queen Anne style home by adding a tower, bow windows and a wrap-around porch. In 1982, the home went through another transformation when it was renovated to accommodate guests. The Hugging Bear Inn was born and continues to welcome families, children, and visitors from all over the world that love Vermont, enjoy a B & B, and most of all have a passion for Teddy Bears. www.huggingbear.com

Clues

Be a Chester Quester! Have an adventure around our Green.
Fill the blanks as you stroll about; let's see what there is to be seen.

Start out at the brick school, built in 1881.
Now it is the Art ___ ___ ___ ___ ___, isn't this fun?
　　　　　　　　　　　9

Eastward on Main Street, there's lots for you to see—
An info booth, a monument the Brookside Cemetery.

Keep on, going on, don't begin to lurch.
Chester's first Meeting House is now the ___ ___ ___ ___ ___ ___ ___ Church.
　　　　　　　　　　　　　　　1　　　　　　6

Cross in the crosswalk—look to left and right.
As you go down School Street, you'll see a frabjous sight.

Past the Rose ___ ___ ___ ___ ___ ___ Tea Room, then the place where they
   made maps,   4

Comes a bridge o'er the water, you'll walk on it perhaps.

But if it's hot and you have time, down to the river you might climb—
And wiggle your toes in the water, you oughta, 'cause the water feels
   so sublime.

There's an old stone school as you journey back.
Turn west at the Green, you're on the right track.

Pointing arches you will spy—
Crowning St. Luke's gothic steeple,
way up high.

Keep on, going on, you may stop to shop—
At the Reed ___ ___ ___ ___ ___ ___ ___ Cream of the Crop.
          10   7   2

Walk on along the Green, store after store.
Misty ___ ___ ___ ___ ___ ___ Bookshop, who could ask for more?
       3   8

Quilts and gifts and music, everything's so neat.
And if you find you're hungry, places where you can eat.

When the end is drawing high, pointed arches you will spy-
Crowning St. Luke's Gothic steeple, way up high.

Cross in the crosswalk, look to left and right.
As you go down Main Street, Chester ___ ___ ___ ___ ___ comes into sight.
                          11   5

Next comes the Hugging Bear, teddies galore.
The chest that holds the treasure is what you're looking for.

Well, oh well, oh! It's your lucky day
What you are seeking is in the ___ ___ ___ ___ ___ ' ___ ___ ___ ___ ___ ___ ___
                             1 2 3 4 5   6 7 8 9 10 11

Created by Jill Dowd and Georgette Thomas in 2002.

"Joanne & Steve were here on a Quest;
For peace & foliage: one of the best.
Saw a partridge, maybe a turkey
& a whole bunch of bees.
From Wilder we came
To travel at ease.
A vulture flew over, and ravens
We heard.
A great place, also, for lovers of bird.
9-29-04"

— Quest sign-in book

8 Blacksmith Covered Bridge Quest

:20

easy

bring: compass

natural
historical

From I-91 take exit 9 toward Hartland/Windsor; turn left onto US-5/VT-12. After 4.1 miles, turn left onto Bridge Street and cross over into New Hampshire—enjoy the bridge! Turn right onto NH-12A. From Route 12A in Cornish, just south of the bridge, head east on Town House Road. In two miles the bridge will be on your right. On your way you will pass the Dingleton Covered Bridge, also built by James F. Tasker.

NOTE: For more Cornish Quests visit our online Quests page at:
www.vitalcommunities.org

Clues

James Tasker lived on Parsonage Road.
He cut down trees by the cartload.
Then brought them here to this Mill Brook,
Built Blacksmith Bridge with posts and nooks.

Enter the portal, walk into this space
You will soon discover an exciting place
It is a very old bridge, 1881 to be sure
Highly prized for its look, Tasker's legacy endures.

"Slab City" was once the name
of this place.
The mill and the bridge
kept an active pace.

Look all around, past the King Truss beams
Names you'll spy carved in wood above the stream
Look north near the hill, there is even a mill
With an undershot wheel that never stood still.

The bridge was built in 1881;
100 years later it was redone.
Milton Graton and his men did labor long
To make this bridge once again strong.
Flooring and sheathing were replaced.
Each side of the bridge was a little bit raised.

When you've crossed the bridge,
Look to both sides.
Past the guardrails, but not to your right
There is a trail down to the old mill site.

You'll be at the mill when you see some stones.
There are good seats here so find your own.
Think what it was like so long ago
When the mill was running both fast and slow.
"Slab City" was once the name of this place.
The mill and the bridge kept an active pace.
If you walk back to and up the road (not down to the mill)
You will spy some old walls at the edge of a hill.
When you see walls ahead and the bridge and road behind,
Look to your left—coppiced birches you will find.

Then on the left a boulder you will see …

The Cornish-Windsor Covered Bridge
Photograph by Jon Gilbert Fox

Built by James Tasker and Bela Fletcher in 1866, this is one of four Tasker covered bridges in Cornish; and the longest wooden covered bridge in the United States.

Now very carefully, listen to me.
With your back to the boulder
Facing 220 degrees SW
Count and then take 17 steps.

You'll be standing tall in the gap of the wall.
Across from you—a wall in view;
Along your left, another wall too!
Where the two walls do meet
There is treasure at your feet!

Created as part of the Cornish Elementary School Valley Quest Exploratory in 2000.

9 The Cornish Flat Village Quest

1:00

easy

bring:
compass

historical

From the Lebanon Green head south on Route 120 until you come to the village of Cornish Flat. Your Quest begins at the Cornish General Store, located on the west side of Route 120 — and adjacent to the Green at the heart of this village. The General Store marks the location of the old Cornish Inn. Park there and begin your Quest!

Clues

The Cornish Inn
In this Inn of a few buildings
28 rooms were for guests
Part was used for dancing
Where people were specially dressed.
Sadly in 1927—it burned to the ground.
The trucks took too long to get around.

Walk north on 120
Then turn left on the Cornish Stage Road.
When you get to the church
You can put down your load.

The Meeting House/Baptist Church
An old building built in 1789
And it is still standing fine.
The bell once rang every hour
In a high, high, tiled tower.
The church is old, very old.
It has lots of mold.
In the summer there are sales
People buy veggies by the pails.
We love this place and you will too.
Keep on going for another clue.

Walk towards the man standing on stone.
Cross a busy road, but don't go alone.
The old Thornton Store is very near.
Pretty soon you will be there.
Walk past the "green" triangle
Where a single conifer stands

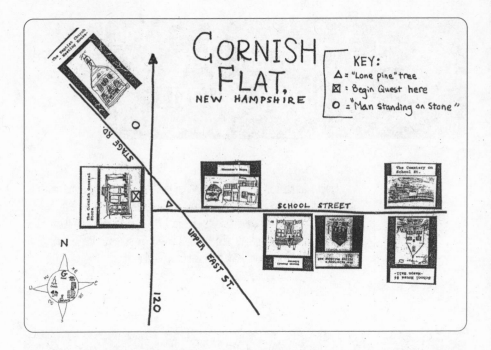

Then turn left onto School Street,
With our map in your hands.
You will also see a STOP facing East.
Look around for a maple
Then count 10 cedars tall.
There's the Thornton Store, on your left,
It's not a bit like the mall!

The Thornton Store
In this store was a chessboard where townsfolk did play.
By an old heating stove they sat part of the day.
Old "Corb," the grocer, sold groceries and grain,
Equipment and tools in the sun and the rain.
He came to your home to see what you'd need,
And return Tuesday noon, his cart loaded with feed.
Look both ways and go east
As you cross School Street;
A concrete stepped building is what you'll soon meet!

George Stowell Library
This building has stood for many years.
When you walk by, it just appears.
On a wall inside is a serious face
Of the famous Judge Samuel Chase.
George Stowell gave money for this place of books,
Right next door is the place for crooks!
To get from the books to the place of crooks,
Turn east, and walk ahead 25 steps.
A golden doorknob you will see,
And triangular window, with panes numbering three.

The Selectmen's Building and Old Jail
Only one person arrested could dwell
In the old iron jailhouse cell.
The office was built in 1888.
It also had a big fire-proof safe.
Then the jail was added on
For people who were punished and let out at dawn.
Look up School Street and head towards the hill
Count 123 steps and then stand still.
Look up and see a big letter, "G."
In front of the old schoolhouse you will surely be.

George Stowell gave money for this place of books, Right next door is the place for crooks!

The Mason Hall/ Old Schoolhouse #6
The big G out front has many lights
Children here learned and reached new heights.
Many children sat inside …
A place to learn, a place to strive.
The schoolhouse bell no longer tolls,
For now this is the Mason Hall.
The Masons have owned it entirely
Since the middle of the 20th century.
The G stands for "God" and "Geometry,"
The noblest of sciences and deity.

Go north from the steps, 23 giant paces
Cross the street safely—check your shoelaces!
12 more giant steps and you will most likely be
At the old Cornish Flat Cemetery.

*(As you enter the cemetery, please, no stepping
on or touching grave stones, and no running.)*

The Cornish Flat Cemetery
Big gate, white paint, 338 stones
Sally Thomas stands out—
Here rest her bones.
She worked for 500 dollars
Through thick and thin,
And her house was close to the Cornish Inn.

She was a servant and very young,
Not aware that her life had just begun.
Many years later, she was 44 years old,
I hope she died peacefully in her Cornish home.

From the gate, head for a large tree.
14 steps is what it will be.
Now step right of the tree,
Walk northeast (diagonally).
16 steps to "Heath" and G.A.R.
Heading north, but not too far.
A split tree in the distance
Is what you will see.
Standing to the east
Of the "potato chip" bark cherry.
It takes 15 steps east to the stone marked, "Electa."
She was the good wife of a man named, "Elisha."
Go along the stone wall another 10 steps
To the stone marked, Thomson (Elizabeth).
Go ahead 5 steps, turn left, down your shoulder,
you should see a large cracked boulder.
The treasure beneath it you should view
Inside is more learning for you to do!
Congratulations on finishing this Quest.
We worked hard and did our best!

Created by Ros Seidel and the Cornish Elementary School 3rd Grade in 2002.

"9/2/02
Beautiful late summer day. Crickets chirping, breeze blowing,
mosquitoes biting, water flowing, all is good!"

— Quest sign-in book

10 CREA Natural Communities Quest

:45

easy

natural

bring:
boots
field guide

From I-91 take exit 9 toward Hartland/Windsor; turn left onto US-5/VT-12. After 4.1 miles, turn left onto Bridge Street and cross over into New Hampshire—enjoy the bridge! Turn right onto NH-12A. From Route 12A in Cornish—just south of the Cornish-Windsor Covered Bridge—travel east on Town House Road. You will pass the Dingleton Covered Bridge and the Blacksmith Covered Bridge, both on your right. Beyond Parsonage Road, you will see the Cornish Fair Grounds on your left, along with the Old Town Hall and Schoolhouse #9. Park by the Old Town Hall. The Quest begins at the trail head across the street. If you reach the Cornish Elementary School you've gone a bit too far.

Clues

With the Town Hall just behind,
A large boulder your eyes will find.
Cross the road towards the sign that reads
"Rodney Palmer Environmental Study Area" amidst the weeds.

To the right of the sign, a trail you will see.
Take 50ish steps to a leaning oak tree.
The tree has been growing since it was small,
This tree likes swamps, but it might fall.

Be very quiet and animals you might spy:
Rabbit, snake, wood frog, chickadee and butterfly.
Here flies the monarch of orange and black;
Birds avoid this poisonous snack!

Up to the double trees (pine and oak) you should go
But not into the water with your toe!
A snapping turtle lives there all year long,
This C.R.E.A. land is where he belongs.

Two pink worm-like wrigglers on its tongue
Lure its prey in where it's no fun!
On your left, red oak, white pine, and white birch you'll see.
White birch is the official New Hampshire state tree.

Here the land is low and flat.
Pine needles make a lovely mat.

Snapping Turtle
Photograph by Ted Levin

Snapping turtles are omnivorous, eating both animals and plants. They live almost entirely in the water, but lay their eggs on land in sunny, sandy locations.

The hemlock forest is there if you seek.
All it takes is just a little peek.

All of these trees have many uses
But the maple is the one with the edible juices.
The others are great for building and timber
And white birch paper makes good tinder.

Along the path twin pines mark your way.
You wish you could linger there all day.
Take 22 steps to the start of a high mushroom trail.
Look to your left for the path, you can't fail.

Here at the "Y," head up the hill.
Keep following the trail and observe as you will.
You'll see holes in trees that are called cavities
And fungus growing, too, on the trees that are diseased.

As you approach the stone steps, look to the right.
I used to be a tall tree … now I'm shortened in height.
Insects and fungus eat me for food.
They need me for nourishment when in the mood.

Nearby the steps find another tree.
With this one what is the mystery?
Its roots are eroded and show off like bones.
These make ideal spots for chipmunk homes.

The sign at the top of the hill has a digit that stands
For the same number of fingers you have on one hand.
The downed white birch marks the last hilltop tale.
Look closer! It's covered with lots of turkey tails.

Turn yourself around and go back down
To where there was a fork on the ground.
Now walk left to the rock past mushroom hill.
See the snapping turtle? Perhaps you will.

Look for three stumps cut by beavers with ease,
Right next to two trees that might be home to bees.

Find five needles per bunch on a nearby white pine.
Hanging on a limb, a rope you will find.
Go next to a rotten balance beam held up by two trees.
This is a good spot for squirrels to eat seeds.

You'll find a baby hemlock in the middle of 3 big trees.
Maybe someday it will grow to be as tall as these.
Now look for the place where dirt makes a small mound.
To hear chickadees and blue jays, make not a sound.

Backtrack to the large flat rock; a perfect place to rest and roost

Walk a while to the "seat stump" where you can lunch.
Nearby are musclewood trees the beavers love to munch.
All along the right is a soggy wetland
Born from the stream and the beaver's teeth and hands.

From the path see a bridge under which the beaver swim.
But don't jump in!
Look left and see stumps with pointed and chewed tips
Feasted on by beaver teeth and graced by beaver lips.

Stay on the path; don't cross the bridge.
No time to get lost on the ridge!
Safety first on Quests or hikes
Don't play on beaver ponds in winter or you might fall through thin ice!

Walk by aging birch trees sprouting hoof-like fungus
Also known as birch polypore mushroom to us.
Mushrooms and other fungus are decomposers,
So are worms and microscopic creatures.

Beyond the birches only a stone wall remains of the farm from days gone by
Upon this spot a Cornish Farmer's field used to lie
And in New England if the farmer doesn't mow
The life cycles will change and a forest will grow.

Ahead a "cradle and pillow" upon the ground to rest your head
Or for a tiny chipmunk it could make a cozy bed.
This mound grew in the spot where a giant tree once stood,
The roots ripped up, made a hole, and left a mound of rotting wood.

Pass two logs with hollow centers
Home to a mole escaping hunting owl dangers?
Daddy mole, watch out!
You better protect your little mole sprout.

Continue to the wild field past goldenrod and milkweed
Replenished every year by many dispersed seeds.
Alive with busy insects on a hot summer day
Dragonflies, wasps and crickets go along their way.

Walk to the mowed grass and feel the sun shining on your face,
An open space where children love to race.
Survey the land where mouse eats seeds and fox eats mouse
Up and down the food chain sun and water matter most.

Backtrack to the large flat rock; a perfect place to rest and roost
Scan the woods to your left, until you see a web of roots.
Break trail to this mysterious place
Walk gently and look down; you may find an orange newt's face.

Creep quietly, with stealth, just like a fox.
You've almost found the Quest box!
When you reach the root-statue explore all the nooks
Then follow the trunk … it points to where you should look.

Keep on hunting, your eyes wide and round.
Where trunk meets ground the box will be found.
Sign into our box, then re-hide it once more
You've learned of this place, now it's time to explore!

Created by Ros Seidel and the 4th grade at Cornish Elementary School in 2003. Special thanks to the Wellborn Ecology Fund of the New Hampshire Charitable Foundation/Upper Valley region for support of this project.

11 The Saint-Gaudens Quest

1:00

easy

bring:
money for
entrance fee
compass

Saint-Gaudens National Historic Site is located off Route 12A, about two miles north of the Cornish-Windsor covered bridge (longest covered bridge in the United States); and is 12 miles south on 12A from West Lebanon, N.H. From Rt. 12A, turn onto and head up Saint-Gaudens Road. The parking lot is a half mile up the road on your right.

historical
natural
architectural

Overview

Discover the beautiful home, studios and gardens of Augustus Saint-Gaudens, one of America's greatest sculptors. This National Historic Park is open daily, late May through late October, from 9:00 a.m. to 4:30 p.m. Admission is $5.00 per person; children 15 and under are free. As a Federal Fee Area, the Federal Golden Passes and the America the Beautiful Pass are honored. A Saint-Gaudens NHS annual pass is also available. For information: www.nps.gov/saga

Clues

This was the place where a famous artist once dwelled
He made sculptures of people and in this he excelled
He grew up in New York City but from Ireland he came
Augustus Saint-Gaudens, you'll see was his name

The entrance booth is where you check in
The ranger there will gladly help you begin
Here you can get a map to aid with your task
And if you have questions, it's a good time to ask

Look for a very large tree in front of a home
it is in that direction that first you should roam
The tree is a honey locust, New Hampshire's largest they say
Once the house was an Inn where travelers could stay

If you look out from the porch, a tall mountain you'll see
It is all by itself and named Mount AS-CUT-NEY
To hike, and to ski, on its slopes you can go,
But it was once a volcano a very long time ago

Saint-Gaudens
Photograph by Jon Gilbert Fox

Visit Aspet, the home, studio and garden of Augustus Saint-Gaudens, one of America's great sculptors. The gardens feature period plantings and casts of ancient sculptures.

Head for the building that has a red wall
There are white columns in front, what does that make you recall?
Saint-Gaudens loved the culture of old Greece and Rome
And he used some of their art to beautify his home

Into this building you now should go
That huge glass window is important to know
It faces due north, the sun does not directly shine in
It's the best light to work with no harsh shadows within

This building is known by a special word; STU-DI-O
It was designed as workplace for an artist to go.
Here Augustus would work with plaster and clay
To create some of the sculptures you see here today

As you walk through the park two kinds of sculptures are found
Ones like Diana the huntress, you can walk all around
Some have just one side, like those on the wall
Called "reliefs" these can be very large or extremely small

Look closely at the art and you'll find great detail
And many you'll see can tell an interesting tale
Look for those of soldiers and presidents, both are on view
You'll find children and painters, and animals, too.

Return outside and past the gardens proceed
Through the hole in the hedge the pathway will lead
A dark wooden building soon will be found
Find your way inside and look all around

There are wagons and carriages and even a sleigh
If the artist went to town, he would travel this way
A strange, dark room with a thick door you will see,
It was very cold inside, why do you think that would be?

Out through the wide gate then a left you should take
Once in that field straight ahead, a right you would make
To the stucco wall with a steep sloping roof
Of the artist's talent you will here see more proof

Find the man on a stone carved with fish and a wave
He was an American admiral and was especially brave
He joined the navy as a boy and the true story is told
How he commanded a ship when just 12 years old!

Find the man on a stone carved with a fish and a wave
He was an American admiral and was especially brave

Find the turtles nearby that seem to drink to excess
Through this space called an Atrium you now should progress
Around the walls of the walkways, relief sculptures are set
Can you find the one with Dunrobin, the sculptor's pet?

In the building beyond are sculptures made of real gold
People carried these in their pockets in days of old
See the small cameo jewelry, he made these as well
As a teenager he carved them from stone and from shell

Here sculptures of people you will see around,
A general, a pilgrim, a famous author are found.
Look closely at one sculpture hanging over a case
Augustus hid his own likeness in the sheepdog's face

Go back to the field—and to the row of trees all of birch
At the first opening in the hedge there continue your search
See a group of soldiers that are marching away
If the men were alive, what do you think they would say?

Led by a man on a horse, as an angel looks down,
On these soldiers of color, who are now quite renowned
In the Civil War their bravery set them apart,
Now their story is told in movies, books, and in art

Follow the birches and the next room you should enter
A mysterious figure sits in the center
It's not meant as a portrait, nor for its meaning to be clear
It was to make people think about life as they were seated near

Continue down the path, well past the last hemlock hedge
Between the field to the left and forested edge
The sculptor once had a golf course in these fields here below
In the winter a long toboggan slide was made through the snow

Keep on walking until a white structure you'll find
When you first saw it, what came to mind?
It is made of marble mined in an old Vermont quarry
And was designed by friends of the artist to help tell a story

A century ago, an outdoor play was staged here
Actors as Greek gods and goddesses did appear
They spoke in rhyme and did dance and sing
At the end chose Saint-Gaudens to be their new king

Turn away from the Temple and look straight across
Search at the base of the pine among grass and moss
The hidden box is there, so write a note that you came
Augustus used this self-caricature when he signed his name

Come back again to the park now that you're not a stranger
You can even earn a patch as a junior park ranger
There is a film you can see, forest trails to explore
Watch a real sculptor work, attend a concert and more

Created by Gregory Schwarz in 2008.

"Aug. 4th, 2003 How fortunate we are to have places like this
on the earth. What an incredible spot. Will come again. "

— Quest sign-in book

12 · moderate · Esther Currier Wildlife Sanctuary · 1:15

Quest: *Exploring Beaver Habitat*

bring:
boots
binoculars
compass
field guide

Take I-89 to Exit 11. Take Route 11 east towards New London, NH. Travel 2.9 miles. A cemetery will appear on your left and a small parking area on your right. Turn right into the parking lot for the Esther Currier Wildlife Sanctuary.

natural

Overview

The **Esther Currier Wildlife Management Area** at Low Plain is preserved for your enjoyment as a result of community cooperation, including the participation of the Ausbon Sargent Land Preservation Trust, the Elkins Fish & Game Club, the New London Conservation Commission and the NH Fish and Game Department. This Department also holds a conservation easement on the property. Financial support comes from the National Fish & Wildlife Foundation, Ducks Unlimited and numerous private benefactors.

Clues

1. Esther Currier knew this land well.
    She envisioned a site of nature and fun.
    Our Quest starts at the gate as you walk down the path
    To a haven of beauty where animals run.

2. As you walk straight ahead you will view lovely trees—
    A garden of pine, hemlock and birch.
    This might have been houses on lot after lot
    But Esther saw better things out on a search.

3. Take the first path that you see to the right.
    Now you're looking for clues of the beavers and such.
    Keep walking, eyes open, for chew marks and stumps
    On your way to an "Overlook" we like very much.

4. What kind of trees do beavers like to chew?
    Using your eyes and a field guide to trees
    Examine the stumps that we're sure you'll find.
    The answer to this question can be learned with ease!

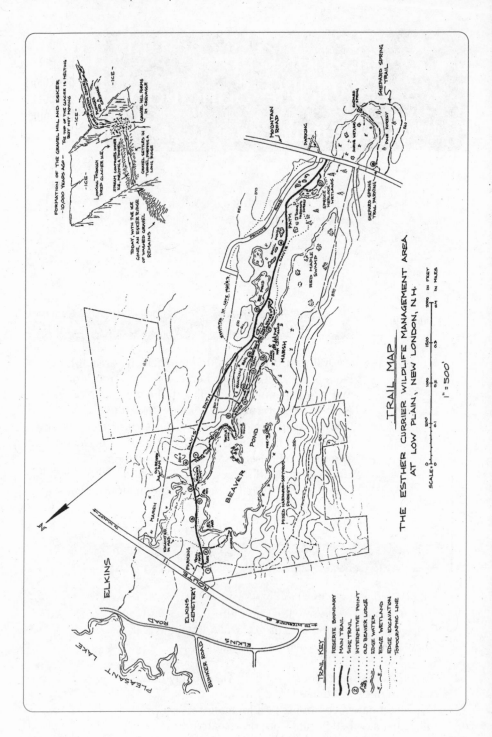

THE ESTHER CURRIER WILDLIFE MANAGEMENT AREA
AT LOW PLAIN, NEW LONDON, N.H.

TRAIL MAP

5. Look out to the Magical Wetland and see
   Reflections of trees, of clouds, and of sky.
   Standing dead trunks—called snags—still pierce this scene
   A reminder of a time when this setting was dry.

6. Head back to the main trail, then onward one hundred steps
   To a beaver's former residence, built of mud and old chew.
   There, a tree like a chimney rises up high
   Taking in the still water with reflective hues.

Beaver
Photograph by Ted Levin

Did you know that beavers are second only to humans in their ability to manipulate and change their environments?

7. Eight-nine or so more steps forward, then spy to the right
    (Two hundred degrees to be most precise!)
    Another lodge of our friend *Castor Canadensis.*
    And a sign revealing beavers built here at least twice.

8. To continue on your Quest head east to the trail
    And follow the path heading south to water flow.
    Where the pond is held back is a wall of debris
    Built by the inhabitants who homes we now know.

Two plus four zeros years ago
Glaciers carved this boggy bowl

9. Cross the bridge, and follow the shaded path
    Past spruce and fir, hemlock and white pine.
    On the forest floor, note the cradles and pillows.
    At "Davis Path" turn right towards "Observation Blinds."

10. Beech understory, white pine high above
    Proceed towards the observation blinds.
    As you travel along this wonderful path
    Keep your eyes and ears open for animal signs.

11. Immediate left past the number eight.
    Do not—No, do not!—go on to the T.
    Towards "Marsh Point" your path snakes
    Please cross on the wooden boardwalk carefully.

12. Two plus four zeros years ago
    Glaciers carved this boggy bowl.
    A glacial ice chunk stayed and melted.
    We call this place a "kettle hole."

13. You're walking on a sphagnum sponge,
    Sheep laurel grows on this moist ground.
    Look for tamarack large and small—
    It's the only deciduous conifer around!

14. Out of the bog, the trail goes up and down
    Ancient glaciers molded these small esker mounds
    Straight ahead spy yet another beaver lodge
    But left is where your Quest is bound.

15. Now you're at the edge of the lake,
    Please step inside the wooden blind
    Look up, look down, look everywhere—
    And see what it is that you can find.

16. Your Quest is done, but look for more lodges.
    There are at least two—and many species of duck.
    If you're patient, these all will come into view.
    What else can we say but this: Good Luck!

Created by the Kearsarge Region Homeschoolers with help from some friends in 2003. The Esther Currier Quest and the Natural Communities Quest Series as a whole were made possible by generous support from the Wellborn Ecology Fund of the New Hampshire Charitable Foundation/Upper Valley region. For more information, please visit www.nhcf.org.

13 Enfield Rail Trail Quest

1:30

bring:
bicycle
compass

easy

natural
historical
vista

Take I-89 to Exit 17. Take Rte. 4 east four miles to Enfield. Take the second right past the Enfield Garage (High St.) just as Rte. 4 makes a sharp left into town. At the first stop sign, go straight through the intersection. Take the first left onto Depot Street. Park at the end of Depot St. in the parking lot to the left of the red building. This building is the old Enfield railroad depot, and now houses the town ambulances. Please make sure not to block the emergency vehicles in any way.

Clues

1. In Eighteen hundred and forty seven,
   Enfield folk thought they'd gone to heaven.
   To this depot they and their cargo could now roll
   To ride the brand new Northern Railroad.

2. Whistle stops and train rides are long gone,
   Victims of highways and air travel throngs.
   Out of sight are rotting ties and rusty rails,
   Now there is gravel and the Northern Rail Trail.

Mascoma Lake, long and deep,
Named after an ancient
Squakheag Indian Chief.

3. Enfield Village is your first destination,
   Hiking or biking, get on with exploration!
   Head to the right or, with a compass, go west!
   All aboard on this historical Rail Trail Quest!

   Before the railroad came, this area, it is said,
   Was mostly farms and a few homesteads.
   The train was a magnet for prosperity,
   Thus the shops, mills and village that you see.

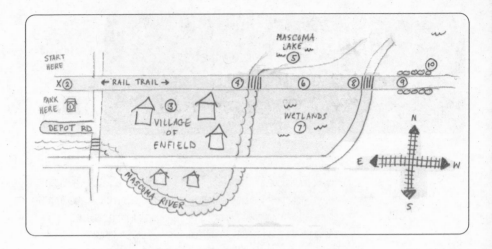

4. Next stop is the bridge over the Mascoma River,
    The bridge or the rapids might make you quiver.
    Instead think back to how water helped fill a hole
    Left behind by a glacier before humans strolled.

5. On the left is Mascoma Lake, long and deep,
    Named after an ancient Squakheag Indian Chief.
    His village was in Mass., far away in those days,
    But his tribe hunted this far North, anyway.

6. The trail up ahead appears flat and straight,
    But look to the sides, you are gaining height.
    You're on top of what's called an embankment
    Built for the railroad's advancement.

    This area was once marsh, soggy and wet,
    With no place to run a train through … yet.
    Rail workers piled dirt high across this wet spot,
    Until it was set and their backs were in knots.

7. To the right of this bank, is a rich habitat,
    A wetland home for many a duck, in fact.
    Explore a little and you may see
    A frog, a turtle, a heron … lucky thee!

8. The next bridge makes us stop and wonder:
    Who built this so cars take turns going under?
    The Shakers built the big bridge across the lake
    To get to the rail depot without effort great.
    Did they tunnel under here and thus this bridge?
    Give a friendly wave to those who way give.

9. The Quest is over, when rock walls appear.
    "Ledges Pass" they are called, the end is near.
    Two gangs of workers, forty men, they say,
    Took a year to carve this cut, with nary a stay.
    Gas or steam engines were not yet the rule,
    Hand drills and explosives their only tools.

Sailing on Mascoma Lake
Photograph courtesy of Valley News

The rail trail offers beautiful views of the lake. Be on the lookout for sailboats!

10. Upon these walls are etched names and dates,
By workers whose sweat this passage did make.
At the end of the pass on the left is a rock,
Behind "1893" you will find the Quest box!

Please don't assume to look right behind,
Cross the path to a twin oak find.
"Root" around as you look for the box
The goal of this Quest is not for lost.

Questers, please note: *At the far end of the pass, there is a trail that leads to the shore of the lake. Once you are on the trail, you are on the private property of Mr. Earl Farnham. Please respect his beautiful property, and be aware that you are passing at your own risk.*

Created by the homeschooling family of Dale Shields, John Auble and their kids Cecilia, Nathan and Devin in 2000.

14 Shaker Feast Ground Quest

1:00

moderate

bring:
compass

Take I-89 south to Exit 17. Travel on Rte. 4 east to Rte. 4A. Turn right onto Rte. 4A and drive south 3.3 miles along the lake shore. Park in the driveway at the Stone Mill: it's on your right, across the street and just beyond the Shaker Museum.

natural
historical

Overview

Imagine a place so beautiful and serene that the Shakers called it "the Chosen Vale." Nestled in a valley between Mt. Assurance and Mascoma Lake, the Enfield Shaker site has been cherished for close to 200 years. On this Quest you will discover the Feast Ground, tucked in the hills of Enfield. After your Quest, consider visiting the Enfield Shaker Museum (admission charged), which is open daily Memorial Day through Mid October.
www.ShakerMuseum.org

Clues

1. Look north toward the hill and you'll see a sign
   That shows Enfield's Conservation line.
2. Follow the path that goes along straight
   Up ahead awaits your fate.
3. You're heading towards the Holy Feast Ground
   Where the Shakers used to sing and dance around.
4. After the meadow the trail turns left. A bridge you'll see
   To a field where merino sheep used to be. (Pass the bridge, keeping on
     the trail.)
5. The trail turns west as up you go. Soon, stop, turn and see
   The remains of the village the Shaker's settled in 1793.
6. Next, travel across the top of the hill and then you'll see
   An old granite post and a big locust tree.
7. At the little white post, take a short break
   For a compass reading you may take.
   Head west at the bearing of 268
   (Hint: due west is 270 degrees).
8. Go a hundred yards heading west.
   You're almost there—at the end of your Quest.
9. Now work your mind while you hike there
   Take on the riddle of the Lord's Stone … if you dare.

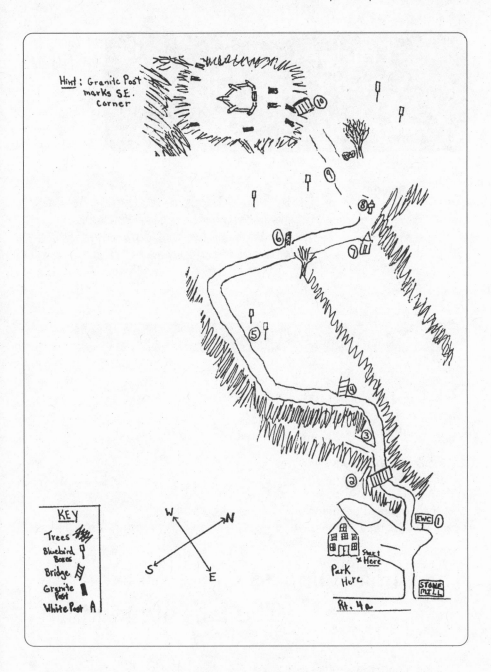

10. A granite slab is still found, but there is a rumor besides:
    Because no one knows where the "The Stone" really resides.
11. The Shakers hid it for safety's sake
    But was it buried in the ground? Sent to the bottom of Mascoma Lake?
12. Now March up the hill like a Shaker would
    And come to a spiritual grove in the beautiful woods.
13. At the southeast corner of this spiritual place
    You'll find our treasure box's special space.

Created by Mary Ellen Burrit's Girl Scout Troop in 1998 and embellished by Julie Orrock Slack in 2007.

15 Fairlee
Glen Falls
Quest

moderate

:30

bring:
field guide

natural

Take I-91 to exit 15. Turn west, and take Lake Morey West Drive 1.4 miles, heading clockwise around Lake Morey to the Boat Launch. Park at the Boat Launch, the Quest begins there. Please do not park in the driveway across from the trailhead.

Clues

1. Park at the boat launch
    Be sure you're all set
    Step o'er the "road-fence"
    And turn to the LEFT.

2. Walk about 70 steps
    (From the BL sign)
    And cross the street
    The woodland opening
    Should be right at your feet!

The trunk points to where
The falls are found.

3. Soon, you'll see a white rock
    But please do not stop.
    If you keep on the trail
    We're sure you'll not fail.

4. A tree broken in half
    Crosses the path.
    Here comes some water
    But don't stop for a bath.

5. Keep on the path …
    You'll see a waterfall.
    But it's just the lower one
    And not tall at all.

6. Just above, a VT HD
    Post is on the right.

1896

Lake Morey Summer Resort...

Glen Falls House, Lake Morey.

OPINION PUB. CO., BRADFORD, VT.

Count them all
As they come into sight.

7. Can you find a big burl?
   On a trunk spy a rounded curl!

8. When you find the 2nd orange
   Marker along your way
   The Upper Falls song
   Should brighten your day.
   But "turn right and 30 steps,"
   Off the beaten path,"
   That's what we say.

9. You'll find a snag
   From a tree blown down.
   The trunk points to where
   The falls are found.

10. Facing toward the Upper Falls
    Turn 45 degrees to the right.
    Walk 22 steps and look down
    To discover our Quest's Treasure Box site.

11. Visitors have enjoyed
    Fairlee Glen Falls
    For more than 100 years.

    After signing our guest book
    Go closer, take a look for yourself
    And give it three cheers!

Created by Linny Levin's 5th and 6th grade class in Fairlee in 2000.

16

Miraculous Tree Quest

1:00

moderate

natural

bring:
field guide
pencil
measuring
tape

Take Route 5 either south from Fairlee or north from East Thetford to the village of Ely. From Ely, take Route 244 west underneath I-91 to Bragg Hill Road. Turn right on Bragg Hill Road and follow it to the end. Park at the cemetery—your Quest begins right here!

Clues

I stand in back with wide, stretching arms,
Protecting everything here from harm.
My family is oak, my color white;
A compatriot stands next to me on the right.
My rounded, lobed leaves can be found
Either upon me—or upon the ground.
Please measure my waist, up four feet
In order to calculate the DBH[1]—hey that's neat!
Record the white oak's DBH here: _____

Leaving the highway noise behind
Seven feet up on Allbee a finger pointing up find.
Next, find a baseball diamond sitting on home
Slink under the line, & left up the road roam.
We're now in a "mast producing" zone[2]
(A fancy way of saying nuts call this place home)!

Road curving to the right,
Peer through younger beech trees on your left.
A road meanders lower, tracing a ravine
Where during the Pleistocene[3]
The Ely River could be seen.[4]

Wires cross above; road curves right
Past a pole (6-SB) and a tall hemlock.

---

1 Foresters use a standard measurement for the girth of trees, known as DBH, or diameter at breast height.
To calculate DBH measure the diameter approximately four feet above the ground.
2 Mast is a noun referring to nuts, collectively: especially as a food source for animals.
3 Better known as the "ice age."
4 The Ompompanoosuc is a descendant of the Ely River which used to drain out through this valley,
approximately tracing the path of Route 244.

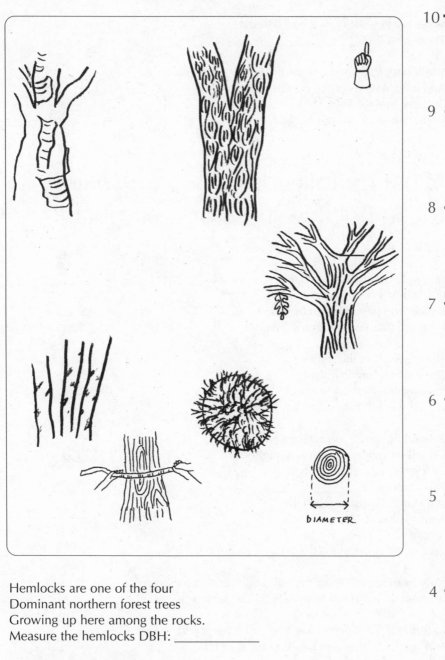

DIAMETER

Hemlocks are one of the four
Dominant northern forest trees
Growing up here among the rocks.
Measure the hemlocks DBH: _____

Onward! Sugar maple, beech
And yellow birch are the other three—
Oh say how many can you see?
Curve left. Threadbare from the years
An old yellow birch stands right near 675
Looking ragged—yet it is still alive.
Calculate its DBH: _____

Our fork holds one and a half poles in its crest—
Veering left I think is the best.
The next large tree on the right is a white ash.
How do we know?
Like muskmelon its bark does grow!
What do folks do with a tree like that?

10
9
8
7
6
5
4
3
2
1

Make hockey sticks or a baseball bat.
The ash's DBH: _____

You'll pass a sugar shack on the left
And a front yard spruce on the right
But stay straight ahead
With your goal still out of sight.

What do folks do with a tree like that? Make hockey sticks or a baseball bat.

An apple tree looms left flanking the road.
In fall it will bear a tasty load.
If soon you pass the numbers 369
I can tell that you are doing fine.

Then, uphill on the right
Three white birch sit tight.
Just past them is a driveway
Which we will turn up today.

Beyond the birch trio is a majestic tree.
Oh tell me what you think it might be?
Despite a very terrible blight
This century old _____
Still stands living in our sight!
A miraculous tree!
A sight rare to see!
Record the miraculous tree's DBH please: _____.

Now examine the nuts, the bark, buds and leaves—
For then you will see how to SEE this rare tree!

To find out the name of the tree you have found
Add up the DBH's and measure the ground.
Taking that distance look 'round for a hole
Where you'll find your answer—but don't tell a soul!

Created by Ted Levin and Steven Glazer in 2000.

17 The Palisades Quest

1:00

difficult

bring:
binoculars
compass
field guide

Take I-89 to exit 15. Go west off the exit ramp, and take a right onto Lake Morey Road East. Turn into the Fire Station; and park in the far, southeast corner of the lot (area closest to the Interstate).

natural

Overview

This Quest is a steep climb to a beautiful south view of the Connecticut River Valley. The cliffs beyond the Quest site serve as an important nesting site for Peregrine falcons, as well. Peregrine falcons are an endangered species—and this is a protected area during the nesting season. Please don't go beyond the Quest box.

Clues

1. Park the car in the lot. Don't stop to rest.
    Follow the fence, there is no bench.
    Walk towards the highway,
    U-turn, and look ahead for the pathway.

2. Along the off ramp, look up on a tree,
    A "Lake Morey" trail marker is what you will see.

3. Travel against traffic, there's a long needled pine branch ...
    Take a turn to the left, giving the highway a last glance.
    Into the woods! This is the path to the treasure.

On your feet, slow and sweet.
    Walk across the stepping stones
you meet.

4. Caution, when you climb this mountain.
    Be careful you do not disturb the falcons.
    These birds are a protected species,
    And are nesting nearby among the rocks & trees.

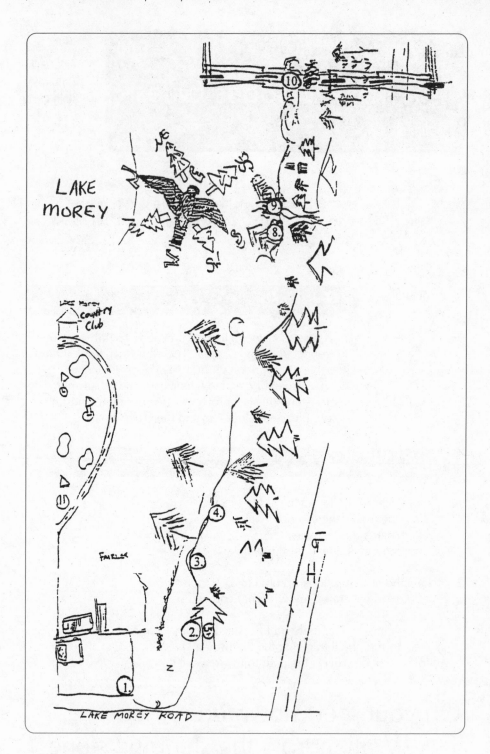

5. Follow the fence; it's on your left.
   The path is steep, so do not weep.
   Through the break, don't let the barbed wire bite.
   Now look, it's on your right.

6. Take a break, to see our lake. It's on your left.
   After a few steps, stop! We don't want you to drop.

a cairn is a pile of stones usually used as a memorial or marker

7. Horray, horray, you're on your way!
    Zig, zag, zig, zag for this part of the day.

8. At this egg, we named her Meg.
    No need to whine, it's time to dine.
    Sorry no diner, this place is finer.

9. On your feet, slow and sweet.
    Walk across the stepping stones you meet.

10. Out of the woods to a clearing,
    Don't touch too high, or you'll fry!
    Stand under the wire. Go to the front support cable.
    Turn to left and walk four steps.
    Turn to view. Walk 12 steps to the rock pile.
    Dig around and you will come upon our treasure box.
    Look inside; it's stamping time!

Peregrine
Stamp by Steve Glazer

Peregrine populations fell during the mid-twentieth century. Rachel Carson's *Silent Spring* helped spark a movement that brightened the Peregrine's future—and ours, too.

Created by Joyce Berube's Girl Scout troop in 1998.

18
Grafton Cave Quest

1:15

bring:
field guide

moderate

Follow Rte 11 east to Chester. Turn south on Rte 35 (by the True Value hardware store) and follow to Grafton. Turn right onto Main Street and then left in front of The Old Tavern onto Townshend Rd. Follow Townshend Road 1/4 mile to the Nature Museum. The Nature Museum building will be on the right, with parking on the left.

NOTE: For another Grafton Quest visit our online Quests page at: www.vitalcommunities.org

natural
historical

Overview

The Nature Museum is a dynamic and educational place to visit. They sponsor many off-site, naturalist-led public programs, and teach classes in schools and libraries across the region. Exhibits and the Second Nature gift shop are open to the public 10:00-4:00 on Saturdays and Sundays year round. The museum is usually open on school vacation weeks, holidays and other special occasions. We are happy to open any other time for individuals or groups by appointment. Admission is charged. For more information: http://www.nature-museum.org/.

Clues

This Quest begins at the Nature Museum. To get the most out of your visit to Grafton, you may want to have two other brochures with you on the Quest. Both brochures are available at the Nature Museum.

- The "Walking Tour of Historic Grafton"
- The "Village Park Interpretive Trail Map"

Built in 1876, this wonderful building, now housing the Nature Museum, began its life as the Grafton Grange. The building was moved to this site around 1940 by Miss Lucy Daniels who worried that it might catch on fire and fall on her small house if it stayed where it was. How do you suppose this big building was moved?

The Grange sold the building to the Nature Museum in 1996, and in 1999 the Museum moved its collections here. The Grange members continue to meet here in this building.

To begin your walk to the Village Park, stand in front of the Nature Museum facing the road. Turn left and head up Townshend Road. Pass the Gallery

North Star and three old-fashioned street lamps, and then note the Daniels House on the left. It was built around 1820.

On the corner of Townshend and Main, see the Phelps Barn and the Old Tavern, built in 1801. The barn carries the name of brothers Francis and Harlan, who bought the Old Tavern in 1865. They added the third story and the porches to the Tavern with money they got from their California gold finds and ran it as the "Phelps Hotel" for the next 48 years.

If you have time, go inside to the front desk of the Old Tavern. Look on the wall above the front desk for the name of the famous Civil War general who once stayed here.

Keeping the tavern on your left, travel uphill through the village until you reach the chapel and the brick church, which will both be on the left-hand side of the street. The brick church was built in 1833 and used to have horse sheds behind it. People who belonged to the church bought stalls for their horses as well as pews for themselves. The two church buildings in town united in 1920 and became the "Church of Grafton."

Just past the church, where brick ends and wood begins, you'll find the Village Park.
Read the stone to see who donated this land to the town … and when. Thanks to them, we may still climb to the rock outcroppings through the forests of hemlock, oak, and large pines that began to grow after most of the sheep had ceased to eat grass here.

Once in the park, follow the red trail for the most direct route to the treasure box.

Take a rest when you come to the second bench you see. It is near a lot of large white pines. Do you know how many white pine needles are in a bundle?

Near the junction where the white trail turns off to the right of the Red trail, can you spot the stone steps that led to an old gazebo? The gazebo is no longer there because a large white pine fell on it in 2002.

Further up the red trail you'll see a square gazebo. Made of cedar, it was built in the 1920's. Before the trees grew up, there was an overlook here, which looked out over the Town.

Keep on hiking. You will know when you are there.
Your legs will be tired. You will still be climbing.
There will not be any more benches or gazebos.
And suddenly you will be saying "Wow!" and then, all jumbled together, you'll hear yourself saying at least as many things as there are needles in the pine bundle:

Look at that rock!
How did it get there?

Look at that rock!!
How did it get there?
Who built that wall?
And why?
Can we go in there?

When all these things are heard from your mouth and those with you, you will know you are in the right place!

If you find the treasure box, please sign-in, stamp your book, and close things right. Others will be coming too, and they'll be happy to find it dry and tight.

When you are ready to retrace your steps, one word to the wise is in order: Go back to the entrance of the Village Park by whatever trail you wish, but please note that if you follow the white "Museum" sign that points down the blue access trail, that path is quite steep.

We hope that you have had a good time and that you will come again.
Our hills, streams, forests and farmland are our real treasures.
Thank you for exploring them and doing your part to take good care of them!

Written in 2007 by Debby Hinman, based on an original created by students at the Compass School in 2000.

19

Balch Hill Quest

1:15

moderate

bring:
field guide
boots

To get there: From Hanover, take Rte. 10 north. Turn right on Reservoir Rd. Go about 1/2 mile and park in the parking lot for the Ray School on the left.

NOTE: For more Hanover Quests visit our online Quests page at: www.vitalcommunities.org

natural

Overview

The Hanover Conservation Council is a private, non-profit organization incorporated in 1963. The mission of the Council is to promote the appreciation and conservation of land and natural habitat in Hanover. Their mission is achieved with programs in land conservation, environmental education and support for conservation oriented public policies. Currently, over 450 households pay dues to the Council in support of its activities. One of the Council's holdings is the Balch Hill Natural Area. www.hanoverconservationcouncil.org

Clues

Along Reservoir Road, east you will go
To a bike path that doesn't quite show …
Unless you look for mailbox #29:
Then to the left of the driveway, your path you will find.

Follow this path to the trail on the right.

So pause and look at the great grandfather trees—Because your treasure is hidden in one of these.

Just be careful, and enjoy all the sights.
Up the hill, follow blazes of white and blue
But be sure not to miss the arrows, too.

Continue on to almost the top
For it is there that you will need to stop.
So pause and look at the great grandfather trees—
Because your treasure is hidden in one of these.

After finding the treasure, continue on to the top.
There's a beautiful view that will cause you to stop.
Nearby, too, is an amazing oak,
17 feet around—this isn't a joke!
See Mt. Ascutney from the top; and Baker Tower, too.
And on your way down just reverse all these clues.

Created by Cathy MacDonald and Pam Graham's Girl Scouts in 1998.

"9/22/02
All these places hidden away from the world. Excellent to wander around this day to discover it all. Thanks for a great Quest."

—Quest sign-in book

20 Mink Brook Quest

:45

moderate

natural

bring:
boots
field guide
swimsuit

Get off I-91 at Exit 13, the Hanover/Norwich exit. Travel east into Hanover, and then, at the top of the hill, turn right onto Main Street. After 0.6 Miles, turn left onto Mink Brook Road. Continue straight for 0.2 Miles. The parking will be on your right. Be prepared to get wet as this Quest crosses a brook! In fact, depending on the water's strength, children may need help in crossing. Be careful, use good judgment and have fun.

Overview

The Hanover Conservation Council is a private, non-profit organization incorporated in 1963. The mission of the Council is to promote the appreciation and conservation of land and natural habitat in Hanover. Their mission is achieved with programs in land conservation, environmental education and support for conservation oriented public policies. Currently, over 450 households pay dues to the Council in support of its activities. One of the Council's holdings is the 113-acre Mink Brook Nature Preserve.

Clues

Open the gate and follow the trail,
Where the mink once walked, waving its tail.
If you happen to see one, don't get too close,
Or of a foul stench you may get a dose.

Wonderful at rodent control, mink can kill and store prey.
You may see mink hunting on these shores one day!

People you might see with dogs at their feet.
Some small, some large, some tired from the heat.
Now on the left, a large house up on a hill is in sight,
Up ahead a little, follow a path to the brook on the right.

Be as quiet as a mouse. Look all around.
Listen to the water's sweet sound.
This sound is made by bubbles breaking.
Under the rocks, animal homes in the making.

Gaze at the pool, ducks love this spot,
Jump in and swim if it's really hot.
Now, return to the trail to continue your walk,
Look up at the sky where some geese may flock.

Look on both sides for the riverbank grape,
A vine with tendrils to climb.
Grouse, fox, turkey and other wildlife
Upon its fruit often dine.

In the last week of April and the first week of May, Suckers move up the brook, jumping up waterfalls so gay.

You must bear right at the crab apple tree,
Walk into the shadows of the forest canopy.
Now you've come to the point where it is time to cross,
You will get wet ... some rocks are slippery with moss.

Alder trees anchor stream banks,
Helping to contain the motion.
Their roots are essential
In preventing soil erosion.

Willow

Alder

Ahead are many trails from which to choose,
But if you don't bear left, you're bound to lose.
Up ahead stands an enormous tree,
Death caused its bark to fall, you will see.

Stay on the trail ... it will twist and wind,
Lots of different ferns here you might find.
Continue on the path along the babbling brook.
When you come to a large flat rock stop for a look.

In the last week of April
And first week of May,
Suckers move up the brook,
jumping up waterfalls so gay.

Gaze upstream. You know the giant log has a story to tell—
It was 1995 when this tree eventually fell.
Dogs, and children, and wildlife alike,
Use this log to cross when taking a hike.

"Horsetail" is another name for *Equisetum* that is not rare.
It is useful for anchoring the soil. Do you see any here?
Check out its jointed stems. Look at it up close.
It can poison livestock if they eat too high a dose!

Three Muddy Kids
Photograph by Ted Levin

Hopefully this won't happen to YOU when you cross Mink Brook!

This log is a dam; sticks don't go too far,
Downstream of the log there lies a sandbar.
Go back to the path, and ahead you will spy,
That here is an island when the water is high.

On the sandbar, raccoons, foxes,
mink ... even bear,
Have left footprints when drinking
that tell they have been here.

At the burnt stumps take a walk up the hill,
This is just a little detour, if you will.
Along the trail, look down at your feet,
Star flowers and Mayflowers grow so sweet.

Return back to the main trail and continue upstream,
The trail is there despite how it may seem.
You will pass by many a boulder,
They were moved by glaciers when it was colder.

Where the trail diverges, stay along the rock wall,
Up ahead is a rock, sitting big, square, and tall.
It sits near the water and is marked with an "X,"
Please listen closely to find out what is next.

At the base of this rock, where it touches two others,
Find a tall birch tree—box is under rock cover!
Congrats to you on completing this test,
Enjoy the walk back along this lovely Quest!

This Quest is an amalgam of two Mink Brook Quests: Mink Brook I was written by Ginger Wallis, Linny Levin and Jay Davis; and Mink Brook II was written by Jessa Berna and Maia Tatinclaux as part of their independent project in Jeannie Kornfeld's Honors Environmental Science class at Hanover High School.

21 Quest to the Velvet Rocks

1:00

difficult

bring:
field guide
compass

From I-91, take Exit 13, and travel east across the Connecticut River into Hanover. At the first set of lights, turn right onto Main Street. At the next set of lights, turn left onto Lebanon Street. There are parking spaces along the street in front of Hanover High School. Park, and walk towards the intersection of Lebanon Street and Rte. 120. The trail can be found behind Co-op gas station.

natural

Overview

This Quest hikes up to the Velvet Rocks Shelter of the Appalachian Trail. This section of the trail is maintained by our partner, the Dartmouth Outing Club. The DOC was formed in 1909 to "stimulate interest in out-of-door winter sports," and quickly grew to encompass the College's year-round out-of-doors recreation. Today the club has over 1,500 student members (about a quarter of the College's student population), and about as many non-student members, making it (to our knowledge) the largest collegiate outing club in the nation (as well as the first). The DOC organizes trips in the out-of-doors, provides outdoor leader and medical/safety education, and maintains over seventy miles of the Appalachian Trail. For more information: www.dartmouth.edu/~doc/.

Clues

As you are walking along Lebanon St.,
A 5-way stoplight you'll soon greet.
To the east, a grocery store, gas station, and field.
Beyond, a forested hill, is where our treasure is concealed.

Behind the gas station, find an opening.
Head east by foot, for a trail you are hoping.
On the far side of the field, look to the right.
Where the forest begins are blazes of white.

For maybe a mile follow white blazes
Over rocks and roots.
You might be glad if you're wearing hiking boots.
When it seems like you've reached a high ridge top,
Keep looking for a blue blaze where you should stop.
Follow these spaced out blue blazes
To another hill top and see
A hole in the middle of a very old tree.

Appalachian Trail
Photograph courtesy of Valley News

More than 250 back-country shelters are located along the Appalachian as a service to all A.T. users. A typical shelter, often called a "lean-to," has three walls and an open door to the world on the fourth side.

If you look to the middle of this welcoming space,
A campfire site you will also face.
A wood shelter for hikers will be here, too.
And a rock outcrop boasts a beautiful view!

From here, all of Hanover used to be seen,
Now it is blocked by trees beautifully green.
But the sky so blue, you might also see.
And where oh where could the Quest treasure be?

From the northwest corner of the shelter
Take a bearing of 290 degrees.
Then walk thirty or forty feet
To a hole at the base of a maple tree.

Sign our book!
Tell us where you are from.
Take an impression of our stamp.
Re-hide our box & you're done.

Enjoy a short rest; then to the right you may wish to go
A few hundred paces to a place you should know.
Now, here on the right, the trees open for you–
A view of Etna, with mountains green, sky so blue.

From here, the blue blazes go vertically down.
Go right at the AT sign you've found.
Follow these blazes onto the right.
When you pick up the old trail–what a welcoming sight!

You will once again pass the velvety rocks,
Pass the forest, the field, the Co-op parking lot.
We hope you hike this on a beautiful day:
And, that you find peace and rest—
and a chance to play!

Created by Mitsu Chobanian's Girl Scout Troop in 1999.

Take Route 4 west two miles from White River Junction. Turn south onto Center of Town Road and proceed to the top of the hill (about 0.8 miles). Park along the green that is on your right. Your Quest begins here.

NOTE: For more Hartford Quests visit our online Quests page at: www.vitalcommunities.org

historical

Overview

This Quest explores the first settlement in Hartford: the mustering ground, an old cemetery and inn, School # 1, and other hidden treasures. Meeting House Common is maintained by the Hartford Department of Parks and Recreation, whose goal is to serve the needs of the community through quality parks and facilities; and by offering life long learning opportunities through recreational and cultural programs. For more information regarding Hartford's parks, please visit www.hartford-vt.org.

Clues

Many years ago, upon this green
Hartford's Center of Town was a bustling scene.
So park your car and come on down
Let's explore this old ghost town!
Start at something red, white, and blue
And about old Hartford we will tell you.

King George the 3rd was no nerd
On July 5th, 1761 he gave us his word
By signing the charter to declare this town Hartford.

Now gaze across the green
And imagine this scene:
Folks coming down from the hills
To practice their drills,
In preparation for fights
To free up our rights.

While imagining the beat of their marching feet
Turn your body to look across the street.
Note the tall trees, so scary and old
They are locust trees we are told.

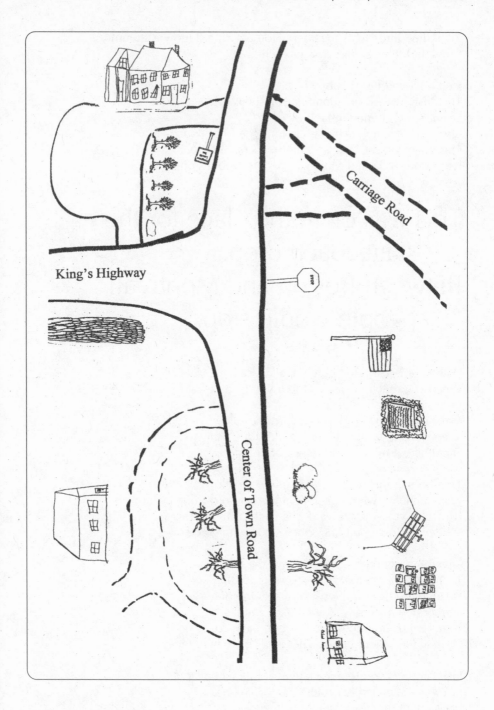

Now turn twice and walk to the sign.
Stop to read it, line by line.
At the back of the sign let's face the woods
Look toward the left please if you could.
Take 35 steps between the biggest tree
And all the picnic tables that you see.

You should soon stumble upon an old road
Now look carefully for a tree with marks of old.

Turn to the left and proceed 70 paces.
Stop at the fork and turn your faces.

Right, find three trees together. Stop & visit # 2.(now a stump)
Cross the street to find your next clue.

Stop and read the sign of white.
The bush by the back porch is your next site.
Leavitt's Inn opened in January of 1794.
Original stenciling is hidden behind the front door.
This once was the place for the stagecoach drop.
Between Boston and Montreal, people would stop.

This was once the place for the stagecoach drop.
Between Boston and Montreal, people would stop.

With your back to the porch, walk past some trees.
When you reach the rock, stop if you please.
Look both ways before you cross.
Make a right so you don't get lost.
Keep walking to the end of the old stone wall.
Stand here a minute and reflect on it all.

The rocks in this wall were an old foundation.
From a church which once held the Hartford Congregation.
Now turn your eyes towards the back corner of this space
Where old town buildings once stood with grace.

Reverse directions and head down the hill
To the sign of red that makes you stand still.
Head to the right and look for the stump of a tree
Further down hill and 2 mailboxes you'll see.
Turn your back to these boxes & go back up 20 paces.
Gaze at the school house where kids once held races.

Josephine Orizzonto once taught at this school.
In 1943 she ended her rule.
Envision all the history we're telling
As you look upon what is now a private dwelling.

Walk back to the green and look for a pipe.
It is also green and an "out of the ground" type.
Then, search for a wooden cross. Then go stand below
For this old cemetery we would like to show.

Enter quietly and look for stones in a line:
3 tall light ones and 4 of the small, dark kind.
With your back to the gate
Go check out their fate.

Welcome friends, meet the Tildens.
Josiah ran a tavern out of his buildings.
Also an authority on the weather forecast
He fought in the Revolutionary War gone past.

Pay final respects to son of Stephen and Abigail
And continue along this historic trail.
With your back to Josiah, put your right hand out
Look for an arcing stone top ... then give a shout!

Here lies Solomon Strong with his two wives
And his many children who lost their lives.
This family we know has many roots here,
Farmers, soldiers, and millers—they were all held dear.

So exit if you would this yard of bone
Take a last look around and keep a low tone.
The final moment is here at last.
It is the end of our story from Hartford's past.

The treasure is hidden down on the ground
If you find a green chimney, then it will be found.

Created by Mary Bouchard's students at Hartford High School in 2003.

"Aug. 28, 2002 We enjoyed getting out of the car and seeing
a village we'd driven thru may times (without noticing
the details)."
— Quest sign-in book

23 Hartford in the Civil War Quest

:45

moderate

bring: pencil

From the Intersection of Routes 5 and 14 in White River Junction, travel northwest (towards West Hartford) on Route 14. Soon you will see I-91 crossing high over Route 14 ahead of you. Look for the Hartford Cemetery on your right, and park in the lot just before the Cemetery, along the chain link fence.

historical

Overview

On this Quest, we travel back in time. Our setting: Hartford, Vermont, in the winter of 1860. The fields have been put to sleep, and in November President Lincoln is elected under the banner, "We cannot be a nation divided, half slave and half free." As southern states secede, President Lincoln calls for 75,000 troops. This Quest begins at the stone of Allen Gilson, one of the first to answer the call.

Clues

Pass one gate, pass two,
Turn in where the driveway waits for you.
Allen P. Gilson, you will see
Who rode in the First Regiment Cavalry.

The last letter of this soldier's name: ___
                                          1

Between the two trees, hydrangeas are these
On through two Hazens, move on if you please
On four stones shaped like a steeple
You will find some Fenno people
Of the plants which decorate this plot
Which of them are native, which are not?

Look left, a tall "trio" of stones you will see
One served in the war, revered was he.

From the obelisk, the last letter of this veteran's last name: ___
                                                                 6

Leave this old tomb that's marked with a shield—

Civil War Memorial
Photograph by Jon
 Gilbert Fox

The population of
Vermont in 1860 was
315,098. 34,238
Vermont soldiers served
in the Civil War. 5,224
of them died, and 100
are buried in the
Hartford Cemetery.

At Ed Blaisdell's stone a rusty star feel.
Ed Blaisdell enlisted at age 24
And went down to Washington ready for war.

His company built strong fortifications
Compared to bloodshed, this was vacation!
When called to Virginia, that duty ended.
On company H, the Union depended.

Ed's second wife survived him by almost 4 years.
Put the 3rd letter of her first name here: ___
                                                  5

Beside Amanda Blaisdell lies Ed's comrade Charles
Who fought for the Union in the 11th Vermont Vols.

Tired, hungry and scared, the soldiers marched into battle
Those shots whizzing by made their weary bones rattle.
One private's canteen was shot from his side—
That bullet just missed him, but not very wide!

Sweet letters from home brought them news and concern
That to vices like drinking and gambling they'd turn.
But these sinful temptations kept cold fear at bay
As the fiddler, the drummer and the piper would play.

What's the 4th letter of Mr. Davis' first name? ___
                                                      9

East of Mr. Davis, many spires you will see.
You seek the one that's shrouded in stone drapery.

From here, many tall shapes reach up toward the sky
Nature's art as a frame will sure catch your eye.
Under shade and shelter for the birds and the bees
Greet the Williamson family and family of trees.

Breathe deep with your noses, and taste the sweet smell
What type of trees are these, can you tell?

What is the first letter of Berkley, Maude, Anna and Mira's last name? ___
4

Turn round and walk past a family of Boyd
On past the Brooks family returned to the void.
Look at two stones and you'll see on the right
Civil War Soldier Orin Watkins, his name barely in sight.

Last letter of Orin's last name: ___
7

Further east; pass the cloth on the obelisk top.
There are some figures on the ground where you should stop.
Marguerite did not serve in the Civil War
But fought for freedom in the Marine Corps.

The 5th letter of our vets' first name is? ___
10

Now, look around for a log that's carved out of stone
Private Pinney survived, from the war he came home.

The letter between Private Pinney's middle initial and his last name: ___
2

(Hint: this one is hard! Need a clue? Think about the alphabet.)

Toward the rusty stone walk, but stop on your way
To linger with Sylvia, but don't read all day.

What is the 1st letter of Sylvia's 2nd husband's 1st name? ___
3

Take twenty steps east, passing two B's.
Stop and ponder these old weeping trees.

The 8th letter of Emily's husband's first name: ___
8

Off to the left, a tiny stone column you'll spy.
Go and discover where Nash's dry bones lie.

The 3rd letter of the organisms growing on this stone: ___
11

Albin Nash signed up for the Mass Volunteers
Not knowing his regiment would fight far from here.
To Louisiana went all the men
To wonder if they would see New England again.

They missed the fresh air and cool summer water
For summer down south got hotter and hotter.
That trip, eleven died from wounds and from shot
But one hundred and one from diseases they got.

While facing old Albin (that's East don't you know)
Take 10 skips forward then right you will go.
Move past all the tablets of Baileys and Browns
At left are the Allens all close to the ground.

Leave SJ behind you and study the land
The tallest of markers a nice pinkish tan
There is but one other its color and height
It blends with the trees and it's up to the right

Go see Mr. Lyman and learn what he's done
At Petersburg, Ed last laid down his gun
If you take a moment to look round the plot
A stone for each story, their own special spot

All except Julia's a letter they share
Read then and you'll find it, you're answer's right there: ___
                                                              12

Retreat to Gilson, who lies in the west,
Head north to discover what's next on your Quest.
Past the stone wall, and over your shoulder
March up to salute the old granite soldier.

Place all your letters in order and you will see
The end of this Hartford Civil War mystery.

___ ___ ___ ___ ___ ___
 1   2   3   4   5   6

___ ___ ___ ___ ___ ___
 7   8   9 10 11 12

This tree is tall. You stand below.
Look for the box on a bough.

Population of Vermont in 1860 = 315,098
Soldiers who volunteered to fight = 34,238
Number who died = 5,224
Civil War veterans buried in the Hartford cemetery = 100

Created with the collaborative participation of Jen Boeri-Boyce's students at Hartford Middle School (2006–7), Upper Valley teachers participating in a Valley Quest workshop, and Valley Quest intern extraordinaire Julie B. Barnes!

24 Jericho Historic District Quest

1:00

moderate

bring:
bicycle

From Interstate 91, take exit 12. Turn left and proceed down to Christian Street, take a left on Christian Street and head down the hill to Route 14. Turn right on Route 14 and after almost one mile, turn right onto Jericho Road and follow it until it ends. Then, take a right onto Jericho Street. Proceed until you get to Sugartop Road on your left. Shortly beyond Sugartop Road is a pullout for parking. Park there and embark on your Quest.

historical vista

Overview

Jericho is a scenic agricultural community floating high in the hills of Hartford. The Jericho Community Club was organized during the summer of 1951 by a group of neighbors in the Jericho District of Hartford, Vermont. Inhabitants of Jericho are automatically members, and those who live elsewhere but who wish to join in the meetings are associate members. The purpose for the club is to promote the best interests of the Jericho community by providing opportunities for recreation, education, and fellowship; by maintaining the Jericho schoolhouse as a community building; and by considering and acting upon all matters which affect the community.

Clues

Join us with our journey
As we make our way through the history
Of Jericho district farms
That you can see in houses and barns.

Thomas Hazen once owned all this land.
It was a gift from the town for lending his hand.
He gave it all out to his children
Who quickly started a buildin'.
Come along and see
Their fine legacy.

Walk past a road called Sugartop.
Pass a field once filled with cow plop.
Head for an old bucket with a post.
In this white house you may find a ghost.
Built in 1788

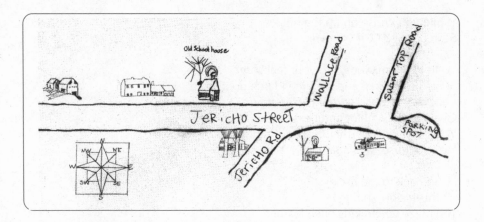

It was owned by son Daniel of late.
Later on, Erminie Nott called it her own.
As a school teacher she was well known
In the one-room school just down the street
Where in a few minutes we'll take your feet.

Now move along to the house of Philemon.
Who was another that Mr. Hazen called "son."
He lived past Wallace Road so fine
In his white house built in 1789.
Note the old wooden latch door.
Long ago this house held a small store.

Cross the street head west and you will see
Philemon's second house built with brick in 1823.
It was later owned and farmed by a Lyman
Seek out the community house while we keep on rhymin'

This was once a one room school.
Look inside, isn't it cool?
Picture Ray Miller in a blast from the past.
He is now a farmer but this was once his class.

Note the old wooden latch door. Long ago this house held a small store.

Neighbor Norman Lyman also went here.
His family has been around for many a year.
Both men spent their lives in this community
And have stories to tell of its great unity.

Go back to the road and finish this trip.
Look for a big red barn and be sure not to slip.
As you travel, check those fields out now.
They once held apple trees, sheep and many a cow.

While you cruise on up the hill
Search for 1912 if you will.

Walk to the mailbox, are your feet sore?
Note the tile roof and the green latch door.
Believe it or not, another Hazen house
Given to a daughter and her spouse.
William Pixley was her husband's name
He, of course, was a farmer just the same.

Head back to the middle
Of this historic riddle.
The place where kids once learned
Is hiding the treasure you've earned.

Look around on the ground
Underneath something round
For rewarded you will be
With the treasure you see.

Created by Mary Bouchard's class at Hartford High School in 2003.

"8-25-01
The sun-dappled floor of the forest
so cool
Is the perfect place to be for
this questing fool.
Thank you for this Quest!

—Quest sign-in book

25 Sally's Salamander Meander Quest

1:00

moderate

bring:
boots
field guide

Take Exit 11 from I-91 and head towards White River Junction, turn from Route 5 onto Route 4 west. Follow Route 4 west for 2.1 miles, and then turn left onto Center of Town Rd. After traveling uphill 0.7 miles, turn left onto Kings Highway. Follow for 0.6 miles, and then turn right onto Reservoir Rd. Proceed 0.7 miles until the road ends at the Hurricane Town Forest parking area. Your Quest begins on Old Reservoir Rd, on the right side of the parking area.

natural

Overview

Vernal pools are seasonal wetlands which fill annually from rain, runoff, and rising groundwater. Vernal pools do not have constant inlets or outlets of water; most pools are dry for at least a portion of the year. This dry-wet cycle prohibits fish from becoming permanent residents in the pool, creating a habitat for the successful reproduction of frogs and salamanders whose larvae would normally be preyed upon by fish.

Hurricane Forest and Wildlife Refuge Park is under the caring umbrella of the Hartford Parks and Recreation Department, who encourage us all to get out and enjoy the great parks in Hartford. For more information: http://www.hartford-vt.org/rec0.htm. This Quest and the Natural Communities Quest Series as a whole were made possible by generous support from the Wellborn Ecology Fund of the New Hampshire Charitable Foundation / Upper Valley region.

Clues

Let's take a trip straight down the Old Reservoir Rd.
In search of a vernal pool
Full of salamanders and frogs—both peeper and wood.

You won't be long on your meander
Until on the right you will find
A pool of sorts, upon which to take a gander.

So: Is this the pool for which we drool?
Nope. Held up by this man-made dam,
To call this a vernal pool would be a scam!

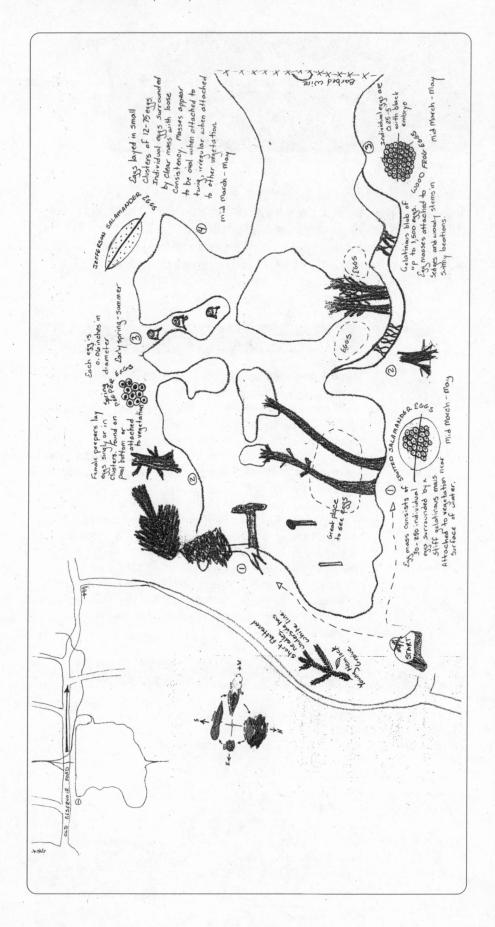

JEFFERSON SALAMANDER EGGS

Eggs layed in small clusters of 12-75 eggs. Individual eggs surrounded by clear mass with loose consistency. Masses appear to be oval when attached to twig, irregular when attached to other vegetation.

mid March - May

④

Barbed wire

Individual eggs are 0.25-5" with black embryo.

③

WOOD FROG EGGS

Gelatinous blob of up to 1,500 eggs. Egg masses attached to sedges and woody stems in swampy locations.

mid March - May

EGGS

②

EGGS

③

Each egg is 0.04 inches in diameter

Early spring - summer

PEEPER EGGS

spring

② Female peepers lay eggs singly or in clusters, found on pool bottom or attached to vegetation.

SPOTTED SALAMANDER EGGS

mid March - May

① Egg mass consists of Spotted Salamander Eggs

Egg mass consists of 30-250 individual eggs surrounded by a stiff gelatinous mass. Attached to vegetation near surface of water.

Great place to see eggs

①

Young Hemlock

Short flattened needles whitish line

START

OLD RESERVOIR RD

N

S

E

Salamander
Photograph by Ted Levin

The name salamander derives from a Greek word meaning "fire lizards." Ancient people linked salamanders to fire as they would crawl out of logs that had been added to fires.

Back on the trail and forward we go
Carry-on with this climb
Putting the reservoir behind.

As you go, don't turn to the left … nor to the right.
Don't be tempted by the next left either.
Another right to avoid is West Side Loop.
Your vernal pool mission carries you straight
To a junction, at which a sign will perform its function.
You've found the green sign, a marker for snowmobiles.
To the right then! And up over the rise.
Just beyond the young hemlocks
Look left, and you'll find a surprise.

Here is the pool which we seek,
Named vernal for the spring treasures
Hidden at its peak.

Start at the mossy stump (found in the open just off the path)
Look out at the pools glow
How is it different from the reservoir seen below?
This pool is a natural depression
Probably caused by a glacier's recession.
You can look for eternity but soon you will see
That no water flows IN from a mountain or OUT to the sea.
Frozen in the winter, thawed in the spring,
Gone in the summer
And returning for fall
The differences in the seasons
Provide this pool's definition and reason.

Turn left from the stump and follow the edge of the pool
Count 42 steps as a general rule.
You'll arrive at a Hemlock attached to the shore
With a mossy "T" extending out from its base.
Look to the right and perhaps you will see

2 poles sticking out of the water
It was right here one March data collection did start.
Hartford Middle School students placed these with care
To discover the patterns of temperature, water and air,
pH, water depth and even live trapping
Help the students create some information tracking.

Continue around this edge,
But, be careful! You might need a leap and a bound
Keep going until you've past the tree that crashed to the ground.

Back to the water's edge
A question does rise:
How does this shallow basin fill to its brim
If there's no water flowing in?
(Which for a vernal pool is the general rule).

Spring and fall rains
And the addition of snow melting
Fill the basin to its brim
Without a stream flowing in.

Pull your thoughts out of the water
Continue to follow the shore.
Two peninsulas of land will soon appear,
One starts narrow and one starts thick
Choose the fat walkway and walk out on it.

Follow the stumps you'll find three in a row.
Circle the second with a look at your feet
And soon you'll find a small treat.

When done with the box place it back in its hole.
Please make sure that it is water tight
And hidden from sight.

Now it is time for the final leg of this wander
Continue along shore with your thoughts to ponder.
Look in the water as you amble and move,
Just be careful not to fall in an unexpected groove.

Stop where you like, what on the bottom do you see?
Everywhere I look leaves have greeted me!
These leaves provide the energy to make this pool function
The base of the food chain, these leaves fuel quite a production.
Combined with bacteria and macro invertebrates
All the nutrients on which an amphibian feeds
Are provided right here for their young, growing needs.

This vernal pool is the key to the amphibian cycle of life:
Egg ⟶ larvae ⟶ juvenile ⟶ adult
At least one, sometimes all stages,
Depend on waters such as these
For their reproduction and protection, if you please.
If it's spring amphibian eggs might be beginning to show.

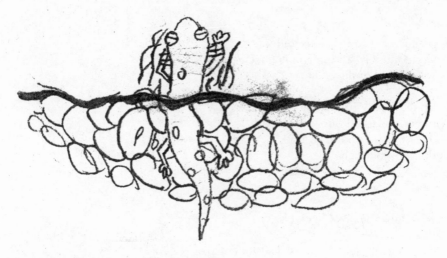

Described as globular, circular, and like jelly,
These eggs are clear or opaque through their bellies.

They are laid in the water, for most but not all,
Piled high and together on the bottom, you will see
Or clustered on the stems of grass they will be.

From here in the spring on the first rainy night
When temperatures creep above 40 degrees—
We could sit in the rain and watch a great sight
The migration of Jefferson's, Spotted and Newts.
Wood frogs and peepers, oh what a hoot!
All seeking this pool to mate and lay eggs.

These adults are returning to complete a circle
Born in the same pool to which they are now migrating
Be careful and watch, but don't keep them waiting.

There are salamanders who like it here in fall.
The Marbled and Dusky prefer their nests dry
Or maybe just damp, but never with water filled high.

A last clue that would confirm this pool be called vernal
Are the obligate species that will stay here eternal.
A look for the mole salamanders
Those which we call Jefferson, marbled, and spotted.
Or listen for songs of wood frogs and peepers at night
The beauty of which takes away any fright.
The presence of these species—considered obligate—
Combined with the seasonal fluctuations of water
Makes us not to forget
That this pool is indeed vernal
And deserves protection for its life eternal.

It's time to return to that mossy stump start.
Along the way take a moment to peak
Under logs you find at your feet.
You're looking for the red back salamander so sweet
The most abundant salamander you'll find in these parts
Its sight is still a great treat.

Just remember to turn logs with great care
And put the logs and salamanders carefully back
Not in a state of disrepair.

From the mossy stump take one last look at the water
Turn your head all the way around.
A pile of brush on the ground
Hides a treasure chest.

Vernal Pool Species Check List

What did YOU see? Hartford MS students have seen:

- ☐ Green frog
- ☐ American toad
- ☐ Spotted salamander
- ☐ Blue spotted salamander
- ☐ Red backed salamander
- ☐ Wood frog
- ☐ Spring peeper
- ☐ Red-spotted newt
  —Red Eft (terrestrial life stage)
  —Aquatic adult
- ☐ Mosquito larvae
- ☐ Diving beetle
- ☐ Daphnia (cladocera)
- ☐ Ribbon snake
- ☐ Backswimmer
- ☐ Isopod
- ☐ Dragonfly nymph
- ☐ Damselfly nymph
- ☐ Water scorpion
- ☐ Caddisfly larvae

_____
_____
_____

This Quest benefited from the participation of Michael Quinn and his students at Hartford Middle School, and Sally Clement, graduate student at Antioch New England.

26 The Haverhill Corner Quest

1:00

easy

Travel on NH Route 10 to the village of Haverhill Corner. Turn east on Court Street (between the two greens) and travel a block and a half, until you see Alumni Hall, with its cupola, on your left. The Quest begins in front of Alumni Hall, and can be completed Tuesday–Sunday from 12–4, mid-June to mid-October.

historical
architectural

Overview

Alumni Hall, the 19th century Grafton County Courthouse and 20th century Haverhill Academy auditorium and gymnasium has been preserved and revitalized through the efforts of Haverhill Heritage, Inc. Haverhill Corner is a place where history, culture, art, the land and community come together. For more information:

www.town.haverhill.nh.us/alumihallmainpag.html.

Along this treasure hunt, you'll learn some of Haverhill Corner's "hidden secrets" as you collect numbers. The number will help you solve a mathematical puzzle and find the hidden treasure box.

Clues

Where four tall columns face the street
Begin our Quest with a counting feat:
Two tall windows point up to the sky.
Count the window panes, it's worth a try.

Number of window panes in the two windows = ☐
A

While this brick building is now called "Alumni Hall"
If its walls could talk, why the stories it would tell.
The Grafton County congregated here
Until 1891 when to the north it disappeared.

West of this is another brick building, now the library.
It tells another hidden story you soon shall read.
This once was the Grafton County Office Building
Housing court records, lawyers and the tax billing.

Note two more chimneys and a seam of brick—
This building was added onto ... can you see the trick?
Count the windows that look shuttered closed.
Secret is they're not real—wonder what you chose.

Number of "shuttered" window on the library = ☐
                                                    B

Turn right and walk east on Court Street to see
Some other historic things that used to be.

Behind a wooden house can you spy a brick addition?
Here was a building with a steep price of admission!

Pass a line of stone posts (one marked low with a "B")
And follow along to our next mystery.

A stump ... a pole ... and then two stone posts.
Stop by the lamp-post to meet your next "ghost."
Behind a wooden house can you spy a brick addition?
Here was a building with a steep price of admission!

This was once the Grafton County "Gaol"
Where one could be held without bail.
New Hampshire's last hanging took place right here
That was long ago – 1868 was the year.

Please take the TOP number off the nearest telephone pole = ☐
                                                                  C

Turn back and start pacing toward Route 10
We'll observe more history on the way again.
Pass 4 stories—three of brick, one of wood.
Next ahead, there's more on both sides of this road.

A stone marker hides down near a garden fence
And tells a part of our story in the past tense.
Judges first owned these twin houses left and right.
Later, guests here were fed well and kept warm at night.

This right one is called Bliss Tavern as we've learned.
Here travelers rested while the fireplaces burned.
The building dates back to Seventeen Ninety
Now a private house with its added property.

Nearby to you is a storm drain—
Count its holes ... yet another number to gain!

The number of holes = ☐
D

Pass 70 south to the end of the common, go right, then
At a spot where there is a green sign cross over Route 10.
Turn direction north, look west and to the ground
Where only a cellar hole of a house may still be found.

That house burned long ago … with a bank and a block of stores.
From here, go a little further, to see the N.H. seal and see more
Of the name "Coos Turnpike" and "Court Street," this had the former.
Where the two met, Charles Johnston called "the corner."

Ahead on your left some chunky stones are all that's left to see
Of buildings lost in another fiery catastrophe.

This treasure hunt is almost as long as it will be
Now turn right toward the towers and see
The dentist's office—once the home of Charles Johnston—
His later home still stands further north, of the north common.

In the figure of Colonel Johnston we can see
An important person in Haverhill's History.
Due to his power, influence and name
A bustling Haverhill rose up here on this plain.

Now see a clock and a sign between two double doors
If you want, you can count numbers, and perhaps floors.
And now onward to the old academy, Pearson Hall,
With its stone steps and columned belfry standing tall.

Now add the four numbers that you have collected,
And then, divide by three, and be a detective.

☐ + ☐ + ☐ + ☐ = ☐
A + B + C + D = E

E divided by 3 = the secret number!

Look for an opening between two standing stones.
Then clockwise around a white fence you should roam.
Count all the posts that you pass, each in turn,
Until you have counted up the secret number you've earned!

There you are. Now take a seat. Isn't this place sweet?
Now, back to Alumni Hall with pillars tall.
Walk in. Greet who is there. Ask and your treasure will appear.

Created by Allinora Rosse, Steve Glazer and Edith Celley in 2002, with support from the Connecticut River Joint Commission's Partnership Program.

27 The Floodplain Quest:

1:00

easy

An Exploration of a Floodplain

bring:
boots
field guide
binoculars
pencil

Take Route 10 to Haverhill. Approximately 1/2 mile north of the village of Haverhill Corner turn west into Bedell Bridge State Park. Park at the bottom of the hill near the barn—your Quest begins there.

natural
historical
vista

Overview

The Connecticut River Valley has been shaped over many thousands of years by the flow of ice and water. First glacial erosion and later river flow deposited a thick layer of sediment on the floodplain, or flat land adjacent to the river banks. Floodplains have been historically important for migrating animals, for Native Americans, and for the early European settlers. To this day, floodplains are prized as important amphibian, bird and mammal habitat, as prime agriculture land, and as natural flood storage.

Clues

From the old stone post look in back of you to see
The end of the forest—a thick tangle of trees.
Then look across west, to a vast, open expanse,
Flat cultivated fields where crops, birds & insects dance.

Follow the road straight ahead between the tilled and planted fields.
Here, a timeless valley tale will soon be revealed.
Seventeen thousand years ago the place that you now walk
Was under water, beneath what is now known as "Lake Hitchcock."

Since the glaciers last retreated more than 120 centuries ago
This land has been continuously shaped by the water's ebb and flow.
Your Quest moves across a river's floodplain: heading west as you go.
The Connecticut River sculpted this earth through cycles of flood, freeze
& flow.

On this broad fertile plain, on the valley's flat floor,
The river can spread where its waters won't roar.
Flooding the fields, bringing richness to soil,
Rather than damage downstream from the roil.

While today this river's flow is altered by many dams
For generations seasonal flooding was the rule of this land.

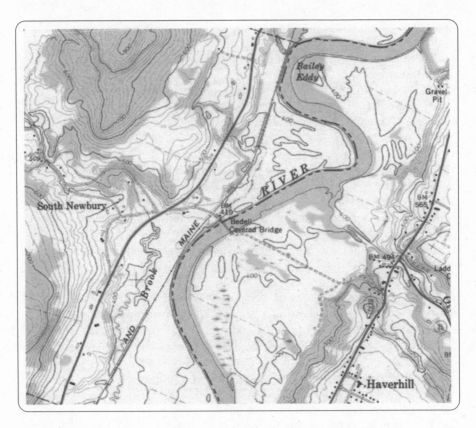

There is archeological evidence and ample documentation
Of more than twenty-five hundred years of human habitation.

In the late 1600s Cowasuck and Sokoki bands
Had seasonal villages and encampments upon these floodplain lands.
With each new flood, a sheet of water covered these broad fields with silt
And on the "river bottom" soil an agricultural tradition was built.

Now the life that inhabits a flood plain has adapted to standing water
   lasting weeks.
So as we pass through the tunnel of trees of the floodplain forest we
   must speak.
Because each year their roots might soak, the only trees that here can thrive
Are trees adapted to saturation—who in standing water can survive.

So, while hiking in the woods we see maple, beech, hemlock and pine
And out here, box elder, silver maple, hackberry and black willow are what
   we find.
Box elders often have multiple trunks; hackberry bark has narrow ridges,
   wide furrows.
Silver maple bark is in long, narrow flakes; black willow has scaly,
   flat-topped ridges.

Before the wooden sign you might see "pot holes" of standing water on
   both sides.
In these temporary, seasonal pools many different species live and thrive.
If you have a bit of time to explore—and a good pair of high rubber boots—
Carefully explore the diverse life forms that live amongst the saturated roots.

River otter, mink, muskrat and beaver, even leopard frogs and spotted
salamanders.
Migrating birds love this kind of place, too. Perhaps you'll see them on
your meander.
Resident birds you might hear ... yellow warblers: "Sweet sweeter
than sweet."
Common yellowthroats: "Whichity whichity whichity." Red-eyed vireo's
nasal "quee."

The reason that we can enjoy this place and conduct our floodplain
investigation
Is the efforts of NH "Fish" & US "Wildlife," and NH "Parks & Recreation."
Now you approach the Bedell Bridge site, a place that has seen oh-so-
many bridges.
Storms have washed and blown them away over 2-1/2 centuries of settler
villages.

The last bridge? It blew away on September 14, 1979.
But even without a river crossing a stop here is well worth your time.
Watch the river flowing south. Look and listen for birds in the sky.
Think of thousands of years of history, of people and animals passing by.

The treasure you seek—the floodplain—has been found
In the flat landscape embracing you all around.
But to find your Valley Quest treasure box?
Carefully search the bridge foundation rocks!

Floodplain Quest Species Check List

What did YOU see?

- Box Elder
- Hackberry
- River Otter
- Muskrat
- Wood Frog
- Yellow warbler
- Common Yellowthroat
- Snow Goose
- Spotted Sandpiper
- Common Snipe
- Hooded Merganser
- Bobolink
- Coyote
- Leopard Frog

- Silver Maple
- Black Willow
- Mink
- American Beaver
- American Toad
- Spotted Salamander
- Catbird
- White-tailed Deer
- Turkey Vulture
- Wood Duck
- Red-tailed Hawk
- Killdeer
- Racoon
- _____
- _____

The Floodplain Quest at Bedell Bridge and the Wellborn Ecology Fund Natural
Communities Quest Series as a whole were made possible by generous support from the
Wellborn Ecology Fund of the New Hampshire Charitable Foundation / Upper Valley region:
www.nhcf.org.

28 Horatio Colony House Museum Quest

:15

easy

bring:
compass

The Horatio Colony House is located at 199 Main Street in Keene, NH. Go north on Main Street from the intersection of routes 12 and 101. Pass Keene State College, go through the roundabout, and then look for the Horatio Colony House, a yellow house—on the left. (Note: the post office is across the street.)

NOTE: For more Keene Quests visit our online Quests page at: www.vitalcommunities.org

historical

Overview

This 1806 Federal style house was the home of Horatio Colony, descendent of one of Keene's historic industrialist families. The old-time New England home is filled with original family furnishings and fabulous collections, which offer a gracious view of a vanishing lifestyle of culture, refinement and travel. A beautiful city garden frames the house with perennial borders that provide antique grace and an array of color throughout the season. The museum is open for tours May 1 to October 15, Wednesdays through Sundays from 11:00 AM to 4:00 PM. Guided tours are offered free to the public. Questers are welcomed any day of the week. For more information, visit: www.horatiocolonymuseum.org

Clues

1. At his house of sticks you will start your Quest.
   It was built in 1806—now go on, do your best.

2. Look at the door and see an object 100 years old.
   You'll see the word "Colony" or so we are told.

3. On the sides of the door are windows with designs.
   Through each window the sunlight shines.
   In 1806 they needed the light,
   No electricity was there to make things bright.

4. Go left, around the corner a faucet you will see.
   The animal on this lives in a tree.
   Horatio Colony added this spout
   In the 1940's to get some water out.

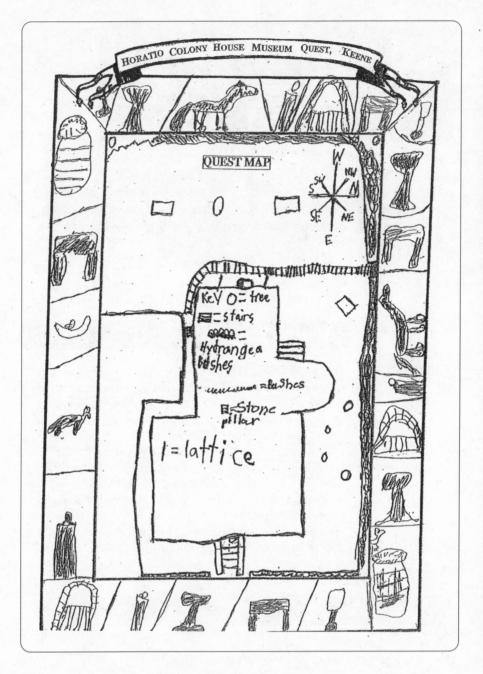

5. If you're at the bird faucet then walk west,
   Until you see two pots with birds at rest.

6. Turn to the left and leave the terra cotta pots behind.
   Above the door an eagle holding two flags you will find.

7. Turn left and leave to see a set of double doors,
   At one time inside you'd find a carriage on the floor.

8. You'd tie your horse to this iron ring,
   Attached to the granite rectangular sort of thing.

9. Walking straight to the narrow brick path can be fun,
   It's only wide enough to go one by one.

10. Leave the bricks that form a path.
    You'll find an iron horse that probably needs a bath.
    Upon his back please wipe your feet.
    Get rid of the dirt you collected on the street.

Leave the bricks that form a path ... Find an iron horse that needs a bath.

11. From the horse about face turn.
    Horatio would plant flowers in the urn.
    On both sides there's a place to sit.
    You can take a break, but you still can't quit.

12. There are window shutters on the back door,
    That start from the top and go down to the floor.
    The shutters act like a screen,
    That keeps bugs out, not to be seen.

13. Go on the brick path heading north, then turn east,
    This is a place you could have an outdoor feast.
    This screened addition was built in 1899,
    By a woman named Emeline.

14. From the screened porch walk northwest,
    To the gate to end your Quest!

Created by Mrs. Field and the Wheelock School 3rd grade in 2002.

29 Stonewall Farm Quest

:45

easy

bring:
compass

At the 'T' intersection where Route 101 ends and Routes 9, 10, and 12 combine to by-pass Keene, take Route 9 west toward Brattleboro. About three miles later, turn right on the Chesterfield Road. Travel up Chesterfield Rd. for a mile and turn right into Stonewall Farm Driveway. Follow the drive up to the parking lot.

natural

Overview

Do you remember when milk was delivered to your doorstep with that thick layer of cream on top? When sheep grazed throughout the fields of New England? When vegetables were picked fresh and you knew where they came from? Step into the past, present and future of agriculture and your environment with a visit to Stonewall Farm, a non-profit, member-supported educational facility and working dairy located in Keene. A wide variety of programs, workshops and special events are made available to the public throughout the year.

Clues

Welcome to Stonewall! We all say 'Hello!'
With a cluck, and a neigh, and a moo, don't you know.
Begin your Quest looking all around, high and low
Do you see some birds clucking? There you should go!

Our chickens are an organic laying flock. They are a mix of different breeds. The most interesting breed is the Turken, which is the chicken with a bare neck. This breed actually has fewer feathers making them easy to pluck. Can you spot a Turken in our flock? The flock is mostly female chickens, called hens. But there is a rooster here too. Can you find him? The rooster watches over the hens while they scratch and peck for bugs all day. He will settle disputes between hens and cluck at them to run for cover if he senses danger. He'll also cluck to his favorite hens when he finds a good spot for eating. Watch and listen closely and you might hear him talking to his "girls."

Just a little bit further you'll see lots of fluff
The cuddliest of creatures. We can't love them enough!
Next door are the birds that quack but don't cluck
No, not a chicken. You're right ... it's a duck!

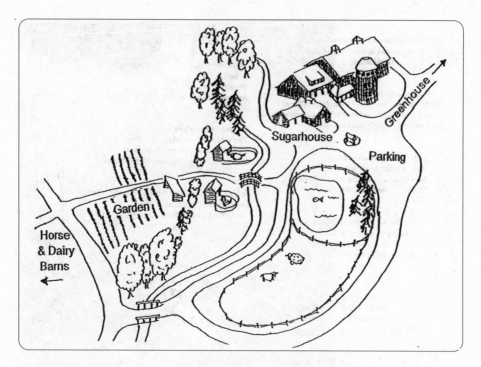

Our rabbits are Angora rabbits, a breed specifically raised for their luxurious fiber. We harvest their fiber by simply giving them a haircut every 3 months. A healthy, high producing Angora can provide nearly a pound of wool a year. Angora wool is lighter and warmer than sheep wool. Angora rabbits have very specific diets to help them digest the wool they swallow when grooming. Please do not upset their tummies by feeding them grass or other items. Careful! Your finger looks a lot like a carrot and if you hold it out to them they might take a nibble to see what sort of treat you are offering!

Now for a hike. Head east down the road
Keep your eyes open for birds or a toad
This is the wetland. There are lots who live here:
Beaver, frogs, turtles and even a deer.
Follow the signs, on the right they should be
Turn off the road and a big tree you'll see
Give her a hug and admire her height
Then on to the boardwalk off to the right

The large tree is called a Bull Pine. Bull Pines are created when a Bull Weevil (a tiny insect) burrows in and damages the upper most bud on a pine tree. The tree can no longer grow up, so it puts all it's energy into growing out, making an interesting branching structure. This tree is probably close to 200 years old and has been here as long as this property has been farmed, maybe even longer. It is much older than the trees surrounding it because all the other trees were cut down at one time for lumber. This tree was left standing because its unusual branching made it a lousy choice to harvest.

This wetland was created by beaver several years ago. Notice on the right of the boardwalk the old beaver dam running along the edge of the pond. If you look, you can probably spy some branches that have been chewed on by beavers. Move quietly and keep your eyes open and you may spy frogs or salamanders living in this wetland. There are also plenty of bugs such as water striders, dragonflies and other aquatic insects.

Sheep and Lambs
Photograph by Jon
Gilbert Fox

Stonewall Farm is home to many animals. The Small Animal Barn was renovated in 2003–2004, and allows visitors a chance to mingle with the animals that live here.

Now back to the road from the direction you came
Past the big building. It all looks the same
Keep walking the road with the brook on your side
The pond on your left to where more animals reside

Our sheep and goats are very friendly and love a taste of dandelion or long grass picked from the side of the path. The sheep are sheared each spring and their wool used for our educational programs. Sheep wool is a popular fiber for making clothing because its insulation structure makes it warm even when wet, and helps keep you cool in hot weather. It is also flame resistant and resists mildew.

Back a few paces, now cross the brook
No time for playing, in the garden have a look
Lots of herbs are growing. Smell their sweet smell
Some crops and some flowers. Do you know their names well?
Walk down the rows, and you might see something you know
Vegetables and fruits, so this is how they grow!

The first rows you come to, farthest from the road, are our herbs. Here you can find lavender, rosemary, basil, oregano, catnip, chives and other herbs. You can enjoy the aroma of many herbs by gently brushing your hand against them and cupping your hand to your nose. Try brushing rosemary, lavender or thyme. You'll find the mint growing near the brush between the playground and garden. Pick 1 leaf per person and smell or taste the mint. All plants in the mint family have square stems. Feel the stem of the mint plants, then see if you can find another 'mint cousin'. (Hint: cats really love a 'mint cousin' herb!)

Let's keep traveling, lots more to see
We must cross the road so look carefully
Now on to the barn and, whoa! You can see
Some big stalls and yards. For whom might they be?

Their manure is precious. We pile it out back
And turn it into compost: rich, moist & black.

The farm is home to several private horses owned by staff members, as well as the farm's own team of Belgian draft horses, Prince and Magic. Prince and Magic pull our wagon and sleigh for hayrides, and also help with farm work such as plowing fields, hauling trees, and harvesting potatoes. Watch the fence near the horse pen. It is electric and can give a startling zap! If Prince and Magic are not in their pen when you arrive, they are most likely working or enjoying a day in the pasture eating grass.

Find another barn, this one also is red
The smell is quite strong many have said
Here you'll see where the ladies each have their own stall
They give milk twice daily, but that's not all!
Their manure is precious. We pile it out back
Turn it to compost, and then it turns black
But we're not done with it yet. You know where it goes?
Onto our fields and our gardens where everything grows!

Our newest dairy girls live in the calf huts in front of the dairy barn. Here they are well socialized by visitors so they grow up to trust people and look forward to a friendly visit. A cow which is not full grown, but no longer considered a calf, is called a heifer. Our heifers live in the small shed behind the dairy barn. Some heifers spend the summer in a pasture way up the hill.

Between the dairy barn and the heifer barn walk back and you'll find the manure pit. Don't fall in! This manure is hauled to the other end of the farm where it is laid out in long rows in the sun to compost.

When a heifer is a little over a year old, she is bred by artificial insemination. Cows have a 9 month gestation, and at about 2 years old they give birth and begin their career as one of our beloved dairy cows. Each cow has her own stall in the dairy barn. The plaque above their stall has information about each cow such as her parents' names, how many calves she's had, how much milk she's produced and the fat and protein content of her milk. It also states when her last calf was born (fresh date), and the due date for her next calf if she is expecting.

Now back to the start, past the garden and brook
Turn left at the pond, and ahead of you look
Ahead is the Sugarhouse. We make sweet syrup, you know
Behind is your treasure. Look high and low!
Time to celebrate, you're finished, you're done!
We hope you learned something, and had lots of fun!

We generally make syrup in March, and celebrate the sugaring season each year with our Sap Gathering event, held the 3rd Saturday in March. For more information about Sap Gathering call the farm. We'd love to tell you all about it!

Created by the Stonewall Farm education staff and revised by Marci Birkes in 2007.

30

1:30

1764—Old King's Highway Quest

easy

bring:
boots
field guide

Take exit 19 off of Interstate 89. Turn west off of the exit ramp. At first light, turn up Poverty Lane and go .9 mile. Parking spots available on left at memorial plaque.

NOTE: For more Lebanon Quests visit our online Quests page at: www.vitalcommunities.org

natural
historical

Overview

This Quest introduces the Old King's Highway, maintained by the City of Lebanon's Recreation and Parks Department. The Recreation and Parks Department's goal is to provide a variety of quality recreation programs and special events, and to effectively develop and maintain recreation facilities for the community's use and enjoyment, which together enhance the quality of life for all residents of the City of Lebanon and surrounding community.

Clues

1. Begin at the rock with a weathered old plaque
    And follow a road that will take you way back
    To a time when the King of England
    Aspired to rule over all this green land.

    King George the 3rd once gave this road its name
    And some of Lebanon's earliest settlers to this place came.
    Walk straight on ahead until you come to a trail
    Stay left on "King's Highway" and you will not fail.

2. This road was planned to be 9 rods wide
    How far would that be from side to side?
    (Here's a clue: one rod = 16.5 feet)
    Most early road builders preferred the hilltops
    As the ground was drier in well-drained spots.

3. Step on a large rock in the middle of the road
    Moving all of these rocks must have been a heavy load.
    Stonewalls line this road, they were moved by hand
    To clear land for crops, hayfields or pastureland.

    Walk on for a while and try to imagine this place
    200 or more years ago, with a different pace

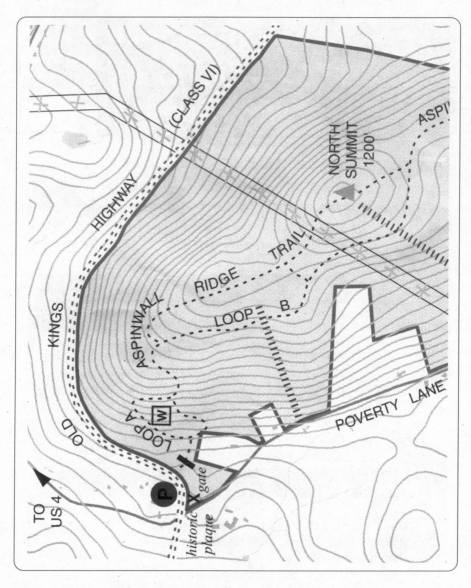

… Horse-drawn carriages rolling by with grace
An animal pound was once located at this place …

In 1767, 162 folks called Lebanon home
By year 2000, to 12,568 that number had grown
Carry on down this road; you don't have to go fast
And under a fallen tree you may have to pass.

A committee of proprietors came here to this spot
And divided this land into 100 acre lots.
Families moved here from far and from near
The Aspinwall family farmed here for 95 years.

4. Walk a ways up the road and look for the snag of a tree
    It's up on the right, and it is full of holes, how can that be?
    A treat for the woodpeckers, when they dig in the wood
    It is bugs they are looking for, would that taste good?

Along this very road was Lebanon's first school
Built in 1768 out of logs, it must have been cool.
Walk past a big tree, broken in half with a thump
And then look out for a tree growing out of stump!

5. Yellow birch trees can take root without much bother
    Ahead on our Quest, you will see more than one other.
    Go on, more than 100 steps to a tree that curves out on the right
    Check out all of the holes, what a sight.

In 1767, 162 folks called Lebanon home. By year 2000, to 12,568 that number had grown.

These were made by a sapsucker looking for sap
And behind in the woods, another woodpecker's trap
Keep journeying along and find a beech tree with bumpy bark
Nectria disease causes this bumpiness, you may see more in this park.

6. Find a tree on its side with roots like a star
    You will know you have come far
    On the left, find a tree that looks like it's growing out of the air
    With a rock stuck in its roots, how unfair

    The other yellow birch tree we promised you'd see?
    What a crazy root system on this neat tree!
    Further ahead on the right,
    Some barbed wire is in sight

    In the late 19th century it was added for clout.
    The wire either helped keep animals in or animals out
    Cross over a brook in the road that is fine
    And pass a giant majestic white pine

7. Walk on into the sun and under some power lines
    A fine view of Mt. Ascutney waits up the hill for another time.
    Look at the stonewalls on each side of this road
    Erosion has caused this road to go low

8. This royal road is now only a trail,
    Along this road, a car or wagon could no longer sail
    Walk under a tree that crosses this highway so good
    Cross another brook and notice stonewalls going up in the woods

    Deacon James Perley Farnum (and family beyond him)
    Had a farm on this road until 1921
    Walk on until you see stonewalls getting taller
    Your treasure is close, but you don't need to holler.

Between the two beautiful walls on your left
Where people and animals walked through the years
Look down low on the left
And spy the box with much deft.

Sign your name in the book and collect your stamp impression
Hope you enjoyed your trip back in time to early Lebanon.

Created by Laura Dintino for the UVTA Trails Day Celebration in 2007.

"I love trees."
— Quest sign-in book

31

Chaffee Sanctuary Quest

:45

An Exploration Through an Alder Swamp

easy

bring:
boots
binoculars
field guide

Take the Thetford Exit (14) from I-91, and follow 113 east to Lyme. From Lyme Village (just beyond the green) follow Route 10 north for 1.7 miles. The entrance to the Chaffee Sanctuary is on the left, just beyond the entrance to Post Pond, immediately after the bridge guard railing. Park in the grass lot where this Quest begins.

NOTE: For more Lyme Quests visit our online Quests page at: www.vitalcommunities.org

natural

Overview

The Alder swamp is a common shrub-dominated wetland found in every town in the Upper Valley region. Alder swamps often occur alongside lakes, ponds, rivers and streams. Because they are often flooded—and their soils are saturated with water—these swamps favor plant species that can tolerate submerged roots, like speckled alder, a variety of willows, and red-osier dogwood. These swamps are important habitat for a variety of insects, birds, mammals, reptiles and amphibians The Chaffee Wildlife Sanctuary, named for the 1st director of the Montshire Museum, is managed by the Lyme Conservation Commission, whose mission is to protect wildlife habitat and native riparian vegetation, particularly for birds; guard water quality in the brooks and pond; and provide low-impact public recreational access to wetlands and trails.

Clues

A sign ,"Robert G. Chaffee Wildlife Sanctuary" says this is the place.
Proceed to the trail marker and to the right you will face.
As you walk along this mowed, grassy trail,
Look to the open field, for it offers a tale.

Can you spy the common milkweed plant?
In this meadow, it is anything but scant.
The monarch butterfly relies specifically on its leaves,
Where it lays its eggs and on which the larvae then feed.

Now approach a curve, and you can plainly see,
Something tall and wooden that is not a tree.
Follow under lines that are attached up high,
Listen carefully for running water, if it's not too dry.

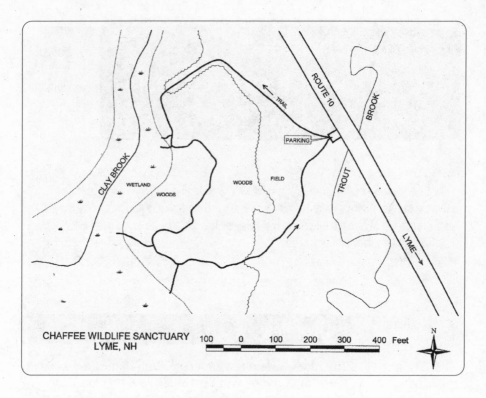

CHAFFEE WILDLIFE SANCTUARY
LYME, NH

100   0   100   200   300   400 Feet

As you're lured by the sound, look for a small sign.
To Clay Brook you will go, to behold an ingenious design.
Beavers built this dam with limbs and sticks,
Creating this pond where many species now mix.

180 degree turn, onward, let the journey continue,
Notice thickets of shrubs and the signs of beaver chew.
These are speckled alder, which designate this wetland community,
Food and shelter for grouse and woodcock, it provides necessity.

Now approach a bridge made of wooden planks,
Lucky 13 in all and for these we give thanks.
To the hands whose effort put them here,
Because of their work, soggy boots are no fear.

The wet ground reminds us of the habitat we're in,
Since it's near a stream, we call it riparian.
A great place to find a diversity of lives,
This ecosystem provides all the elements in which they thrive.

Keep a watchful eye and keen ears as you follow along,
And you may be treated to a variety of song.
Many birds nest here or pay a visit to this marsh,
Where they find food, water, and shelter from the harsh.

Some species that are common for you to hear or see,
Include the yellow-rumped warbler, catbird, and black-capped chickadee.
And perhaps—if you visit as the day fades into the night—
You may be treated to the display of a male woodcock in flight.

Milkweed
Photograph by Ted Levin

Milkweed seeds are attached to soft filaments known as silk (or floss), which allow seeds to be dispersed over great distances by wind. An experiment to try: How many seeds are in a milkweed pod?

When you come to yet another sign for Clay Brook,
Follow the arrow and go have a look.
Several wooden boxes appear along the waters edge,
To entice the handsome wood duck to nest among the sedge.

Take in the view and then about-face
And onward to where the sign is in place.
From here we continue our journey down the trail
Next stop, "Little Post Pond," will soon avail.

Raccoon, otter, beaver and deer,
    If you are watchful and quiet,
their presence is near.

Gaze out from the boardwalk at this lush wetland site,
For many kinds of wildlife, the conditions are just right.
Raccoon, otter, beaver and deer,
If you are watchful and quiet, their presence is near.

Yes, you guessed it, to the main drag you go,
For our Quest has so much more for you to know.
As you approach a stand of tall pine,
Look for its needles, which reveal the kind.

Count 5 in a bundle, that means it's a white,
They provide shade, yet let in enough light.
For the ferns you see thriving in the soil below,
It is a moist, protected niche they require to grow.

Now look about you for small trees other than pine,
What you seek has opposite branching, straight across in line.
The red maple has simple leaves, 3 points, and edges with teeth
Where these trees thrive there is usually poor soil underneath.

Look ahead towards the light, the field plainly in view,
In its direction you'll travel, your Quest nearly through.
But first you must find the location of the treasure,
In doing so, I know you will find such pleasure.

It is a pine whose trunk branches thrice that you seek
Once you spot it, look to its crotch for a peek.
Take a moment to sign in, sketch, or write.
I hope this Quest has provided some useful insight.

And now, as you undoubtedly know,
It is back to the parking area you will go.
Admire the old field as you make your way back,
It's managed so wildlife will feel less impact.

Chaffee Sanctuary Species Check List

What did YOU see?

❑ Milkweed	❑ Monarch Butterfly
❑ American Beaver	❑ Speckled Alder
❑ Ruffed Grouse	❑ American Woodcock
❑ Yellow-rumped Warbler	❑ Catbird
❑ Black-capped Chickadee	❑ Wood Duck
❑ Raccoon	❑ American Bittern
❑ White-tailed Deer	❑ White Pine
❑ Red Maple	❑ Otter
❑ _____	❑ _____

The Chaffee Sanctuary Quest and the Wellborn Ecology Fund Natural Communities Quest Series were made possible by generous support from the Wellborn Ecology Fun of the New Hampshire Charitable Foundation / Upper Valley region. For more information: www.nhcf.org

Created by Andrea Lewis, with assistance from Bill Shepard and the Connecticut River Birding Trail.

32

2:00

Pinnacle Hill Quest

moderate

bring:
field guide

Take Route 10 north out of Lyme. Just after you pass Post Pond (on the left), turn right on Pinnacle Hill Road. After 1 mile turn right on Cutting Hill Lane and then bear right at the fork in the road. You can park in the turn around, where Cutting Hill Lane is blocked, just past the grey cape on the left.

natural
vista

Overview

The upper most portion of this land (the actual Pinnacle itself) has been conserved by the Upper Valley Land Trust. UVLT is a regional land conservancy working to protect farmland, forests, wetlands and waterways, wildlife habitat, trails and scenic areas in the Vermont and New Hampshire towns of the Upper Valley. Since 1985, UVLT has protected over 380 parcels of land encompassing more than 34,000 acres. UVLT is a non-profit organization and is supported primarily by contributions from local individuals and businesses. For more information visit www.uvlt.org, or contact UVLT at 603-643-6626.

Clues

Start your hike by following the old road uphill.
Keep the meadow on your left.

Soon you will be joined by a stone wall on the right.
Think how much work it was for the farmers to build this stone wall!

Wow!
Look at the views!

As you climb the hill, the road passes between large 3-trunked oak trees. Further along, watch for evidence of the windstorm of April 2007.

Soon after the stone wall becomes close at hand, on the right, you reach the place you will leave old Cutting Hill Lane.

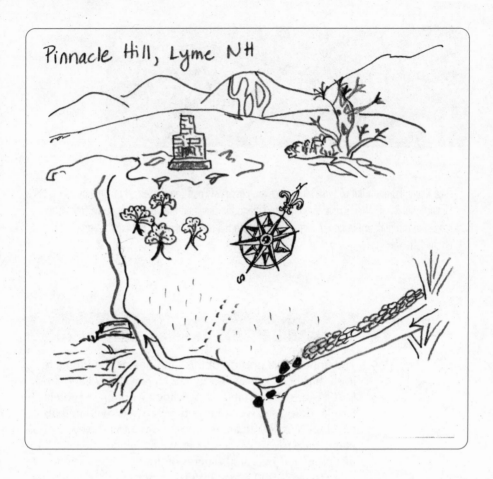

Pinnacle Hill, Lyme NH

On the right is a row of five large boulders and a gate with wooden posts.
Turn right, passing between the boulders.

Look to the right. Can you find the spot where Mrs. Cutting used to live
  in her house?
The house is gone, but if you look carefully you can find the old cellar hole.

Look to the left. Can you find a path along the line of trees and up the
  big meadow? That's the way to go!

Walk uphill along the meadow.
Can you see the footsteps of other visitors?

When you reach the stone wall on the other side of the meadow
you have to find a way through—search at the left end!

Keep climbing along the edge of the next meadow,
keeping the forest (or what used to be a forest!) on your left.

Wow!
Look at the views of Vermont out across the meadow.

At the far left corner of this meadow you turn left, and climb steeply uphill.
Follow this trail upwards as it bends to the right.

You encounter and old apple orchard just before the summit.
Can you find any tasty apples? The deer love to eat them.

On the summit is a stone chimney—all that is left of what was once a
  hilltop house.
Find the three chains that once held down the cabin; what were they for?

Can you see Smarts Mountain and Dartmouth Skiway to the east?
Can you see Post Pond and the Connecticut River valley to the west?

To find the box, stand at the fireplace and face Post Pond.
Turning slowly to your left, look for a cluster of birch trees at the edge of
  the clearing.

Search for the box there,
Floating high in the air.

Created by the Crossroads Academy 5th grade, 2008 with help from David Kotz and
Mark Valence.

"My first bear sighting here ... a big, dark form helping him/herself
to apples high in the tree on the east side of the Pinnacle."

—Quest sign-in book

33 Porter Cemetery Quest

:45

bring:
compass

easy

historical

Two miles north of Lyme on Route 10, turn west onto North Thetford Road. Follow this road to the end, and at River Road turn right (north). After 0.4 miles park on the side of the road at the intersection of River Road and Gregory Road—your Quest begins here.

Clues

Start at the intersection of "Gregory" & "River."
An event here in 1944 made the whole town shiver.
Mr. Frank Gregory's farm here met with disaster,
As a fire's orange flames burned higher and faster.

The house and red barn burned down to the ground;
But thankfully, there were three men around.
Frank Gregory, Elbridge Jenks & Howard DeGoosh
Worked together to save all the cows that they could.

For the next chapter of our story, walk north up River Road.
At the white house the next episode will unfold.

Asubah Heaton's story is with us still, Recorded in "The Writings of Pony Hill"

In 1794, eight Lyme school districts were created;
And here, land from the Stetson Farm was donated.

This house became the "Stetson School" of District # 7
Built by John Tomson for $136 back in 1807.
Lillian Gregory (Mrs. Elbridge Jenks) started here in 1919.
She is the 2nd generation of Gregory's that we've seen.

Continue on River Road, keeping the barbed wire on your right,
Until a driveway on the left comes clearly into sight.
Up the driveway, about 68 paces hence,
You'll see a small plaque on a white fence.

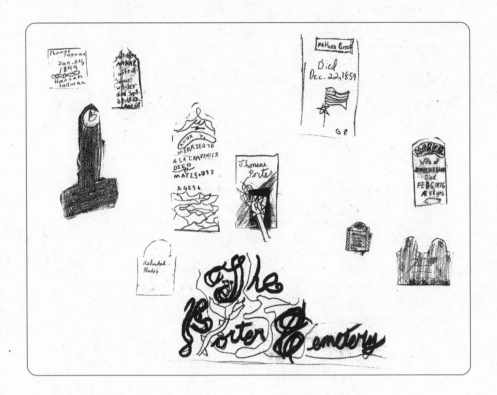

Enter the cemetery gate, and go up the hill 20 paces towards the river.
Look right to see leaning David Turner … there's is no need to shiver!
Look west, towards Thetford, and see High Peak.
Now, continue on your journey to the treasure you seek.

See the North Thetford Church steeple in the southwest?
10 steps towards it to a "death mask" is your test.
Continuing south, count 6 stones on your right and look to the ground.
Thomas Tallman's grave—that's what you should have found.

Face due west and look for a stone.
There you will find Hannah Tallman standing alone.
The cemetery's tallest grave is clearly in sight.
The Wadleigh hand is pointing up to heaven's light.

With your back to the north edge of David Tallman's stone,
40 steps to the north is where we want you to roam.
There, four arched willow stones
Mark the Turner Family's tomb.

Back toward the south, laying flat upon the ground
A cracked gravestone will certainly be found.
This stone has 2 "candy canes"
And an angel up above Abraham's name.

Now look to the biggest of all the pine trees,
You may see it sway in a penetrating breeze.
On the way there find the Porters' 4 "half circle" graves.
Go there, friend, if you are really brave.

You've visited the Turners & the Tallmans;
And the Porters and the Perkins.
Further south, uphill from 2 small pines
Asubah Heaton is the one you will find.

Asubah Heaton's Story is with us still,
Recorded in "The Writings of Pony Hill."
Written by a 3rd generation of Gregory,
Listen to Vivian Gregory Piper's story:

> *When Vivian and her sister Edna were kids,*
> *They had lots of chores, as all the farm kids did.*
> *One night they went searching for Curly Nose, a cow—*
> *Who should have been in the barn, but wasn't somehow.*
>
> *They searched for Curly Nose, round and round,*
> *And then stopped to rest in this burial ground.*
> *An incredible story began to unfold …*
> *And at a nearby stump the rest of this tale is told.*

Created by Steve Dayno and the Lyme 4th grade in 2003; and revised in 2007–2008.

"The steam was flowing
The trail was nice going
Christian made it here
Found the box, and was of good cheer."

— Quest sign-in book

34 The Bridge & Beyond Quest

1:00

easy

bring:
field guide

From West Lebanon take 12A south past shopping plazas. Turn left on the Brook Road. Follow the Brook Road into Meriden. Turn right on Bonner Road and then right again, into the Plainfield School. This Quest begins at the school.

natural

Overview

This Quest is written in haiku, a Japanese verse form. The three lines have 5, 7 and 5 syllables respectively.

Clues

Welcome to this Quest
Written by our 4th grade class:
Composed in haiku.

From our school's front door
Please go to the parking lot
And then the garage.

OUR FIELD
Follow the path towards woods
Stop in the middle and look.
Listen: field haiku.

Small dragonfly nymph
Swimming under the water
Watch out for the fish

*I sweep through the grass
Try to catch colorful bugs
Sweep again, no bugs.*

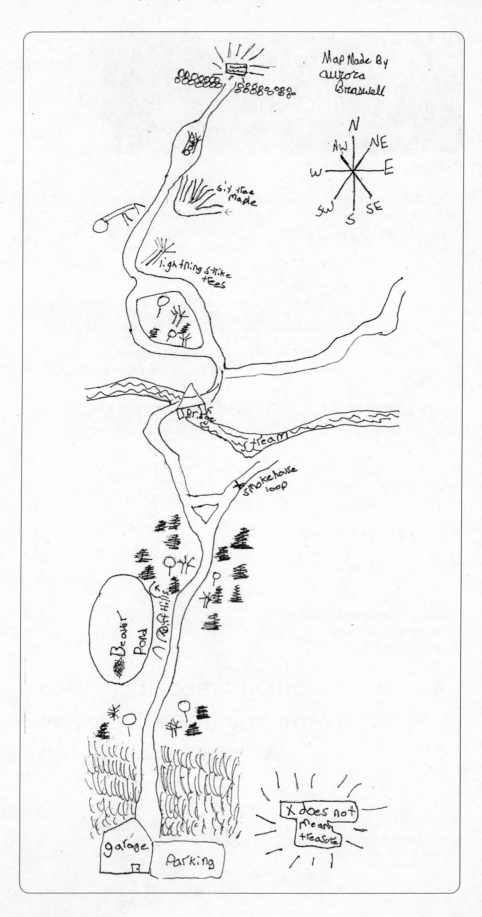

Map Made By aurora Braswell

six tree maple

lightning strike tees

N
NW NE
W E
SW SE
S

bridge

stream

smokehouse loop

Beaver Pond

garage

Parking

X does not mean treasure

The grass smells leafy
The wind makes dandelions fly
Soldier bugs eat slugs.

Out looking for bugs
I caught a common housefly.
The moth won't eat it.

We caught at the field.
We found a lot of insects
Then we let them go.

The edge of the field
What a peaceful place to be
It helps me feel calm.

Take last look around
See field, field edge and forest
Three habitats merge

INTO THE WOODS
Walk down woodsy path
Look! Stumps marked with beaver teeth
Pine needles on ground.

Climb up a dirt bank
Look for beaver's stick-built hut
Return to wood's path.

At fork look for sign
Don't take Smokehouse Loop; bear left.
See bridge through tall trees?

AT BLOOD'S BROOK
Watch the flowing stream
Listen to its babbling
Explore, listen, learn.

We studied the stream:
Temperature, flow, who lives here.
Hear *Blood's Brook* haiku:

The water would flow
Shiny wet rocks in the stream
I think there were fish.

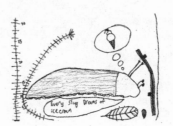

The brown newt swims fast.
The green trees sway in the rain.
The black bug—long, big.

Small dragonfly nymph
Swimming under the water
Watch out for the fish!

The water hit rocks.
I throw big rock in water.
Splash went the big rock.

Ferns blow in the wind.
Swish wish ferns blow in the wind.
Ferns live in peace, mmmmm.

Mosquitoes buzzing.
Buzzing up, down and all around!
Soon they will bite me!

Over the river
Walk across the Townsend Bridge.
Beware of the troll!

Walk straight from the bridge
At the fork, go left, right now
Take no Townsend Loop.

Go straight toward the sign
Walk where the sign says to go
Pace toward the arrow.

Look for the skinned tree
Walk across the bridge of logs
Ahead beaver marks.

Then go straight from there
Seventy-three steps to stone.
Enjoy the green ferns.

THE COOL FOREST
Here we studied things
That inhabit the forest.
Now, forest haiku:

Green ferns growing here
In the sunlight birds are singing.
Trees grow new fresh leaves.

Spring hemlock fresh air
Bright green trilliums swaying
Loud morning birds chirp.

Black cherry trees sway
Cloudy weather in my sight
Peaceful birds fly by.

Trees, beautiful folk
One, a soft-skinned little girl
Pigtailed leafy hair.

I like hemlock cones.
The small cones are on the ground.
The cones are pretty.

The eft is winding
Under pine and maple trees
Orange on brown dirt.

From the mossy rock
Follow to twin hemlock trees:
One alive, one dead.

"Earl," the living tree
Has sapsucker holes in it.
"Al" is the dead one.

Across, yellow birch
A few steps … tall tree with scar.
Did lightning do this?

Keep on. On the left
You'll find a surprise: a burl
Can you find some more?

Continue to walk.
Find a six-trunked maple tree
And then walk some more,

Through a fern-filled space.
Next look for beaver signs.
An oak blocks your way!

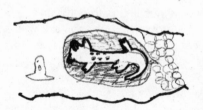

Go around the tree,
Continue to the stonewall.
Your treasure is near!

The wizened old tree
Twisted and old with crannies
Guarding the stone wall.

Go to the left wall.
Look behind fallen bark.
You will find our box!

The Quest is now done.
Sign in! Tell us you were here!
Re-hide for others.

Created by Mrs. Pullen's Fourth Grade Class at Plainfield Elementary School in 2007.

35 Sargent / Hayes Farm Quest

1:30

moderate

bring:
boots
field guide

natural
historical

This Quest begins at the bottom of North Pleasant Street in New London. Take Exit 12 off I-89 north or south. Take Newport Road east into New London. Remain on this road, which becomes Main Street. After passing the fire station on your left, turn left on North Pleasant Street at a yellow blinking light. Follow North Pleasant down the hill to the base, where you will cross a small bridge over a brook. The road becomes Lakeshore Drive at this point. Park in the parking area on your right immediately after the bridge. Your Quest begins here!

Clues

1. Of the "pioneer" marker take note
    Between pasture and road
    Beginning in the wooded glen
    A trail sign is found within.

2. Follow needled path between
    Moss-grown stumps and rock wall seen
    Bearing left at the three-trunked pine
    "Coco's Path" you shall find.

3. At the rocky crossing, look right if you choose;
    Frogs and salamanders breed in this springtime pool.
    Cross old stone wall to brook and clearing
    Splashing water is what you're hearing.

4. Crossing the stream to sandy cover,
    Find there a mossy border.
    Cobble shore, sand and gravel,
    Rolled by Great Brook, onward you travel.

5. Stand still there and look for a mighty birch (yellow).
    Brook forks ahead, to the right you follow
    Toward a pool deep where fish try to hide.
    Continue along brook, white blaze ahead, trail to your right.

6. Your Quest continues along this wooded trail
    Under hemlocks tall but not frail.
    When small, these trees grew in the shade
    Of other trees, long to rest laid.

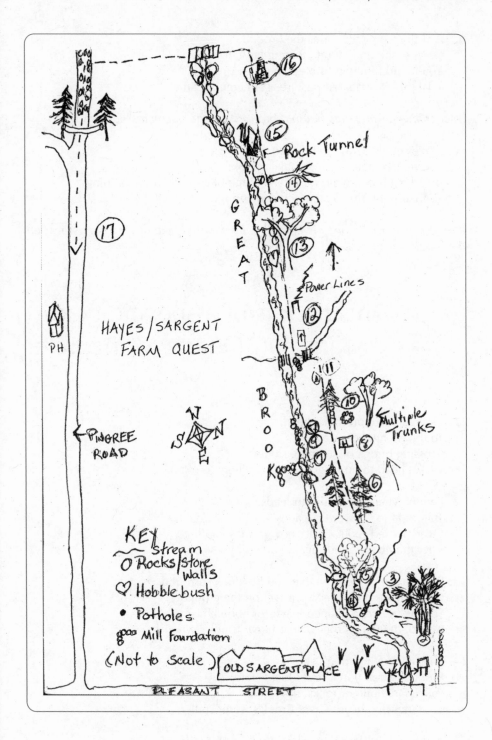

7. Stand by water, corner wall of rock up across the brook;
    An up and down sawmill was the form it once took,
    Herbert Hayes in the deep pool scrubbed;
    "Grandpa's Bathtub" it was dubbed.

8. You've walked Sargent farmland (owned over 100 years' time),
    Now come along to the "Hayes Farm" sign.
    Owned by the Pingrees six generations ago,
    Daughter married Hayes; still she loved this land so.

9. A wall of stone confines the brook,
   Years of toil and labor, clearing land, it took.
   You'll find multiple-trunked trees—a sign
   That this was cleared pasture, 19th century time.

Note: *Triangular rock juts out into brook. A bridge once crossed here.*

10. Blazes move away from brook.
    Above, tree types change, take a look.
    By a long brook wall, for three orange blazes you are searching,
    To their right, find a stone-circled spring.

Note: *A squatter who once lived on the land would take water from here when the brook was frozen.*

This rock is of a specific type— Kinsman Quartz Monzonite.

11. Orange blaze on rock ahead,
    To the stream you are led.
    Crossing bridge or stepping stones
    Walk ahead to trail sign, showing where to roam.

12. Follow where the trail sign leads,
    Trail right to "Lower Cascades."
    Over crossed roots, under power lines you'll go,
    After the lines, woods again you will know.

13. Smooth beech trees, maple and hemlock surround
    Over stream bed, keep your feet on the ground.
    See the big heart shaped leaves of hobblebush;
    Ahead, the trail is rocky, hear Great Brook's whoosh.

14. Through a felled tree's gate
    Along the trail you'll find Quest's fate.
    Past a large pile of rocks, up a hill,
    Cascades up ahead, Great Brook's water spills.

15. A glacial boulder to your left, ahead water falls,
    Find a tunnel of rock through which many hikers have crawled.
    This rock is of a specific type—
    Kinsman Quartz Monzonite.

Heifers on the Road
Photograph courtesy of
Valley News

———

This was once a farm.
Try to imagine the trees
gone; and the stone
walls as borders keeping
the animals in.

16. This was a Colby College site many years ago
    With trails, a bridge and a fireplace also.
    If you stand on the bridge and the brook is low
    Below water spins out a natural pothole.

17. Cross the bridge, take a left on this old road,
    Follow it out to Pingree Road; continue along, straight as told.
    Now, look at the homestead on your right. A wall of rocks
    And what is behind it? It's your treasure box!

Created by Meredith Bird Miller and dedicated to the spirit of Linny Levin in 2000.

"Started out cool,
ended up sweating.
Great hike +
beautiful path."

—Quest sign-in book

36 Wolf Tree Quest

1:30

difficult

bring:
binoculars
field guide

natural
historical

This Quest begins at the bottom of North Pleasant Street in New London. Take Exit 12 off I-89 north or south. Take Newport Road east into New London. Remain on this road, which becomes Main Street. After passing the fire station on your left, turn left on North Pleasant Street at a yellow blinking light. Follow North Pleasant down the hill to the base, where you will cross a small bridge over a brook. The road becomes Lakeshore Drive at this point. Park in the parking area on your right immediately after the bridge. The Quest begins across the street at the trailhead.

Clues

1. Follow sky river above and pine needle road beneath
   Surrounded by trees—hemlock, birch and beech.
   Wolf Tree is the trail on which you will stay;
   Uphill and ahead your Quest does lay.

2. Cleared pasture was this land end of nineteenth century.
   If you had been here then you'd see naught a tree!
   You can read this land that early farmers held dear:
   Multiple-trunked tees are clues this land was once clear.

3. Walking on up at the first hill's crest
   You'll see boulders large both to the right and left.
   An old stone wall is found along the curve
   Stay on the wide path as to the right you swerve.

4. A "Webb Trail" sign to your right is on display.
   Go straight beyond it or you'll be led astray.
   Move to a warm clearing beneath power lines
   From cool beneath hemlocks, maples and pines.

5. Rocky road between stone walls winds;
   Up this hill your Quest climbs.
   Benjamin Bunker farmed this land for a reason.
   The south-facing hill meant a long growing season.

6. Benjamin Bunker carried up the hill, it is said,
   Two hundred pounds of cornmeal for his family to be fed.
   In the late 18th century he had the will
   To cut, clear and farm on this rocky hill.

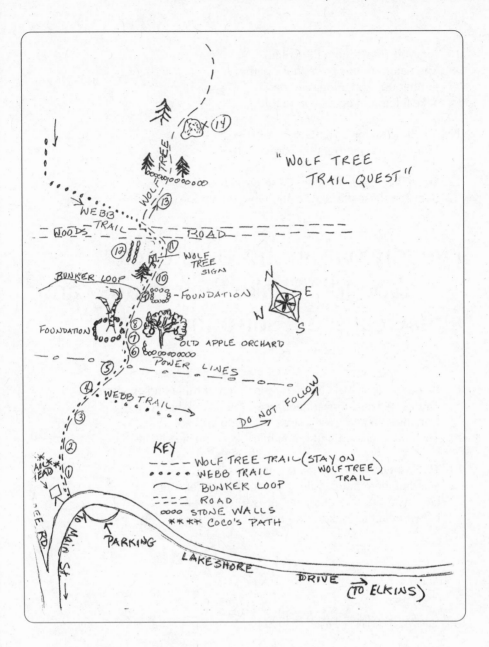

7. On your left: can you find the place?
    It is the stone foundation of the "Old Bunker Place."
    During WWII this foundation held a tower
    From which volunteers watched for planes by the hour.

8. Follow orange blazes* into the woods straight ahead
    As along this hill top farm Quest you are led.
    On your left you'll see the "Bunker Loop" sign
    Across the trail on your right a second foundation you will find.

9. Once cleared pasture on your right
    Go straight on as the trail gets tight.
    Friendly balsam firs on the left abound:
    "Shake their hands" and a magical scent surrounds.

---

* Some of the orange blazes are faded; you may also follow the SRK (Sunapee, Ragged, Kearsarge) Greenway white trapezoid shaped signs. They also indicate the correct route.

10. A "Wolf Tree" sign will explain
    The nature of this great trail's name.
    Further on, find a logging road.
    Take a left and do as you're told.

11. You'll be taking a right on "Wolf Tree."
    From the trail across the road you'll see ...

12. Stone walls, side by side, these provide a clue:
    Between these, farmers' cattle were driven through.

Friendly balsam firs on the left abound: "Shake their hands" and a magical scent surrounds.

13. Bear right on "Wolf Tree," through glen of moss and evergreen.
    Orange blazes follow, fallen trees you'll walk between.
    Continue on and over a stone wall you will go,
    The trail winds up and on awhile—keep on steady and slow.

14. The last glacier rocked and rolled this boulder
    Standing here much taller than your shoulder.
    Lichens are a clue that here air is so clean—
    Now circle the rock to find the box in-between.

Created by Meredith Bird Miller in 2000.

*"Our homeschool group was
here on a lovely summer day.
Our 1st Quest—a real treat!"*

—Quest sign-in book

37

The Fells Quest

1:00

moderate

bring:
money for
  entrance fee
pencil
field guide

Take I-89 south to Exit 12. Take a right off the exit ramp. Make an immediate left onto Rte. 103A and follow it for 5.6 miles to The Fells. The Fells will be on your right. Park just inside the gate. Grounds open year-round. Admission fee charged.

natural
historical

Overview

Located in Newbury, New Hampshire, on the shores of Lake Sunapee, The Fells was the summer retreat for three generations of the Hay family: Secretary of State John M. Hay, who also served as private secretary to Abraham Lincoln; Clarence Hay, a noted archaeologist, who developed the gardens with his wife, Alice Appleton Hay; and nature writer John Hay. The estate is now open to the public and operates as a historic site, public garden, and wildlife refuge. It is named the Fells, because the land reminded John Hay of his ancestral homeland in Scotland, where rocky upland pastures are referred to as "Fells."

Clues

1. Horse and buggy once drove through the gates.
    Now you bring your car.
    As you start the Quest today,
    This is where you are. __ __ __ (__) __ __ __   __ __(__).

2. The little gatehouse is just the start
    Of the grand __ (__) __ __ __ __ this used to be.
    Then head down the driveway, wide and long.
    To see the wildlife, walk very quietly.

3. At the fork in the road you'll see the house,
    And a field of shrubs whose fruit is blue.
    A food to make and serve with these,
    Is a __ __ __ __ __ __ __ (__) __ __ muffin clue!

4. Go left on the road and behind the house,
    Then through the gate in the high
    __ __ __ __ (__) wall.
    Follow the sound of a fountain's splash,
    But be careful, we don't want you to fall!

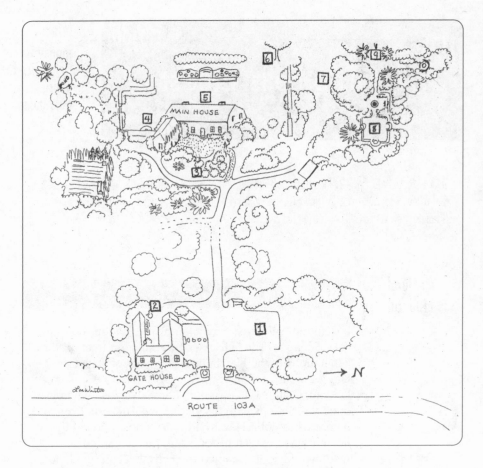

5. Now turn and walk to the wide brick porch,
    And count the columns all in a row.
    These (__) __ __ __ __ pillars of grace and strength
    Make quite an impressive show.

6. From the lawns, gaze out to the field,
    And look to the end of the wall.
    Since 1902, when the 26th __ (__) __ __ __ __ __ __ __ was here,
    Teddy Roosevelt's Maple has stood tall.

Now turn and walk to the wide brick porch
And count the columns all in a row.

7. Now climb the steps on your right to the forest edge,
    And walk back to the back of the row.
    Notice the leaves of B __ __ (__) __ and B __ __ (__) __.
    How tall and silently these trees grow.

8. Turn left on a path to a magical place,
   By the wooden bench that's painted __ __ (__) __ __.
   Enter a forgotten garden of shady rooms
   Behind the big leafy rhododendrons' height.

9. Now find a shaft of marble quite tall,
   Once a portrait head of half-goat and half-man .
   He graced this garden of whispering trees,
   The Greek God of the woodland named __ __ (__).
   (Hint: his name rhymes with "fan.")

10. Take the circled letters from your answers true,
    And write them down in a line.
    Scramble them all into two new words.
    Near that structure the Quest box you'll find.

    (A clue for those who need some aid:
    It's what the moonstruck mason laid.)

    B _ _ _ _   C _ _ _ _ _ _ _

Created by Maggie Stier and Loa Winter in 1998.

"Our Quest continues
for stamps galore.
We are so happy
To be romping
On this valley's floor.
Students of RRC!"

—Quest sign-in book

38 Sleeper's Meadow Quest

1:00

moderate

bring:
binoculars
compass
field guide
pencil

Take I-91 to Bradford, VT (Exit 16). Travel east to get to Route 5, then travel north on Route 5. As you pass Oxbow High School click your odometer and count off 3.7 miles. Sleeper's Meadow will appear on your left, with a big brown barn. Park near the barn.

natural
vista
historical

Overview

This farm has been conserved by the Upper Valley Land Trust. UVLT is a regional land conservancy working to protect farmland, forests, wetlands and waterways, wildlife habitat, trails and scenic areas in the Vermont and New Hampshire towns of the Upper Valley. Since 1985, UVLT has protected over 380 parcels of land encompassing more than 34,000 acres. UVLT is a non-profit organization and is supported primarily by local contributions from individuals. For more information visit www.uvlt.org, or contact UVLT at 603-643-6626.

Clues

Note: *During the Quest, you may cross beneath electric fences meant to contain grazing cattle. Do not be concerned—but please **do** be careful! You may also come across grazing cows. Proceed gently with awareness, as this Quest explores a working farm.*

Welcome to Sleeper's Meadow and South Newbury.
We hope you enjoy the beauty, and our local history.
The Upper Valley Land Trust conserved this farm
So that we—and others—might enjoy its charm.

Along your journey, we ask that you collect words and letters.
Collect them all to find your Valley Quest treasure!

1. In front of you is a very large __ (_) __ __.
    It was built about 1785.

2. Looking west from Route 5
    Count the paned windows on the barn's second floor.
    Please write that number here: __ (_) __   (spell out)

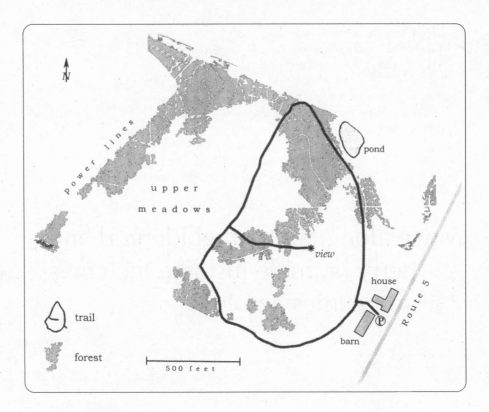

3. Find a big wooden sign.
    The first word starts and ends with the same letter.
    Write that letter here: __
    Note: A Tory is one who supported
    the "Red Coats" during the American Revolution.

4. This house was built in 1785, too.
    How many columns are on the front porch? (__) __ __ __   (spell out)
    The windows to the left of the front door
    Open to the office where Doctor Samuel White worked.

5. Now allemande left! Look for something red with two numbers on it.
    This used to be the South Newbury Post Office!
    The number on top is the year the Post Office was established.
    Write the first number here: (__) __ __   (spell out)

6. The number to the right was our zip code.
    Please write the third number here: __ (__) __ __   (spell out)
    Mail came here for 144 years, it is true.
    Until the very last letter in 1982.

    Mrs. Isabel Whitney saw a lot of letters
    For she was postmaster here for 40 years.

    Now walk uphill between barn and shed.
    The next part of your Quest lies up and ahead.

7. Follow the mowed path up to a "T"
    Turn right and proceed to the fruit trees.

They give us cider, they give us sauce!
They give us pie, they reach up to the sky!
What kind of trees are they? __ __ __ (__) __

8. Dogleg left past a straight tall maple.
   Find a small white sign if you are able.
   Write the two words here: __ __ __ __   __ (__) __ __ __

   These cabins were used by guests starting in the 1930s.
   Right is white ... left is a forest path. Take the path through the trees!

Move along, through goldenrod and berry bramble just like the cows that sometimes amble.

9. Cool beneath the shady grove
   "Ah! These woods I do, do love!"
   Said Selenda.
   Ms. Selenda Girardin
   Made this special place "open"
   For you and for me to enjoy and to see.

   On the ground to the right of the path is a square grey __ __ (__) __

10. Straight ahead is a metal __ __ (__) __.
    Beyond it lies your fate.

11. To your right see an open field; in the center a small rise.
    Cattle were buried there long, long ago, when TB took their lives.

    Now a choice of paths. Which is right?
    Follow the blaze when it enters your sight.
    What color is the blaze? __ __ __ __ (__) __

12. Move along, move along,
    Through goldenrod and berry bramble
    Just like the cows that sometimes amble.
    An electric fence is now in view,[*]
    Slink under one, slink under two.
    What are these fences made of? __ (__) __ __

    The fences help to keep the cattle in alternate
    Pastures, minimizing erosion and impact.

---

* Fences may be active; pass through carefully.

Jersey Calf
Photograph courtesy of Valley News

In 1952, Sleepers Meadow was brought by the Whitney family. Roscoe Whitney was drawn to the size of the barn—large enough for the 100 head of cattle he needed to support his large family.

13. Stand beneath the white birch.
    What is wet and lies beyond? A (_) __ __ __
    Now search for a yellow blaze
    Then off that-a-ways.

14. Up the hill and under the pines
    The forest's shade is cool and fine.
    Take note of the Questers sign.

    Into the meadow you go,
    Moving between two fence rows.

    Off to the right you will spy
    Where hawks like to roost and fly.
    "Our family called this place Hawk Island," said Selenda.
    Can you see why?

    Follow between wires, higher and higher
    Up the trail to a small knoll.
    At the top
    Find a big white rock
    And then please do what you're told.

First, take the 13th letter of the alphabet and put it here: ___
2nd, stand on top of the white rock and turn around slowly three times.
3rd, pretend your standing not on rock but on a clock.

The path ahead of you is 12 o'clock
And from where you have come from is 6.
Carefully cross wire towards 8 o'clock – that's the trick.
Seven dozen steps. Then stop to see …

15. Look closely: was it love that brought these two together?
Search hard to find the Valentine Trees,
For that is the place that I want you to be.

Continue east between two thornapples,
And over a mossy stone.
Proceed slowly & carefully to "higher ground."
Past wire, and where "The View" can be found.

An incredible scene, with mountains stretching in-between.
From left to right (if it is clear) you should see:
Lafayette, Kinsman, Black, Sugarloaf and Moosilauke.
Take the 1st letter of the 3rd mountain: (_) __ __ __ __

This would be a good place for a picnic!
If you have one, ENJOY!

16. Now make your way back to the "Three turn rock"
and I'll tell you how to find your treasure box.
Facing the unknown, 12 o'clock, make like a rolling stone down and left.

Follow the row of pines.
A crooked pasture pine left means you are fine!
Under the last wires, almost back to the old barn
And now you know well the Whitney-Cole Family Farm.

So how do you know where to find the treasure box?
Well in all treasure hunts an ___ marks the spot.
That's your last letter—so fill in the blanks,
Then go find your treasure, and for this place give thanks!

__ __ __ __   __ __ F __ __ __   __ __ __ __
13 8 3 10   11 4   2 9 6   14 1 12 7

__ __ __
15 5 16

Created by Selenda Giradin, John Taylor and Steve Glazer in 2002.

39 The Historical Newport Quest

:45

easy

bring:
compass

historical
architectural

Take exit 13 from I-89 toward Grantham/Croydon. Turn right onto NH-10. Head south on Rte 10 to Newport. Turn right into Richards Free Library parking lot. From Claremont, follow Rtes 11-103 east to Newport. Turn left onto Rte 10. After the traffic circle, continue north on Rte 10. Turn left into Richards Free Library parking lot.

Clues

1. Park at a place filled with books
   Then get out and take a look.
   The Richards family donated this house
   In here you have to be as quiet as a mouse.

   Head north to a building where kids are taught
   In the summer the classrooms are wicked hot.
   This used to be Newport's High School
   Some kids who went here did not find it cool.

You might just hear
the ringing of a bell made by
Paul Revere

2. Head east across the street to the Baptist church
   Admire the beauty then continue your search
   Follow the sidewalk and don't be nervous
   On your left see the stone church for Episcopal service.

3. Cross to the common, find a statue most grand
   Remembering times when others threatened our land.
   Newport answered the call to fight and defeat them
   Some gave up their lives defending our freedom.

4. Next go to the post office to continue the way
   Notice the white church where the Methodists pray.

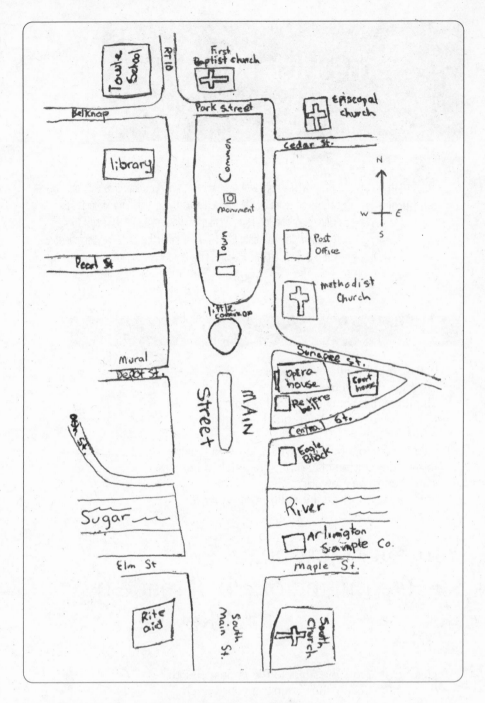

5. Now continue south, crossing Sunapee Street
    Notice the red brick buildings that can't be beat.
    Soon you'll come to some steps where you might wish to linger
    Where people once listened to opera singers.
    In a case to your right you just might hear
    The ringing of a bell made by Paul Revere.

    Just a little more south and look up the hill
    Is a place where now your stomach will fill.
    A judge and a jury once worked here without fail
    Considering whether to send people to jail.

6. Back on Main Street cross to the opposite side
   There's a mural showcasing our historical pride.

7. Cross back to the other side of Main Street now
   And travel south to a structure we consider a marvel.
   The Eagle block once was an inn of renown
   A few years ago was nearly torn down.

   Continue on south and cross a small bridge
   The water below is as cold as a fridge.
   Our town might not exist without the Sugar River
   From Lake Sunapee flow those waters forever.

8. Pass a brick building once called "Arlington Sample,'
   Where moms and dads used to work, and Grandma and Grample.
   Cross the road now but stay away from the drug store
   Keep your chin up and continue a little bit more.

   Up in the sky you will notice a steeple
   You're almost at your treasure so don't you dare weeple.

9. In front of the church you'll notice a sign
   Investigate closely we're sure you will find
   Maybe under a bush or down on the ground
   The object of your Quest you sure will have found.

Created by the 7th–8th grade South Congregational Church Faith & Nature Camp Group, assisted by their leaders, July, 2005.

40 Gile Mountain Hawk & Haiku Quest

1:00

difficult

bring:
field guide
binoculars

natural
vista

Take Interstate 91 to Exit 13. This is the Hanover/Norwich exit. Go west towards Norwich. Pass Dan and Whit's store and continue for approximately 1/2 mile. Take a left onto Turnpike Road. In 2.6 miles, the paved road turns to dirt. In 5.3 miles you will see a sign for the Gile Mountain Trail and Parking.

NOTE: For more Norwich Quests visit our online Quests page at: www.vitalcommunities.org

Clues

Wood sign names this place
And the trail meanders right:
Proceed, eyes open.

Tiny turkey tails
Like little fuzzy brown ears
Mark stump on the left.

See tree tops snipped off,
White birches doubled over:
Signs of ice and wind.

Wires marching south.
Kestrel perch on them waiting
for the grasshoppers.

Trail turns to the right—
Not a conifer in sight—
At two blazes blue.

Stop at tiny bridge:
Sensitive fern spore cases,
Each spore a new life.

Turn up hill. Look up
For a three-crotched tree and see
Where a hawk might be.*

---

* Hawks can't weave nests but can lay sticks down. They need a sturdy place like a 3-crotched tree.

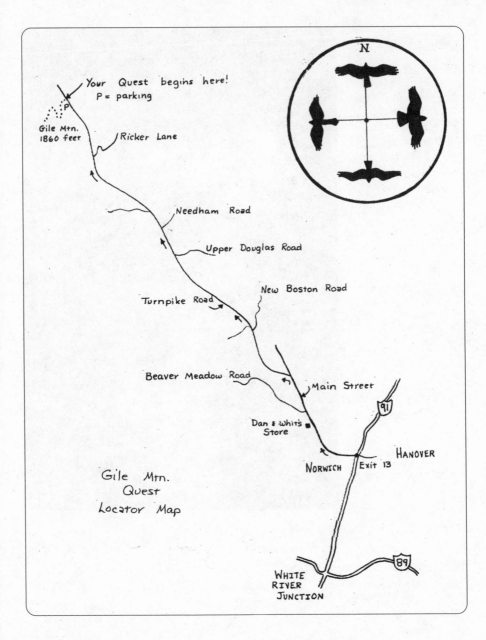

Gile Mtn. Quest Locator Map

Wires marching south.
Kestrel perch on them waiting
For the grasshoppers.

Steeper. Trees again.
Hawks migrate above these trees—
Come in fall and see!

Uphill. The thermals
Lift off the land in columns.
The hawks rise with them.

Look: ice storm central.
Sheared trees and blown down branches—
The storm left its tracks.

Red Tail Hawk
Photograph by Ted Levin

The Red Tail Hawk has a raspy cry, "kree eee ar." This vocalization has been featured in movies worldwide to represent an eagle or a hawk.

An empty shelter
Waits for you rain, sleet or snow.
Thank you, volunteers!

Climb up the tower
For seven stories of view,
Migrating hawks, too.

And for your treasure:

North from tower: spruce.
Within find a standing snag.
Behind, sugar can.

Created by Steven Glazer and Ginger Wallis in 2000.

41 Grand Canyon of Norwich Quest

1:15

moderate

natural

bring:
compass
field guide

Take Interstate 91 to Exit 13. This is the Hanover/Norwich exit. Go west towards Norwich. Turn left on Beaver Meadow Road just past Dan & Whits. This Quest is on the Bill Ballard Trail which is located on the west (left) side of Beaver Meadow Road about 4 miles from the Norwich Inn in the center of Norwich.

Clues

As you go on the Quest, I hope you will see
Forest disturbances, there are more than just three.
Clues of blowdown, logging or fire you may find
Because our forests are changing all the time.

Walk north up the road after parking your car.
Turn on the trail that is left and not very far.

Leave ruins of pond and foundation of mill,
Then cross the bridge and walk up the hill.
Pick up needles. They'll be on the ground.

The "mound" is made from
decomposing roots and debris
While the "pit" shows where
a tree used to be.

Needles together in two's and five's will be found.
The two's are red pine, with rough scaly bark.
Were these trees planted in rows in woods so dark?

A red oak up ahead has a story to tell.
The four trunks grew after its ancestor was felled.
So pass #6. Look left after 100 feet more,
then imagine the diameter of this tree's original core.
To calculate: Note the center of each trunk.
Connect them in an imaginary circle near the ground.

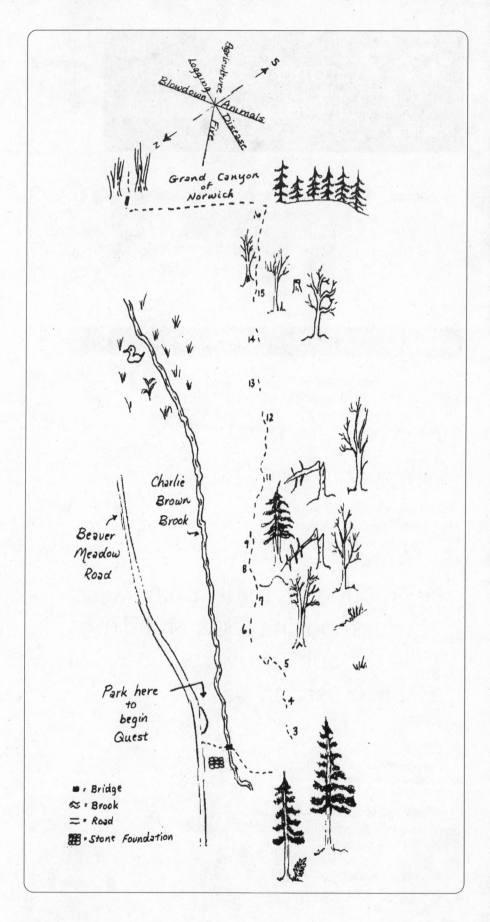

Dan & Whit's General Store
Photograph courtesy of Valley News

When you finish your Quest, stop in at Dan & Whit's for refreshments. There has been a general store serving the community here for more than 110 years.

Cross the stream at #7 and on the right you will find
a "pit and mound" that will boggle your mind.
The mound was made from decomposing roots and debris
and the pit shows where a tree used to be.
So if you find a pit right next to a mound,
then evidence of a very old blowdown you have found.
The tree fell to the southwest so it was a
northeasterly wind that blew the tree down.

On the left after #15, a poplar was scarred long ago.
Was the basal scar from fire or log skidding? Can we know?
Note that a collection of leaves on an uphill side
provides the fuel for a fire to thrive.

Stop to look at the rock walls in the canyon nearby.
Continue left on the trail and cross where a bridge of stone lies.
Bearing from a multi-trunked birch near a pit and mound,
go 230 degrees to a multi-trunked tree. Here, the box will be found.

Created by Ginger Wallis and Linny Levin in 1998.

42
Montshire Quest

:30

easy

natural

bring:
money for
entrance fee
field guide

Get off at Exit 13 from I-91. Head east towards Hanover. Very quickly you will turn south at your first opportunity. Follow the signs into the Museum's parking lot. The Quest begins inside the museum. Please note: The Montshire Museum and property is open 10-5 daily. Admission is charged for non-members.

Overview

The Montshire Museum of Science is a hands-on museum offering dozens of exciting exhibits relating to the natural and physical sciences, ecology, and technology. The building is located on a 110-acre site near the Connecticut River, and the Museums' outdoor environment is a large part of the visitor experience. Science Park is a two-acre exhibit area in a beautiful, park-like setting. Also outside is a network of easy-to-moderate walking trails for visitors of all ages and fitness levels. For more information, check www.montshire.org.

Clues

Begin your Montshire Quest with a trip up the stairs,
A climb up the tower as you lose all your cares.
Take a look around and enjoy the view.
Can you spot the Connecticut River and the Ledyard Bridge, too?
Make sure you turn and see all around,
Over the railroad tracks and down to the ground.

Back down all the stairs and out the backdoor,
Checking for seasonal notes on the white board
Walk out the back door and to your left you should head,
Follow the path as you carefully tread.
Towards the granite globe you should slowly wander.
Your place on it you should carefully ponder.

Follow the trail into the woods is my hunch,
Through white pines with needles, five in a bunch.
Past a hanging boulder too heavy to lug,
All it really needs is a very gentle tug.
Soon signs of animals you might want to learn,

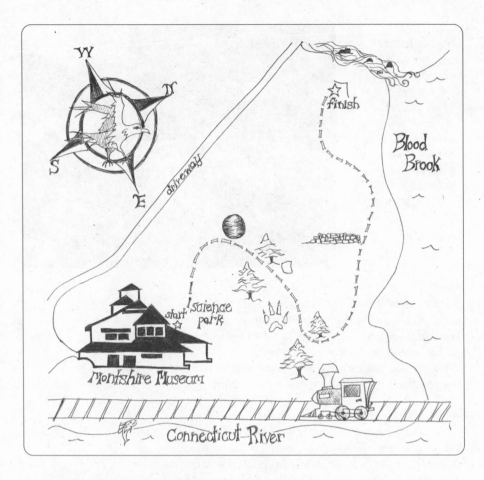

Soon signs of animals you might want to learn,
As you go round the very next turn.
The smell of the mink is not so nice to discover,
But as you continue on look for signs undercover.
A fox up the hill in her den may be sleeping,
While a red squirrel may be scampering with nuts he is keeping.
In winter, look for the tracks of the fisher,
Or the scat of the coyote even though you'll miss her.

Towards the granite globe
    you should slowly wander.
Your place on it
    you should carefully ponder.

Down the hill into hemlocks you'll enter,
With short flat needles, faint lines down their center.
Look up through their needles as you ponder their beauty.
Then take a sharp left, for that is your duty!
To follow the trail along the edge of the water,
No matter if you are the son or the daughter.

Montshire Museum
Photograph courtesy of the Montshire Museum

Did you know that the word Montshire is a contraction of the words Vermont and New Hampshire? So is Vershire!

Soon there will be a sign of people long ago.
A old rock wall that is now terribly low.
Watch for signs of a beaver or a little bird's nest,
And continue on till you need a rest.
What do you notice as you crouch to the ground?
Do you hear anything here making a sound?

When given a chance go right to the overlook,
Observe all around you from the turn you just took.
Go till you see a brook that was once called Bloody.
When the water is low the lagoon may look muddy.
A train sometimes travels over the arched bridge of stone,
Or if you are lucky you might see a duck in a group or alone.

The platform is this Quest's final destination.
So look for the box attached at this station.
Look down in the bottom for the stamp you might need.
Congratulations on following this lead!
So leave us a note on all that you found,
And return to the Montshire where discoveries abound.

Created by Amy Vanderkooi for the Montshire Museum in 2000. She updated it in 2008.

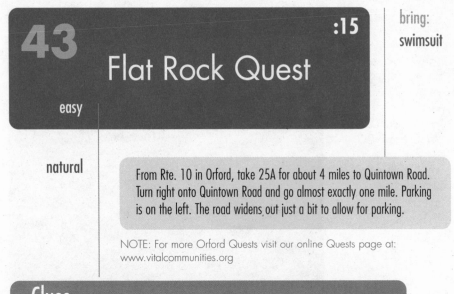

43

:15

Flat Rock Quest

easy

natural

bring:
swimsuit

From Rte. 10 in Orford, take 25A for about 4 miles to Quintown Road. Turn right onto Quintown Road and go almost exactly one mile. Parking is on the left. The road widens out just a bit to allow for parking.

NOTE: For more Orford Quests visit our online Quests page at: www.vitalcommunities.org

Clues

1. Start where you park.

2. Go to the big boulder
    Beware it's colder.

3. Go to the pool
    and you'll be cool.

4. Go to the bank
    and don't get spanked.

5. Go to the upper edge of Flat Rock.
    Don't slip and take a dip.

Go to the pool
and you'll be cool.

6. Go to the culvert and
    try not to take a slide ride.

7. Go to the middle
    of Flat Rock, Doc.

8. Go to the steps
    but don't get wet.

Holding a Frog
Photograph by Ted Levin

Frogs are wild; but if you are careful and gentle, you can meet them close up. Be sure your hands are clean; they have sensitive skin. Be gentle: you are a lot bigger than a frog!

9. Go back to the bank—
    duck your shoulder
    so you don't hit the boulder.
    Under those rocks
    you'll find the box.

Created by Sue Kling's Second Graders at Orford Elementary School in 1998.

"5/11/03 It is Mother's Day and I am sitting by the Flat Rock with my husband Joe and our 18 month old son Max. My gift is time with my family in a beautiful, peaceful spot away from the hectic pace of 'real life.' It's a lovely, sunny day spent sitting in a lovely, sunny spot."

—Quest sign-in book

44 French's Ledges Quest

1:00

difficult

bring:
binoculars
field guide

natural
vista

Take Route 120 about 3.5 miles south of Lebanon and make a right onto Main Street in Meriden. Turn left onto Colby Hill Road and cross a Tasker Covered Bridge (see Quest 8). Make a left in about 1 mile onto Columbus Jordan Road. Go almost 2 miles to a pull-off. The trail will be on your left.

Clues

There's a sign
you can find
on the tree
near the trail.

Be polite, there could be a bee
in the tipped-over tree.

Follow the blue marks on the trees.
Near the top, climb up the rocks on your hands and knees.
As you climb higher you feel the breeze.

Way up near the top,
Blue blazes stop.

Climb up the rocks on your
hands and knees.
Get to the top and feel the breeze.

Follow red today
A new sign points the way.

When you get to the top annoy the fox.
Slide down the rocks, then find the box.

How? Get to the tippy top, then stop.
Point to the school and the radio tower.
Follow your faces and go twelve paces (or more).

Spider Web
Photograph by Ted Levin

Spider's strong and flexible silk creates magnificent structures, utilized for both protection and predation. A magical sight ... unless you are stuck in it!

It's hard to find 'cause
It's under a pine.
Look for a log that fell down on the ground.
Under the rock the box will be found.

Going down, when red changes to blue,
The Columbus Jordan Road Trailhead is for you.
If you miss it and go too far,
Go back and find the blue trail, or you won't find your car!

Created by Betsy Rybeck Lynd's second grade class in 1997.

"This place is really cool.
I came here with my aunt and uncle."

— Quest sign-in book

45

Coolidge Quest

1:00

bring:
pencil

Boyhood Home of the 30th U.S. President

moderate

Plymouth Notch is located on VT 100-A and can be reached via VT 4 (from Woodstock and I –89) or VT 100 (from Ludlow, Rutland and Killington). Turn at the entrance sign into the main parking area. See map. PLEASE NOTE: The roads through the historic site are public rights-of-way. Look both ways when crossing the roads and wait for the traffic to pass before you cross. After completing this Quest, you will most likely want to visit the historic site, so bring some money for the admission fee.

historical
architectural

Overview

This Quest at the President Calvin Coolidge State Historic Site is free and stays outdoors. The historic site buildings are open from late May to mid-October. The Quest may be done in the off-season, but some clues will be missing and the Treasure Box will not be accessible if snow is on the ground. Another, in-depth building Quest is available with admission to the Visitor Center. For more information, visit www.HistoricVermont.org/Coolidge.

Clues

Complete the verses below as you walk through the village of Plymouth Notch and learn about the life of Calvin Coolidge. Use words from the following list to fill in the blanks. Some blank spaces are numbered. Finally, put the letters in the correct sequence to reveal the location of the hidden treasure box at the end of the Quest.

WORD LIST (*Note: One word is used twice*)

shop	Cilley	continuous	White	July
gasoline	whirligig	cheese	foundations	barn
school	store	Cemetery	notary	presidential
seal	garden	pine	slope	

A. Walk from the parking lot to the stone Visitor Center
When the door is open, we invite you to enter.
It is from these exhibits that you can learn
Much about Cal Coolidge and his presidential term.

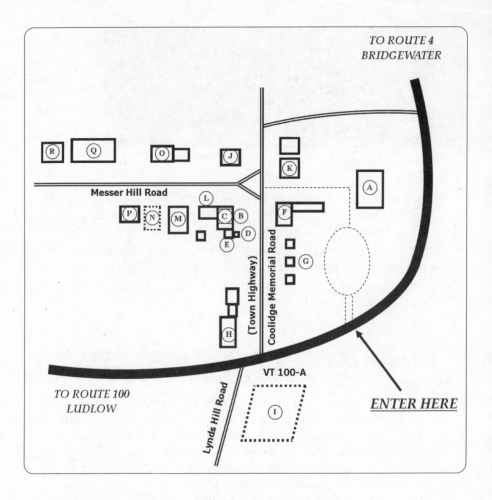

B. From the Center head up the path and you'll see
An old-time store once run by Florence ___ ___ ___ ___ ___ ___ .
                                                        8
Here folks could buy sundries and just sit a spell
To chat about neighbors—there was much to tell!

C. Above the store is a large, high-ceiling hall
Held here were dances and sometimes fancy balls.
As the President's office this room reached great fame
When to Plymouth the '24 Summer ___ ___ ___ ___ ___
House came.   13

D. Right in front of the general store
Is a ___ ___ ___ ___ ___ ___ ___ ___ pump where according
to lore   4

You could fill up your brand new Ford Model T
For under a dollar—how nice would *that* be!

E. To the left is the post office, still serving Plymouth town
Its first woman postmaster was Carrie Coolidge, formerly Brown.
When Calvin was born in the house that is near,
His grandfather was postmaster that very same year.

Summer White House
Photograph courtesy of
Vermont Division for
Historic Preservation

———

Calvin Coolidge used the
dance hall, located
above the general store
at Plymouth Notch, as
his presidential office in
August 1924.

Independence Day in Plymouth is special in one very, big way -
Calvin Coolidge is the only U.S. president born on this day.
It is here every year on the Fourth of __ __ __ __ ,
14

Commemorative stamped envelopes you can buy.

F.   Just across the road and next on your way,
Was a fine business in Calvin's day.
The Aldrich House, sheds and barns joined together,
Is a fine example of "__ __ __ __ __ __ __ __ __ __
architecture."   9

G.   Here Midge Aldrich opened a tea room and gift __ __ __ __
16

And three cabins out back where tourists could stop.
Called "Top of the Notch" after the lay of the land
This business even had a roadside souvenir stand!

H.   Go south down the road and away from the town
On a knoll sits a large house built by a farmer, James Brown.
Brown was a partner in the making of __ __ __ __ __ __ .
18

This house is private, so view from the street please.

I.   When you get to Vermont Route 100 A
Cross the road carefully and look both ways.
Walk down Lynds Hill Road and on the left you will see
On a very steep hillside,
Plymouth Notch __ __ __ __ __ __ __ __
11

Not suitable for farming; the hill was too slanted.
Because of its ___ ___ ___ ___ ___ no crops could be planted.
          2

So buried here are Coolidges from seven generations,
Calvin, of course, the most famous relation.

Climb up the stone steps – it hardly seems real
To find a simple grave bearing the

___ ___ ___ ___ ___ ___ ___ ___ ___ ___ ___ ___ ___ ___

___ ___ ___ ___ .
    19

Thousands have come here from far and wide
To show their respect at this Vermont hillside.

J. Now it's back to the village—you still have more clues
Still watching for traffic, but enjoy the fine views!
Straight ahead, a gold-colored house across from the store

Independence Day in Plymouth is special in one very big way: Calvin Coolidge is the only U.S. president born on this day.

Was the childhood home of Cal's mother, Victoria Moor.
It was here that she married John Coolidge in the front sitting room
In 1868 they surely made a lovely bride and groom.

K. This home later owned by the Wilders, Cal's uncle and aunt
Their farm included the two barns built in the earth's slant.
Known as bank barns, the
___ ___ ___ ___ ___ ___ ___ ___ ___ ___ ___ serve as first floor
             5

Then at street-level you will find the main door.

L. Turn around and now look at the back of the ___ ___ ___ ___ ___
                                              1

Attached is a small house filled with early décor.
Calvin Coolidge was born here on July 4, 1872;
A future U.S. president—but who then knew?

M. Easy to spot and the next on your search
Greek Revival in style is the Union Christian Church.
The inside remodeled in Carpenter Gothic design
By Willie Pierce, craftsman, who did this in hard ___ ___ ___ ___ .
                                                    3

N. Cal's stepmother Carrie kept a ___ ___ ___ ___ ___ ___ nearby
                                            17
    That still has bright flowers that catch the eye.
    A spinning ___ ___ ___ ___ ___ ___ ___ ___ ___ is near the gate
                                    7
    It shows the wind's direction and its rate.

O. Across the road in the house painted white
    History happened one hot August night.
    Sworn in by his father a public ___ ___ ___ ___ ___ ___
                                            12
    Calvin became President here in 1923.

P. Opposite the Homestead is a small weathered ___ ___ ___ ___
                                                            6

    Kept here were hand tools needed for a then-modern farm.
    Hammers, axes, chisels, wood planes, and vises,
    Young Calvin was taught how to use these devices.

Q. Up Messer Hill Road you now will travel
    But stop before your path turns to gravel.
    Here at the factory you can buy Plymouth ___ ___ ___ ___ ___ ___ .
                                                    10
    It's a granular curd type that is sure to please.

R. Next door to the factory is the one room ___ ___ ___ ___ ___ ___ .
                                                    15

    Each student brought logs for the woodstove's fuel.
    Calvin's sister, Abbie, received her teaching degree
    At age twelve – that's pretty amazing, don't you agree?

    Now from your answers, fill in the blanks below
    With the letters that are numbered, and then go
    To the side of this building with windows of height
    Here the treasure box waits if you've done it all right!

    ___ ___ ___ ___ ___ ___ ___   ___ ___   ___ ___ ___ ___ ___
     1   2   3   4   5   6   7   8   9   10 11 12 13 14

    ___ ___ ___ ___ ___   🍁
    15 16 17 18 19

Created by the Vermont Division for Historic Preservation in 2008.

46 Quest for the Right Words @ Quechee Gorge

1:00

moderate

bring:
swimsuit
pencil

Take Route 4 toward Woodstock and pull into the Quechee Gorge Visitor Center on the left. Plenty of parking and lots of great information! Your Quest starts at the gate next to the visitor's center.

natural
architectural

Overview

Quechee Gorge State Park is owned by the US Army Corps of Engineers. It is part of the North Hartland Flood Control Dam Area. The 612 acre park is managed for recreational use by the Vermont Department of Forest Parks and Recreation. Quechee Gorge is considered the most spectacular river gorge in the state of Vermont. It was formed thousands of years ago when a giant ice sheet began to recede and the flow the Ottauquechee River resumed but took a different course through ancient Glacial Lake Hitchcock. As the ice continued to melt, the Rocky Hill Dam eventually broke and Glacial Lake Hitchcock drained. The Ottauquechee River changed its course and turned south and flowed through the soft delta left by the lake. Meanwhile, a great waterfall was migrating up the Connecticut River from the breached dam. Eventually, the waterfall reached the Ottauquechee River and began eroding rock. Over thousands of years, the waterfall carved its way northward, creating Quechee Gorge.[*] In 2005, the new visitors' center at Quechee Gorge opened. It is staffed and run by the Hartford Area Chamber of Commerce. It is open from 10 am until 4pm, seven days a week, year round, but closed for holidays.

Clues

Welcome to Hartford's Quechee Gorge.
We promise that you won't get bored.
Fill in all of our blanks with the words that you choose
There are no right or wrong answers; just follow our clues!

_____

[*] Adapted from David Laing, Consulting Geologist, 152 Christian Street, White River Junction, Vermont 05001, from www.vtstatepartks.com.

This Quest should be _____ .
                                                          adjective
You don't have to run.

When you've finished walking, writing & all the rest,
You will have created your own personal Quest.

Start at the _____ gate
                         adjective

There is no need to wait.

Go down the _____ steps.
                         name of material

Pass through a door.
Inside, you will find a store.
This is the Visitors Center:
Have no fear! Please enter.

When_____ is done, head out back.
            name of person in group

Quechee Gorge Bridge
Photograph courtesy of Valley News

This bridge is the oldest standing steel arch bridge in Vermont. It is an early example of steel-arch construction—and was an impressive engineering challenge.

Yes, go back outside and read the plaque.

_____ the blue trail and you will be right back for more.
    verb

A great switchback trail made by the Youth Conservation Corps.

Soon you will come to a bend,
But this trail—it will not end.

Turn right, not straight
And do not _____.
     verb

Up ahead you will find a _____ fence
             adjective

Read the sign and please do what it says.

The trail has _____ blazes marked on the trees.
     color

Use your eyes, you can _____!
        verb

This is not a test.
But if you look, you might even find a bird's nest.
At the trail merge, turn stop a bit along the ridge
And look up and you will find a _____ bridge.
            noun

It is a _____ bridge, off to your _____,
    color   direction

Stop, look & listen: enjoy this sight.

_____ down to the bottom of
verb
the gorge
A new trail you
need not forge!

The bridge you have spotted was originally built with train tracks in 1875.
John Storrs designed this unique structure, where cars now drive.

OK—Get going down the _____ trail.
adjective

You will pass many_____ roots, veiling the sides of this everlasting
trail.   adjective

Coming right down the path, there will be a _____where you may
want to rest.   noun

Pause for a moment and think of what a _____place for this kind of
Quest.   adjective

And down the slope you will continue your part
All this walking is good for your _____.
part of body

Beyond 0.2, at the Quechee Gorge trail, stay right ...
Unless you are camping here for the night!
Another fork follows, soon in your sight
Remain on the trail on the route that keeps right.

We hope you are enjoying this _____ trail.
adjective

You're doing great. If you work together you will not fail!

Long, long ago a _____, a thick sheet of ice
noun

Covered this place, leaving a natural treasure we think is _____.
adjective

_____ down to the bottom of the gorge
verb

A new trail you need not forge!

Stroll _____ by the ferns on your left
       adverb

Listen to the _____ in the Ottauquechee River singing best.
       liquid

At the DANGER sign, stop and look around
The _____ rocks, river and much more are there to be found.
       adjective

Walk down the stone stairs on the right,

Scramble on_____, you'll enjoy the sight.
       plural noun

If the water is low, and the temperature is high
Go in for a dip—look up at the sky.

When you're done with your scramble
And ready to ramble,
Go back up to higher ground
Your treasure box still to be found.

Past the stone stairs is a bench. Keep on, look low!
You are looking for our hidden loot! .
A tree that has fallen is where you must go.
Once you are there—look into the _____.

Created by Alex and Amelia Good in 2007.

47 Vermont Institute of Natural Science Quest

:45

moderate

bring:
field guide
pencil
money for
entrance fee

The VINS Nature Center is located on Route 4 in Quechee, VT just west of the Quechee Gorge. The Quest begins at the Nature Store.

natural

Overview

The mission of VINS is to protect our natural heritage through education and research designed to engage individuals and communities in the active care of their environment. The VINS Nature Center is open 10 and to 5 pm 7 days/week in the summer season. Winter hours and programs are available on a seasonal schedule. Visit www.vinsweb.org for hours, admission pricing and program details; or call 802-359-5000. General admission to the VINS Nature Center also includes access to all trails, programs and exhibits.

Clues

Leave the Nature Store; you're on your way.
Have you tested your wings on "Flap" today?
Behold in front, a natural arc sculpture,
Which could represent the flight of a vulture.
Follow the path to the large white stone.
During your adventure, you won't be alone.

Find the third letter of the last name of the man honored on this stone. _____

Bear right at the fork, down the path from the stone.
Find the big sign displaying a skull and a bone,
That tells why birds are different from bears.
Believe me, it's more than just feathers and hairs.
Look at the bird, but don't be tempted to stay.
Bear right for the map that shows you the way!

Find the last letter of the name of the river on the big map. _____

Find the third letter of the biggest word on the big map. _____

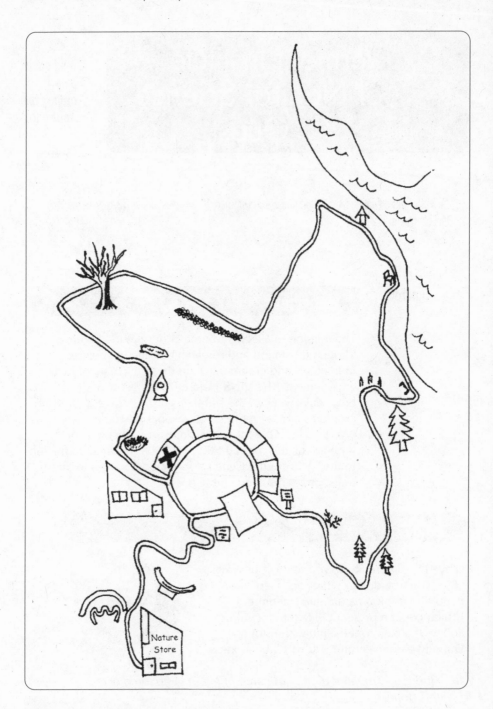

Follow the path; you've nothing to fear.
Look to your left; there's an alien here!
This thorny invasive doesn't belong,
So stick to the path and move right along.
Around the bend, ask the pines if you may,
Slip between and head on your way.

These trees with needles grouped five all together,
Stay green on their branches, no matter the weather.
With sun and open land, white pines love to sow.
These pioneer species are the first to grow.

Barred Owl
Photograph by Ted Levin

A medium-sized, gray-brown owl streaked with white horizontal barring on the chest and vertical barring on the belly. An opportunistic hunter, Barred Owls eat voles, shrews, mice, rats, squirrels, birds, fish, frogs and more!

As you trek down the path take a look to your right,
For a pine you can't hug; try as you might!

Find the first letter of the name of the beaver's large front teeth. _____

Glance to your left, some holes you will spot.
Woodpeckers dined here on insects they caught!
Be on your way to find a special mark.
Beavers snacked here on a tree's inner bark!
Now take a rest with Jen Lingelbach,
And read her poem that's found in a rock.

Find the third letter of the month this bench was dedicated. _____

Continue left down the path, in summer it's key,
To listen for blackbirds' "Kon-Ka Reeee!"
Countless creatures call this place home,
From turtles and frogs to deer that roam!
A bunch of small beeches lead your way down the trail.
When you find a wood bench you can rest your tail.

Walk slowly here and take in the views,
Of a wetland that can make one muse.
Ahead in the woods a shelter you'll see.

Make your way there, oh so quietly.
In the blind you will find many pictures that aid,
Seeing creatures that soar and others that wade.

*Find the fourth letter of the first word in the Osprey's
scientific name.* _____

Find the fifth letter of the state where all these birds can be found. _____

Notice a nest box built for a duck.
You'll find it among all the reeds and the muck.
The cattails fill an important niche,
Like trees rooted in soil so rich.
Amble along toward the wall made of stone,
Full of places for chipmunks to make their home.

Seek out the rotting log so nice.
Inspect it for fungi, insects, and mice.
Once a towering sugar maple tree,
Many people got their syrup from me.
Stroll through the woods 'til on the hill high,
Where below lies a pool with no fish fry.

*From the sign on the left, find the sixth letter of the word for the group
of animals described on this sign.* _____

*From the sign on the right, find the last letter of the name of the
nymphs illustrated.* _____

Head out of the woods past the nest on your left.
It's the size of an eagle's; think of the heft!
Find the Quest Box near that bird's enclosure,
But only for now is your Questing over.
Go visit our birds; your learning never ends.
Please come back soon to VINS with some friends!!!

Now unscramble the letters you've been collecting,
To find one group that VINS is protecting.

____ ____ ____ ____ S ____ ____

____ R ____ ____ .

Created by the VINS education staff in 2008.

48

Quest for the Rockingham Carvers

:45

easy

bring:
compass
pencil

historical
architectural

Take I-91 to exit 6. Travel west on Rt. 103 about one mile until you see the Rockingham Meeting House sign. Turn left and then the meeting house will be on your right, about 0.3 miles in, at the top of a steep driveway.

Clues

Note: *A pace equals two steps*

1. Start at the most prominent house of white,
    With colonial architecture it is quite a sight.
    The building went up in 1787,
    The folks in back are now all in heaven.
    As you Quest you will travel into the past;
    Collecting clues that will lead you to our box at last.

2. Use the map, and head west from the meeting house.
    You will find the Divoll monument near the gate.
    One of the Divoll family members suffered a terrible fate.
    His birth and death months have the same second letter,
    You will need this letter. It's a clue to your treasure: ___
                                                        2

    Look around: Tall obelisks are plainly in sight.
    This stone is called marble. It is clearly white.
    Other stones are grey; solid and shiny.
    That kind is called granite, and is quarried in Barre.
    The oldest stones here you can tell by date.
    These grey or black thin slabs of stone are called slate.

3. Now, go a little north of west and walk twenty paces.
    Turn right and go 30 more.
    The Eldridge grave is the thing you're looking for.
    This grave has a tree engraved on its back; on the front are names.
    How many are not dead as of the year "Y2K?"
    That number is part of your Quest today: ___
                                                3

4. Travel southeast and look up to the grave with the books
    That cannot be read. As you face the open books,
    a name is what you are looking for; use the last

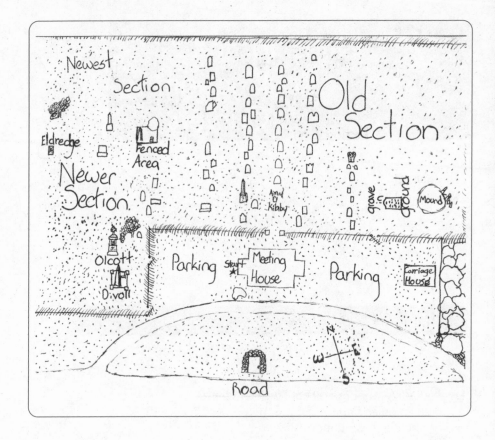

of the first and the first of the last:
Be sure to write these letters down.
These two will surely help you out later on: ___ ___
                                                                 4   4

5.   Go east to a little old grave by the open gate,
     Amy Kibby is underneath, her age was
     98 when she died. In the fifth line use
     the 6,7,9,10,11th letters, they are in spaces
     5,6,8,9,10. ___ ___ ___ ___ ___
                     5   5   5   5   5

6.   This grave has a spherical face
     That sits up high in a central space.
     The next stone found?
     Its mouth's corners are turned down.
     Then, Patty's stone with wide open eyes
     Gazes out to Rockingham's skies.
     Three stones left you will see
     a Whiting stone carved so beautifully.

7.   From Mary W. look over your shoulder
     To find John Harwood, Revolutionary soldier.
     Further down this row are other stones we'll show.
     On a 2nd Mary Whiting stone
     Two soul discs rise to heaven's home.

A few more stones to a shining sun
Watching over Patty, a little one.

8. Two rows west on stones of slate
    Other beautiful carvings await.
    John, with a furrowed brow ...
    Charlie, eyes wide open, even now ...
    Sally's stone with a single one ...
    Betty and her twins: 3 rising suns.
    Take some time to slowly look around:
    So many other beautiful stones can be found.
    Maybe you will find the Park family tree ...
    A beautiful memorial of much misery.

9. As you exit from this resting place,
    Where many stones hold a circular face
    Please note this special "Rockingham Style"
    Was unique to this region—but only for awhile.
    A Rockingham shop, started by Moses Wright
    Carved these special stones with a style just right.
    Moses, Alpheus, and Solomon, three Wrights;
    A. Burditt , S. Adams: all their work still delights.

10. Go east to the little house of white. And within?
    Inside is an old hearse for the dead to ride in.

11. If you followed the clues correctly and
    filled in the blanks, then you now know
    where to go to find the box. Go, go, go!

    Soon, you will have reached the end of your Quest,
    Sign our book. Then, go home and rest!

    Final clue:

    ___ paces ___ ___ ___ ___ ___ from h___ ___ ___se.
     3   4   4   2   5   5   5   5   5

Created by the 7th and 8th grades at the Compass School in 2000; edited and adapted in 2007.

49 Kidder Brook Quest

1:00

moderate

bring:
compass
boots
pencil

From I-89 take Exit 12 and head east toward New London. Take a quick left onto Little Sunapee Road. Bear right at the fork on Little Sunapee Road. Bear right again onto 114. Turn left on Twin Lake Villa Road. The parking area is on the right after you cross a little bridge over the brook. Note the stone bridge just beyond the parking lot.

natural
historical

Overview

This Quest begins on the site of Twin Lake Village. Twin Lake Village is an old fashioned vacation resort with 200 acres on Little Lake Sunapee. The Kidder family has been welcoming guests here for over 100 years. For more information, check out their website: www.twinlakevillage.com. The Quest continues on into the Gile State Forest which is part of the New Hampshire Department of Resources and Economic Development, DRED. DRED was established in 1961 and consists of four divisions: Forest and Lands, Parks and Recreation, Travel and Tourism Development, and Economic Development. For more information: www.dred.state.nh.us.

Clues

1. Embark upon your Quest,
   Stones arc over the stream.
   Scramble up sundry ___ ___ ___ ___ ___ steps
   Before you run out of steam.

2. When you're cold and you tire
   Come down by the stream
   And warm up by the ___ ___ ___ ___ ___ ___ ___ ___ .

3. Follow the blazes of orange beside the water
   Listen as the babbling brook calls
   Check out all of the ___ ___ ___ ___ ___ ___ ___ ___ ___ .

4. Then turn to the left
   And you shall see
   25 feet long

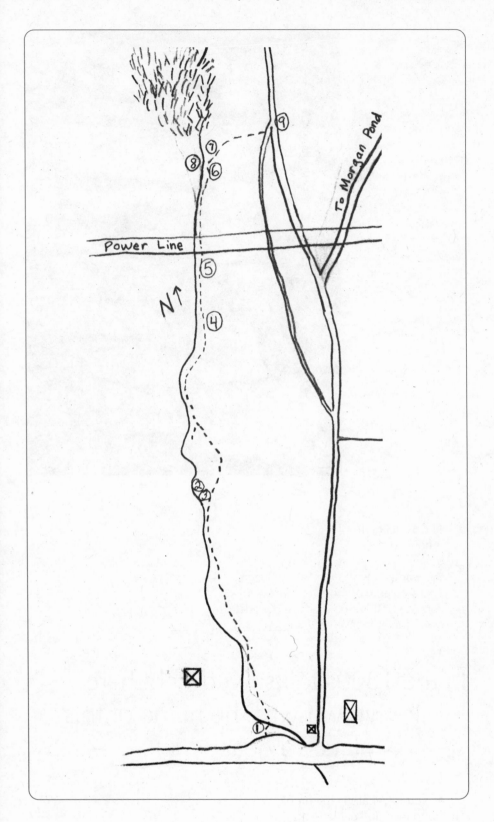

To Morgan Pond

Power Line

N↑

Stonewall
Photograph courtesy of Valley News

For an excellent education regarding stone walls, enjoy "Of Junipers and Weird Apples," the second chapter in Tom Wessell's book *Reading the Forested Landscape: A Natural History of New England.*

And 10 feet tall
A boulder ___ ___ ___ ___.

You come down to the Sandy Beach.
There's plenty of moss and rocks.
You can bask in the shade and wade.
Don't forget to take off your ___ ___ ___ ___ ___.

In the 1800s folks lived right here.
Perlytown was the name of this
place so dear.

5. As you travel along the brook,
    Up to the left, keep a look.
    A big stone wall is in sight,
    a reminder that this land once looked very different.

6. As you approach the power line
    notice a pile of sticks and mud.
    ___ ___ ___ ___ ___ ___ ___ made this with their big teeth.
    Have you seen them eat? I wish I could.

    Cross under the power lines through the land that is clear.
    Follow the trail to the left, your treasure is near.

7. Traverse above a stone wall
    20 meters along the path
    turn left and climb on top of the boulder
    Don't go too far, or you'll fall in with a ___ ___ ___ ___ ___ ___ .

8. Three hundred ancient rocks stand
    the remnants of a hand-made ___ ___ ___.
    Imagine almost 200 years ago
    A farm with a millpond spread out below.

    This was the site of an old shingle mill.
    It was run by the Kidder family long ago.
    Further down this brook at Morgan Pond,
    there used to be a lumber mill.

    In the 1800's folks lived right here.
    Perlytown was the name of this place so dear.
    Abandoned mills and cellar holes,
    are all that is left of the departed souls.

9. Go back off the boulder.
    As you, head back down the trail, look over your right shoulder.
    In the stone wall, find a nook.
    Your treasure box, sign the book!

Created by Phil Major's class at Kearsarge Regional Elementary School in 2000; additional information was added in 2007 by Jan Kidder of Twin Lake Village.

50 Black River History Quest

50

easy

1:00

bring: boots

Take I-91 to Exit 7 for Springfield, VT. Follow Route 11 east through town, toward Chester, traveling 4.5 miles. Turn left at the Springfield Shopping Plaza, go over a small bridge, and make an immediate right into the parking lot of Riverside Middle School. Follow the parking lot around the school next to the athletic fields, park at the tennis courts. Walk the path between the woods and the courts, till you get to the football field at the back.

natural
historical

Overview

This Quest was created by the Black River Action Team (BRAT) to help celebrate the powerful, beautiful Black River. The Black River Action Team began in 2000 as the concept that "someone ought to do something" became energized into action by the realization that everyone is a "someone." Since that first cleanup of the Black River's banks and bed by three volunteers, BRAT has grown to include more than seventy-five "someones" of all ages, working around the watershed. With the support of the CT River Watershed Council as its umbrella organization, BRAT continues this annual tradition of rolling up sleeves to get down & dirty in order to clean up the Black River and its tributaries. For more information check: www.blackriveractionteam.org.

Clues

Start your Quest at the stone of Horace Brown;
Visit one of his paintings at the Hartness House, downtown.
A generous man with talent galore,
He died in 1949, after the Second World War.

With your back to the school, you'll be facing the forest;
Walk past the stone and say "goodbye" to Horace.
Follow the field up the right-hand side;
That's the Black River down there, rolling by.

Her history's marked with some epic flows,
Part of the cycle of a river, you know.
The Plaza and bridge were once but a marsh;
Heavy storms swelled the river, and flooding was harsh.

Someone Ought to Do Something!
Photograph courtesy of BRAT

Keeping our rivers clean can be fun. Visit the Black River Action Team's website to learn more.

Hardship and loss were the Black River's yield,
Until a dam was installed up in Weathersfield.
Homesteads and farms were lost to the project;
Some families let go so that others could prosper.

In the center of Springfield roars big Comtu Falls,
With houses and factories built high on stone walls.
Invention and industry made the town prosper,
Good fortune was made with the power of water.

Earl Aldridge once kept this as pasture
for bovine;
Now it's a forest, all planted
with pine.

Do you spy the tall pines, at the edge of the field?
Look for the path, keep your eyes peeled!
The carpet of needles will cushion your feet;
Watch for squirrels in branches, they play hide-and-seek.

The pines drop their needles, but it won't hide your way;
Watch for chickadees as they sing and play.
Acid in the needles keeps other plants from growing;
What used to grow here, there's no way of knowing.

Earl Aldridge once kept this as pasture for bovine;
Now it's a forest, all planted with pine.
When winter was blowing, Earl cut ice from the river;
He'd sell it in summer, when you needed a shiver.

Cross a set of wood planks—two streams does it hide,
Which drain all year 'round the far mountainside.
Snow melts and rain falls, water moves through the soil—
It carries nutrients and microbes, or road salt and oil.

Your path winds along through the pines and then out;
The end lies not far, have never a doubt!
The plants grow thick here, slowing your motion.
That ravine up ahead might be the work of erosion.

Above you runs traffic on old Fairground Road;
Down here in the gully, you could see a toad!
Tree stumps are common, out here in the woods.
Do you see a trio, 'neath which lies hidden The Goods?

Find the Quest Box and stamp your book well;
You've seen all the sights on this walk through the dell.
As you pick your way back to Horace Brown's stone,
Think back to the time when the cows called this Home:

Big blocks of ice, covered in sawdust;
Fishing with bobbers in the heat of late August;
The marsh at the bend full of ducks and bull-frogs,
And a turtle or two hanging out on the logs.

The Black River's story runs powerful and deep,
We hope you'll come back and fond memories you'll keep.
Discover her wonders, by paddle or shore;
If you learn a little, you'll want to know more.

Created by Kelly Stettner of the Black River Action Team in 2007. This Quest and the Wellborn Ecology Fund Natural Communities Quest Series as a whole were made possible by generous support from the Wellborn Ecology Fund of the New Hampshire Charitable Foundation/Upper Valley region. www.nhcf.org

"Grampi made it up the hill, now he has to make it down!
With a little bit of luck he will have earned his crown!"

— Quest sign-in book

51

easy

Springfield Mills Quest

1:30

bring:
pencil

natural
historical
architectural

Take I-91 to Exit 7. Take Route 11 west into downtown Springfield. Just after the second traffic light, make a right into the parking lot at Chittenden Bank. Your Quest begins here. NOTE: This Quest can only be successfully completed at the following times: Monday through Thursday 9am until 8pm; Friday 9am until 5pm; Saturday 10am until 3pm; and Sundays June through August from 10 am until 1 pm.

Clues

From your parking place look downtown
Until you see the steeple brown.
Cross Main Street and walk through the light
Our library is on your right.

The Bank Block is across and down
For a long time it's been the heart of town.
It housed the phone exchange and jail
A radio station and 2 banks as well.

On this Quest you will need to collect
Some numbers that are correct.
Count the letters in the Bank Block name
This is how you start our game. ___
                                 10

Keep strolling and soon you'll see
A big building that is still a factory.
It's Lovejoy's machine tool shop
And this is where you've got to stop.

On the front of the building left from the door
Is a sign with numbers for the ISO.
Take the last number on this sign
And double it, you're doing fine ___
                                   11

The community center is attached to Lovejoy's
It's where we keep our many toys.
It used to be part of the factory
But now it is used by you and me.

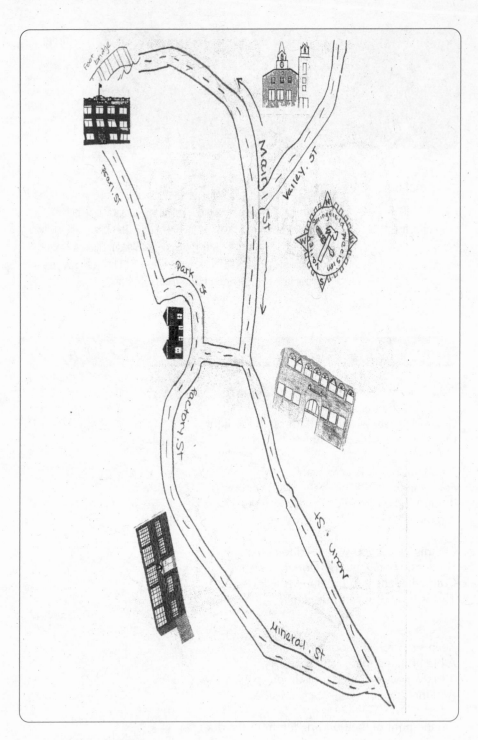

On the side are games we like to play
Look at the bingo board on display.
Take the top number under the "N"
And reverse the two digits and minus 2 ___ to get your end.
9

Now cross the bridge over the River Black
It's been the heart of our city all the way back.
This river gave power to all of our plants
The dams and the turbines cranked out the amps.

On the corner is a light
That is where you will take a right.
You must walk down Mineral Street
Don't go left, it's too steep.

On this road there are a few
Places where you can stop and see the view.
But one is better than the rest
From here you will see your whole Quest.

Now cross the bridge over the River Black
It's been the heart of our city all the way back.

Look far and wide across our town
Add 3 to the number of steeples you can count. ___
5

Now walk on down the street some more
To Jones and Lamson's three and four.
Here is where they made the machines
That made Springfield tops in the industrial scene.
It's where the state now keeps their books
Inside are murals that are worth a look.

To your right is the river park
It used to be the train yard.
The dam was built to harness power
During J & L's finest hours.

Now on you go to Comtu Falls
It's around the corner and not so small.
Its name in Abenaki means "great noise"
Go to the bridge and hear its voice.

The next numbers for your Quest
Are the first two of the bridge date—forget the rest. ___
1

On the Comtu building is your next clue
Take the address multiplied by two plus 5. ___
15

Turn until you see the bowling pins
This is where the next part of your Quest begins.
You must climb the hill in front of you
It will lead you to your next clue.

Look at the building with the blue trim
It is one of the oldest with lawyers within.
Its date of construction forms your next clue
Use the first numbers, not the last two. ___
7

Past Parks and Woolson you'll now have to walk
They made machines for the cutting of cloth.
Now the Big Elks Lodge will appear on your path
Take the first and the third number for the math ___
                                                    2

Across the street is Park Street School
Where we learned the golden rule.
On its front there is a date
Your next clue is to the left of the eight. ___
                                                3

At Pearl Street make a right
Soon your target will be in sight.
The last house on the right's for you
Count the porch posts for your next clue. ___
                                               4

Right away on this same street
Find a fire hydrant at your feet.
Turn right and carefully walk downhill over 100 paces
Turn left until the tan building front you're facing.

Count the number of windows on the entry way door
___, that's right for sure.
8

This whole complex was the Fellows Corporation
They made gears and gear shapers that built our nation.

Go across the footbridge to your right
Now turn around a see a circle white.
The first number of the date is what you need ___
Write it down and then proceed.   13

Now you're back on our Main Street
Walk right until Valley Street you meet.
Cross over to look at the Methodist's place
Take the first two numbers from the date. ___
                                              12

Now walk back to Main and make a left
Pass your car which you have left.
Count the number of letters in the first name of the bank
Now add that to 5 to fill in the blank ___ + 5 = ___
                                                       6

Across the street is a building green
It's the home of a pretty odd scene.
The International Order of Odd Fellows was there
They did good works in our City Fair.

Your last clue is in their construction date
Take the first two numbers without delay. ___
Now you're ready to find the spot   14
Where we've hidden the Valley Quest box.

Take your numbers and match them to
Their letter partners to make your clue.
Now fill the letters into the blanks below
To find the name of where you must go

If you need one last little hint from us
Keep on walking down Main past the bus.
Then cross at the light and walk until you're finding
The name of your goal—it's on their building.

SOLVING THE QUEST

You can find out which numbers match which letters by filling in this little chart. A = 1, B = 2 and so forth.

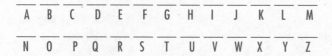

A	B	C	D	E	F	G	H	I	J	K	L	M
N	O	P	Q	R	S	T	U	V	W	X	Y	Z

Now, place the correct letter in each numbered space to find the location of the Valley Quest treasure box.

1	2	3	4	5	6	7	8

9	10	11	12	13	14	15

p.s. Ask at the desk!

Created by Susan Dreyer and the Springfield High School CHOICES students in 2003.

"Vermont is a wonderful place."

—Quest sign-in book

52 Springweather Quest

:45

moderate

bring:
compass
binoculars
field guide

natural
vista

From the junction of Rte. 11 and Rte. 106 in Springfield, continue north on Rte. 106 for approximately 1.8 miles. Turn right onto Reservoir Road, and go 1.5 miles take the second left and turn into the parking lot for the reservoir. To find the Trailhead, face north and find parking lot barricade. Walk through the gap and between two picnic tables. You will find yourself on the path to the information kiosk.

Clues

Start in the information area. Follow the railing to marker #1.
Take the red trail, your Quest has just begun.

Walk the plank to marker R2,
I'd take the right if I were you.

At marker R4 don't bear right,
Or you might go out of sight.

Follow the path to marker R5,
Don't take a left-hand dive.

Go around the corner to the bench with a view.
I'd go slowly if I were you.

To continue your outdoor thrill,
Walk on to the top of the hill.

Don't turn into pine tree heaven,
Stay to the left of marker R7.

Go past the bench to the left of pine tree heaven's gate,
Proceed through the clearing to marker R8.

Stand on the left of marker R8,
Head to the bench where you can wait.
(350 degrees)

Follow the trail to marker R9,
Stay on the green trail and you'll be just fine.

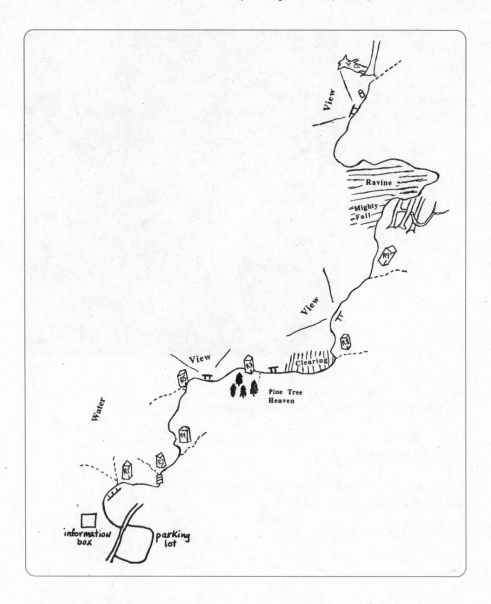

Watch out for the mighty fall if you please,
And go by the branch that weaves between two trees.

Follow the trail around the ravine, And continue to the bench where a view can be seen.

Follow the trail around the ravine,
And continue to the bench where a view can be seen.

Facing the water, find the man-made stump with the bluish-green hat,
About 34 degrees to the right from where you sat.

Birch Bark
Photograph by Ted Levin

All parts of this native tree have practical uses. The bark has played a key role in the manufacture of canoes for transportation and wigwams for shelter.

To find the treasure if you please,
Put your toes to the stump, and face 8 degrees.

Search near the moss on the decomposing tree,
The prize is there for you to see.

If you found the treasure—now you're done.
We hope you had a bit of fun!

Created by the 7th grade students of Marita Johnson and Mike Frank at the Riverside Middle School in Springfield, Vermont, in 1999.

53

Justin Morrill Homestead Quest

:45

easy

bring:
compass
boots

From I-89 take Exit 2 at Sharon and drive northeast on Vermont Route 132 for six miles to South Strafford Village. In South Strafford, take a left at the stop sign onto Justin Smith Morrill Highway. Drive two miles to Strafford's "upper village." The homestead will be on your right, just before the library. The Quest begins in the parking lot of the Morrill Homestead. Admission is charged to enter the House. (You do not need to enter the house to complete the Quest, but you will want to once you are there!) The Homestead is open from late May through mid-October from 11:00 a.m. to 5:00 p.m. on Saturdays, Sundays, and Monday holidays.

historical
architectural
natural

Overview

Senator Justin Morrill (1810–1898) was a self-educated native of Strafford, Vermont. Inspired by his own lack of formal education, Senator Morrill was the chief sponsor of the Land Grant Act, signed into law by President Abraham Lincoln in 1862. The goal of the Act being to create a land grant to each state to provide an education to farmers, mechanics, artisans and laborers. The Morrill Homestead is an example of Gothic Revival Architecture. It was designed and built by Justin Morrill before embarking on his political career. The Justin Morrill Homestead is a Vermont owned Historic Site. Find out more about this place and many others at: www.historicvermont.org.

Clues

If you stand between two landmarks
One very tall, one very short, and look to the rising sun and the bay
Into which the setting sun does stray
There you will find the very first clue …
But try as you might you can't peek through!

Next turn in place to where is featured
The horse rising from within the four lions' heads,
A parking place for four legged creatures
Visiting the Senator's homestead.
And there you will find the second clue,
But don't get tied up, there is more to do!

Justin Morrill
Homestead
Photograph by Jon
Gilbert Fox

This prime example of Gothic Revival architecture (in rosy pink!) was designed by Morrill himself. Built in 1848, the house is furnished with original family pieces.

Next head up the hill to a door without a house
Where without a roof plants will get doused.
There you will see some rusty pipe
That kept the plants from getting frostbite
And now you have found the third clue,
You're just warming up, there is more to do!

Look uphill again to the red door in midair,
What could have ever lived up there?
Downstairs lived the bacon, upstairs lived the beef,
Aren't you sorry they aren't here still to eat?
And thus you have found your fourth clue
Don't stop now; keep on the "mooo"ve.

Head to the smaller of the storage places
Where the outside wall has lots of vertical spaces.
Peek in the crib, you won't find a baby
Unless it's a baby ear of corn, maybe.
Now you've found the fifth clue
Are you ready to go where the ice blocks grew?

Now climb up the hill almost to the trees
But watch your step, you might fall in and freeze.
No fishing, no swimming,
No boating, no floating,
And in the water there's probably no otter.
Now you found the sixth clue
Used for making ice cream for me and you.

Roll down the hill to the first two buildings
"Baa" lived on the left, horseshoes forged on the right.
Next is the home of Jim, Charlie and Ruth
Each in their own spacious booth.
Now we'll move on to the next clue

Don't horse around there is more to do!
Go to the stage where games were played
To get there head left towards a high castle wall.
Here they played shuffleboard
And hoped to get a really good score.
Now we'll meander on a path of gravel
For our very next clue to unravel.

To the front of the castle you should perambulate
And spy the oldest Norwegian in the state.

To the front of the castle you should perambulate
And spy the oldest Norwegian in the state.

Spend a moment on the tour
To see plants that have been here before the Civil War.
Last and least there is a building we missed
For your last clue cross any bridge.

Now that you've done your very best
Look for a box that ends your Quest.
On a post much like Morrill's fence
Lift up the lid that you have sensed.
Stamp your journal; you're on your way
Hope you have a very great day!

Created by children and adults partcipating in "Family Nights" at the Morrill Library in 2001.

54 The Town House Quest

:45

easy

historical
architectural

Take I-91 to the Norwich Exit, #13. Drive straight through Norwich.
After 5 miles, merge onto Route 132 West. Continue to South Strafford
(8 miles) where you will leave 132 and stay straight toward Strafford
Village. Park behind the Town House. Face the stream.

Clues

Seventeen-eighty was the year
Enoch Bean has his mill dam here.
Walk around front, to the present green,
Where only his log house could then be seen.

There, ten times Town Meeting met,
With surveys made and roadways set
So folk could get to Enoch's mill,
Though routes were rough and rugged still.

With Revolutionary War's alarm,
Bean's Quaker Beliefs cost him his farm.
For trumped-up debts, his land was sold
While he was away and was not told.

Buyer, Daniel Robinson, in'88,
Walked from Foxboro to Vermont State—
One hundred-fifty miles with wife, eight children,
Bringing his handmade desk and Bible with him.

Cross the green to a house, the mustard-yellow one,
Daniel built in '90, with two of his sons,
A dwelling, an inn, public tavern and more.
Then, together, they built a store next door.

Follow the Brook Road on your right,
Past bridge, and stones piled "half-wall" height.
Joel Hatch used to walk this way
When he ran Daniel's inn and store each day.

His home (#34) is our destination.
First tiny half-cape with foundation,

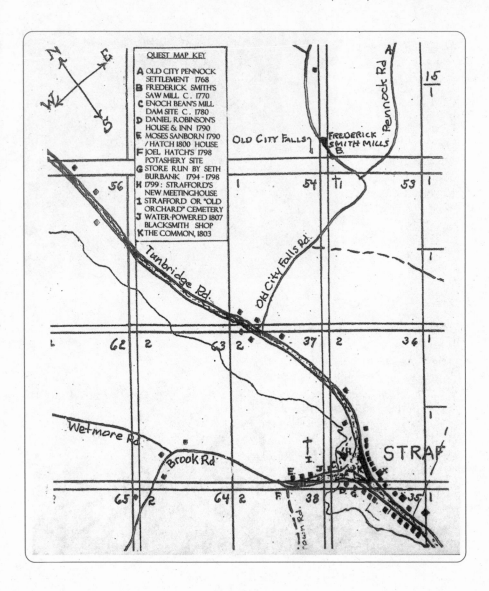

That Moses Sanborn built so well,
Joel enlarged to full-cape and ell.
Across the road was Joel's potash,
Where folks brought hearth ash in for cash,
Or "outdoor ashes" from clearing woods
That paid the bill for store-bought goods.

Walk back now, down the Brook Road, straight
Up to the cemetery gate.
Then through the ancient turnstile pass,
To climb a smooth, steep slope of grass

Before the first big tree, turn right—
At infant Sanborn's dove in flight.
A pink granite spire lifts up the soul
Then a gray spire—Royal, son of Joel.

Strafford Meeting House
Photograph by Jon Gilbert Fox

Built in 1799, Strafford Town Meeting has been held here every March since 1801. The 50x60 foot meeting hall has 20 over 20 windows, a clock tower, and elegant spire.

Follow flagstones by an iron fence,
Plus five more paces, turn right and thence
Seven stones to Moses Sanborn's space—
The man who first built Joel's place.

Exit left and the hill's crest follow
A drive, goes right back to "The Hollow."
Where, left, this '07 Blacksmith Shop
Used Enoch's dam for power nonstop!

Seventeen-eighty was the year Enoch Bean had his mill dam here.

Back on the Green, face Daniel's door.
A "long room" across the second floor,
For gatherings or Masonic Hall,
Revelers and dancers had a Ball!

A tavern and lodging, victuals as well,
And next door, Daniel's store (the brown ell)
Seth Burbank ran it—'94 the date—
Joel Hatch took over in '98

That year, Strafford met at Daniels's inn.
To see whose meetinghouse plan would win:
"The City's" site near Smith's Falls and Mill,
Or "Upper Hollow's" on Daniel's hill.

The people chose to set the stake
On "The Hollow's hill—and that would make
The name "Old City," the City's lot
And "Upper Village," the chosen spot.

The inn was roof over builders' heads,
The tavern kept them wined and fed,
The store sold hardware and supplies,
While Daniel helped to supervise!

But three years passed before the Town could get
Title to where Common and Town House set.
Not 'til Daniel sold his two sons his lands—
On the deed, it was THEY who set their hands.

Still, with money from pews, all ended fine,
The Town House was raised in '99
Your Town House Quest, too, will turn out well—
At the box outside, 'neath the clock-tower bell.

Created by Strafford Historical Society in 2005 to celebrate the Strafford Historical Society's 50th Anniversary.

"A beautiful, peaceful place."

—Quest sign-in book

55 Sunapee Harbor Quest

1:00

easy

bring:
compass
binoculars
swimsuit

Take I-89 south to Exit 12A. Make a right onto Springfield Road and proceed approximately 1/2 of a mile to the intersection of Route 11. Turn right again and proceed along Route 11 for 3.5 miles. Take a left at the sign and yellow flashing light into Sunapee Harbor. Park near one of the public parks on either side of Main Street.

natural
historical
vista

Overview

LSPA (Lake Sunapee Protective Association) is a member-supported, non-profit environmental educational organization founded in 1898 that works year-round to maintain the quality of Lake Sunapee and its watershed. LSPA's educational outreach is to all residents, lake users, students and visitors in the Lake Sunapee region. For more information, please check their website at www.lake-sunapee.org. Sunapee Harbor offers many recreational opportunities including boat rentals, lake cruises, evening band concerts, restaurants, shops and great ice cream! Close proximity to Sunapee State Park and State Beach for hiking and swimming.

Clues

At the tan House Knowlton, upon the hill,
on the paved road's edge, stand so still.
Look to the wall and its majestic rock,
here is where you begin your walk.

Crossing Garnet and Main on a ladder of white,
lean over green rails; water shimmers with light.
Relax and take some time to see,
Sunapee Harbor of large Lake Sunapee.

A right turn you make,
on your left is the lake.
Cross ahead to the dam, and if you are able,
stand by the building that once was a stable.

See the lake join a river so sweet.
Sugar River it's called; again cross the street.

Sail Reflected on Water
Photograph courtesy of Valley News

Lake Sunapee is the fifth-largest lake located entirely in New Hampshire. The lake is approximately 8.1 miles long and it contains eight islands.

Stand over water and find a stick white
used to measure the lake's water height.

Class A lake on your left, follow the walk
'tween buildings and boats where folks often talk.
When you reach the boat ramp, south you shall cross
to a park where there is much grass and some moss.

Which way do you think the
     water is moving?
Pick up a leaf fallen and
     set it to cruising.

Walk to where sand and soil join a wall,
careful now, don't you fall!
As you admire the beauty of this lake,
there are choices we each make
to keep the water clean and clear.
It is a treasure we hold dear.

Go north and cross Main to a Real Estate Office.
Straight ahead now, a road will suffice,
called "River," which is aptly named.

Follow this now to the source of its fame.

Which way do you think the water is moving?
Pick up a leaf fallen and set it to cruising.
Following now as your leaf floats along,
go ahead, loosen up, and just burst into song!

Across the river, see clock and tower,
you've been moving along by your own power.
A large white birch by the river grows,
on this side of the river, stop, stretch your toes.

Along the Sugar River, we take tests,
to make sure the water is at its best.
Conductivity, turbidity, pH are a few,
Samples like these give water quality clues.

At the stop take a turn east.
Cross over the river and, last, but not least,
South, follow the water's edge on the River Walk.
Up toward the street and parking lot

Back to the start, the House on the hill,
Now full of water science and history still,
Climb the long drive that leads to the rear,
You're almost through, the reward is near.

You'll see the glistening harbor
Standing just near the door,
Outside LSPA find the prize you seek,
North, South, East, West 'neath the goose take a peak!

Created by Meredith Bird Miller in 1998. Revised by Kathleen Legnard Stowell in 2008.

56

1:00

Bill Hill Quest

moderate

bring:
field guide
binoculars

From Exit 14 off I-91 follow Rt. 113 west up over Thetford Hill and down into Thetford Center. Turn left onto Tucker Hill Rd. Just past the covered bridge turn left into the driveway and park at the "Trailhead Parking" sign.

NOTE: For more Thetford Quests visit our online Quests page at: www.vitalcommunities.org

natural
historical
vista

Overview

The farm on Bill Hill was established in the early nineteenth century and cleared for cultivation, pasturage, and hayfields. In 1963, Thetford writer Noel Perrin bought the Bill Hill property and, leaving his New York City roots, began a dual life of teaching and part-time farming. Over the following four decades, Perrin learned from his land as he worked to shape it, harvest from it, and maintain the open view from the top of Bill Hill that he loved so much.

Noel Perrin wanted to assure that the land would exist in its undeveloped state in perpetuity. In 1984, he placed his property under a Grant of Conservation Restrictions to the town of Thetford. Fifteen years later, he transferred the grant to a conservation easement under the Upper Valley Land Trust (UVLT). UVLT is a regional land conservancy working to protect farmland, forests, wetlands and waterways, wildlife habitat, trails and scenic areas in the Vermont and New Hampshire towns of the Upper Valley. Since 1985, UVLT has protected over 380 parcels of land encompassing more than 34,000 acres. www.uvlt.org

Clues

Before you start just look around
What near this Quest trail can be found?

A sugar house, ready to go
Which might be envied by Thoreau!

In feet, it counts eight by eleven,
In syrup, sometimes twenty-seven

Gallons per year for Mr. Perrin,
Who for the maple trees was caring.

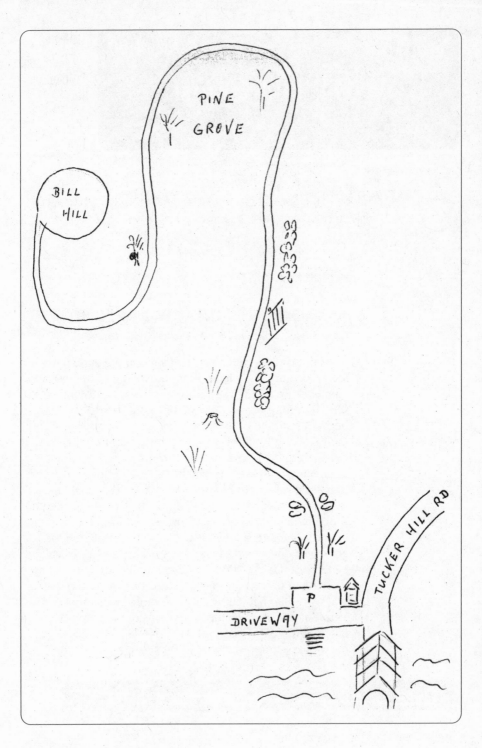

Across the driveway steps lead down
(Invasive knotweed covers ground),

And straight ahead, without a hitch
You see the falls and the covered bridge.

This path follows the river's bends.
And at Union Village Dam it ends!

But YOU go back: The Trailhead Parking leads
To an old gearbox in the weeds.

Who used it? Maybe Henry Bill,
Who gave the name to our hill?

No, he lived in the eighteen hundreds.
The land was cleared and sheep here wandered.

Now start your Quest where you can name
"White Pine"—"White Birch", they form a frame.

Light blue blazes you will have to follow.
They guide you through a grassy hollow

Until you reach a rocky cleft.
Twin spruce trees guard it on your left.

The trail climbs up along barbed wire,
Then joins the stone wall a bit higher.

These walls, once built to keep sheep in,
Restored they were by Noel Perrin.

Stumps on the left are soft and spongy;
How many years the tree rings tell ye?

Beyond the metal gate in the wall,
A stand of red pines straight and tall

Was planted on the steeper slope.
The trail goes round it and your hope

For better views is soon rewarded:
The open pasture does afford it!

Caused by a fungus, you'll soon see
A "Black Knot" on a cherry tree

Before the upper field you round,
Where weeds, berries & wild flowers abound.

"A lump of glacial debris" way up on top
Marks where your Questing will stop.

T'was Noel Perrin's favorite view,
Conserved for people just like you,

Who wander up and always will
Enjoy the sights from old "Bill Hill."

Created by Inge Trebitz and her grandchildren in 2004.

57 Quest for the Lonesome Pine

1:00

moderate

natural

bring:
field guide
binoculars
swimsuit

Take I-91 to Exit 14. Travel west on Route 113 two miles towards Thetford Center. Just as you enter Thetford Center—at the foot of Thetford Hill—turn left onto Buzzell Bridge Road and proceed to the Union Village Recreation Area. Travel 0.4 miles and then park in the large lot on your left. Your Quest begins there.

Overview

The Mystery Trail at Union Village Dam is an Army Corps of Engineers facility. It encompasses approximately 1,400 acres situated on the Ompompanoosuc River, four miles above its confluence with the Connecticut River. The Dam provides flood protection for Thetford, Norwich, White River Junction, Wilder—and countless spots downstream, too.

Clues

Walk to your west along this peaceful country road.
The east branch of the Ompomp. may be good for a toad!
After beach, ferns & locusts, find "Mystery Trail" to the right
Then follow my lead with all of your might.
Pick up a trail map guide in the box.
We are on our way, so pull up your socks!

Mysterious clues do abound—they just need to be found.
Whether human history, or giving nature a chance
This Quest will do part of the loop; look deep—give more than a glance.
Before the bridge with buds alternate and red brown,
Look for an American Basswood, the carver's tree.
It has heart-shaped leaves, and coppice wood
(four big stump sprouts) for you to see.
Let's cross the river. Be sure to notice its sparkle and quiver.
Kingbird may be chief, but it is the Blue Jay who cries "thief, thief."[1]

---

[1] During the late spring and summer, the Blue Jay's diet includes baby birds and eggs. In no way, however, are they a threat to the survival of other songbirds. They are a principal planter of acorns.

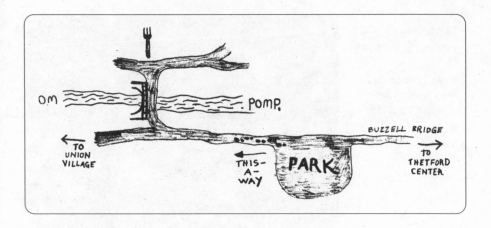

At the fork we will bear right. Look for the Red Oaks, sturdy with might.
Having flat-topped ridges and salmon colored grooves in the bark
The leaves are big and pointy. Acorns are clues to this tree in the park.
You will pass Hemlock, with needles so tiny and green
Maybe a Red Squirrel will chatter—begging to be seen.
Thriving in soil so poor, find one which reproduces by spore.
It can be up to three feet high, and has 3 branching parts the same.
With fronds widest at the base it is "Bracken" by name.

From the days of yore, an old town road you roam
Look and see if you can find a few fence posts made of stone.
The quacking and peeping that you may hear?
It might be frog's music reaching your ear.[2]
Bear right at the fork for treasures are near. What could they be?

Can you hear the "laugh" of a Robin?
Or the "wrock" of a Raven?

Look and see!
Can you hear the "laugh" of a Robin?[3] Or the "wrock" of a Raven?[4]
Both of these birds inhabit this haven.

Follow the path and you shall see a specimen from days of old—
If only this lofty White Pine's stories could be told!
Be they natural or human, mysteries and wonders are abundant.
Just how was the old stone farm gatepost relevant?
Can you find a cellar hole, a silo pad, or stone foundations?
Being a history sleuth you will have many investigations!

Now find yourself nearing the pond's soft edge
Graced with alders, with cattails and sedge.

---

[2] Spring peepers can be heard here from late April until early June.
[3] Robin arrives in late March, has two nesting cycles and departs by fall.
[4] Ravens enjoy this setting year-round.

Fiddlehead Fern
Photograph by Ted Levin

Did you know that the fern is one of the first plants on our planet? Fossil remains have been found dating back 450 million years!

Listen for the bubbly Song Sparrow's
"Madge. Madge, please put on the teakettle" song.[5]
Or the "wichity, wichity" of the Common Yellowthroat (a warbler)[6].
You just can't go wrong!

Dragonflies dart and zoom. Do milkweed dance and spin?
We have a wetland with lots of room—and Wood Duck boxes ready to go in.
Look close, for there may be a painted turtle, heron—
even a migrating Green-wing Teal.
Were it me that was here, Aye, I'd surely give a squeal!
Butterflies do flutter and yearn, and have nary a care.
Tree Swallows bank and turn—the acrobats of the air.[7]
Perhaps you might find a berm built of twigs, sticks and mud?
Keep an eye & ear for the beaver, which whacks his tail with a thud.

Ah … there is so much more to this story,
Like the hillside in fall in all its glory.
So many mysteries waiting to be solved
In a place so far away from the maddening crowd.
Let the peace feel its way in … 'cause there's so little that is loud.
Spring, summer, fall—which time is the best?

---

[5] Season: Late March through October.
[6] Season: May through July.
[7] Springtime visitors

Come again and again, and experience the rest.
And for the last mystery: find your treasure chest.
Remember how you looked for the "Lonesome Pine."
Make your way to that tall tree and the last clue you will find.
From that Pine make your way to another fallen tree.
To a big ole stump is where your treasure box will be!

Species Check List

What did YOU see?

[ ] American Basswood
[ ] Eastern Hemlock
[ ] Locust
[ ] Red Oak
[ ] White Pine
[ ] Bracken Fern
[ ] Kingbird
[ ] Blue Jay
[ ] Robin
[ ] Raven
[ ] Song Sparrow
[ ] Common Yellowthroat
[ ] Wood Duck
[ ] Painted Turtle
[ ] Blue Heron
[ ] Green-wing Teal
[ ] Tree Swallow
[ ] Red Squirrel
[ ] Beaver

Created by Bill Shepard in 2000. Quest for the Lonesome Pine and the Wellborn Ecology Fund Natural Communities Quest Series as a whole were made possible by generous support from the Wellborn Ecology Fund of the New Hampshire Charitable Foundation/Upper Valley region. www.nhcf.org

"The sounds at this place
put a smile on each face.
Thanks for leading us here."

— Quest sign-in book

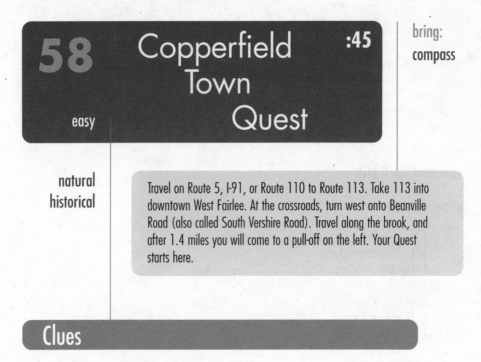

58 Copperfield Town Quest

:45

bring: compass

easy

natural historical

Travel on Route 5, I-91, or Route 110 to Route 113. Take 113 into downtown West Fairlee. At the crossroads, turn west onto Beanville Road (also called South Vershire Road). Travel along the brook, and after 1.4 miles you will come to a pull-off on the left. Your Quest starts here.

Clues

This Quest begins after you park,
Turn left and head north in order to embark.

Please follow the road carefully—
Because of cars that you might see.

On both sides are cellar holes.
These were dug by people, not by moles.

One thousand people lived here
One hundred and twenty years ago.
They had a big coal smelter
And small houses built in rows.

Turn back uphill and proceed to
The corner of the "great wall."

The holes, you see, were houses
Inhabited by people—also by mouses.

One hole a church, another a store,
Mr. Ely's mansion and many more.

Pass four telephone poles
Then take twenty paces
And turn left to the cellar hole
With your smiling faces.

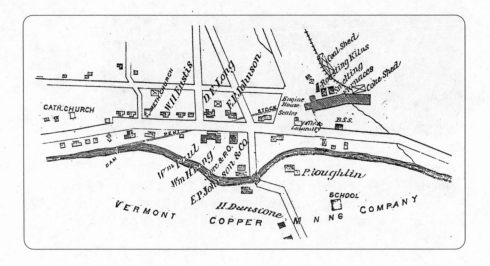

Take a look but don't go in
Then back to road and left again!

Across from the fifth pole.
Look for a path
And an old cellarhole.

On the downward path is
a cluster of birches
(Something often found
On Valley Quest searches).

You might see traces of
A beaver or an otter—
Giving you a clue
That you are near to water.

After you have seen our
Splendid, rushing waterfall
Turn back uphill and proceed to
The corner of the "great wall."

Now slowly north along the wall
Eyes open for our box (which is small).

Beneath a tall balsam fir tree
The wall continues—don't you see?
Look in the gaps between the rocks
And if luck would have it, you'll
find our box!

Created by Barbara Griffin's 2nd and 3rd grade at Vershire Elementary School in 2000.

59 Quest for the Raven

1:30

difficult

bring:
binoculars
compass
field guide

From Exit 14 on I-91, take Route 113 west to West Fairlee. 4.5 miles beyond the Westshire School in West Fairlee turn right on Eagle Hollow Road (a paved road heading toward Corinth, Goose Green and Bradford). Travel 1.4 miles, up and over a knoll, to a small parking area on your left.

natural
vista

Overview

The Northern Hardwood Forest is the most common forest found in the Upper Valley region of Vermont and New Hampshire. It is a transition between the boreal (spruce/fir) forest to the north and the deciduous forests further south. In this type of forest, four tree species tend to dominate: sugar maple, American beech, yellow birch and Eastern hemlock. Because these trees can reproduce in their own shade, this forest is self-perpetuating. Dappled light penetrating the forest canopy allows for a rich diversity of understory trees and shrubs. The species that thrive here, however, tend to be those that can tolerate the shade. Pioneer species like paper birch and white pine seed-in when opportunity arises in the form of a disturbance: an opening created by a windstorm, perhaps, or by a logging operation. Northern Hardwood Forests are important habitat for many species. Mammals likely to be seen include red squirrels, Eastern chipmunks, porcupines, black bear, and moose, among many others.

Clues

Cross two lanes to the forest road
But then into the woods is where we'll go.
After 10 steps or so, right onto the trail
As I begin to tell you a small forest tale.

If you look to the trees it does seem to me
That you'll find quite a species diversity.
There are beech trees here, with shiny grey bark
And paper birch peeling, bright white like starch.

White ash can be seen, its bark a lattice of diamonds.

Raven
Photograph by Ted Levin

These large, loud birds are very intelligent, and have successfully adapted to arctic, desert and temperate climates.

Red and sugar maple, too, you will certainly find.
These dominant trees make our storyline clear—
We're in **Northern Forest,** a place we hold dear.

Bear right where the beech tree has blown down.
Disease & strong winds brought it to the ground.
Next, with big boulders left, look way up to see
The trees' tippy-tops—also called the "canopy."
(Off to the left you may see a cairn—pile of rocks and limbs,
Placed by the Mountain School to mark where they climb.)

Keep up the trail until you find a pair of white birches
This is the next place to conduct a quick search.
Trees grow *beneath* the canopy, 10' high or so
An "understory" it's called 'cause it grows below.

This understory—of sugar maple, beech and hemlock—
Another clue that Northern Forest is where we walk.
Your trail climbs up across a wet and muddy place
There at the ground is where to place your face!

In this forest many ferns choose to live:
Christmas, marginal, hay-scented, lady and sensitive!
These ferns are intricate, things that we adore
In Northern Forest you'll see them on the forest floor.

At the fork you can follow either left or right

As both trails come together just out of sight.
Where they rejoin you can find four clues
About this land's history—clues we can use.

The first clue is the stump of a tree
The 2nd a six-foot scar you can surely see
The next is birch trunks lying on the ground
And last is a stone wall ... but can it be found?

As you keep walking, heading up the trail
About each clue I will tell you a small tale.
The stump of a tree? Why that's a plain fact
Someone was here with a chainsaw or axe.

The six foot scar at the bottom of the tree?
Was left by loggers and their machinery.
The birch trees prostrate with bark so white?
This tree only grows where there's lots of light.

All these birches call out: "this land was clear"
Stone walls reinforce that it once was pasture here.
The walls are another clue: this is a boundary mark
Letting us know we're in EAGLE HOLLOW PARK.

When you reach the crest of the rise
Two new trees are a treat for our eyes.
They are trees with needles, both conifers:
One's called red spruce, the other balsam fir.

Spruce needles are smaller, and to touch are "spikey"
The "furry" fir needles lie flat, and smell oh-so-nicely.
Now that you know the trees of this habitat
Listen and look for animals ... for calls and for scat.

Moose like to munch on the twigs and buds of fir
Red maple's new growth? Winter food for deer: high in fiber!
Sugar maples savored by squirrels and grosbeaks.
Hemlocks hold sap that the hummingbird seeks.

Calls you've probably heard ... a loud "wrock, wrock?"
This is a great site to hear the boisterous raven talk.
And signs that we've seen? Why scat of deer,
Lots of tracks of moose, bobcat, and signs of little bear.

Stay on the trail, enjoying the fine view
For awhile proceed forward, without any clues,
Until you come to an alley of young saplings
Almost forming an arch where a choir might sing.

"Striped" stripe maple, "shiny" yellow birch and "dotted" pin cherry,
This tunnel may find a new home within your memory.
At the top of the rise, just to the left of the trail
Find a 12-foot rock outcrop ... there's no way to fail.

Stand with this rock's face touching your back

Then ahead through woods on a 230-degree track.
Keep on straight, yes, go on through the wood
At 55 steps: a 3-trunked yellow birch sign for the good.
(Do you see it? Go to the birch for your next clue.)

Now, 150 more steps in the very same direction,
And the top of the ledges for your inspection
Perched atop of this rocky place, see many things,
Like our friend the raven, with his jet-black wings.

Of all of the wild places, ravens like cliffs best
Often it is up here they choose to build a nest.
Listen closely, quietly. Can you hear them sing?
Across Eagle Hollow their voices often ring.

Now, in order to find the Valley Quest box
Meander the top of the ledge: a long grey rock.
At one end of this rock, find a small cavity
For this is where the box must surely be.

Enjoy your stay up here for a good long time,
A wild place and view like this, both precious finds.
To get back, reverse your steps back to the rock
Then take the trail downhill left on a leisurely walk.

Quest for the Raven Species Check List

What did YOU see?

☐ American Beech	☐ Paper Birch
☐ White Ash	☐ Red Maple
☐ Sugar Maple	☐ Christmas Fern
☐ Marginal Fern	☐ Lady Fern
☐ Sensitive Fern	☐ Red Spruce
☐ Balsam Fir	☐ Eastern Hemlock
☐ Common Raven	☐ Moose
☐ Striped Maple	☐ Yellow Birch
☐ Pin Cherry	☐ Red Squirrel
☐ Eastern Chipmunk	☐ Porcupine
☐ Black Bear	☐ Bobcat
☐ Hermit Thrush	☐ Rose-breasted Grosbeak

Created by Ginny Barlow, Andrea Lewis and Steve Glazer in 2003. The Quest for the Raven and the Wellborn Ecology Fund Natural Communities Quest Series as a whole were made possible by generous support from the Wellborn Ecology Fund of the New Hampshire Charitable Foundation/Upper Valley region. www.nhcf.org

60 Crystal Cascade Quest

2:00

difficult

bring: binoculars

natural overlook

From Exit 8 off I-91, travel west on Route 131 for 3.2 miles to Cascade Falls Road. Turn right onto Cascade Falls and take an immediate left at the fork onto High Meadows Road. At the last house, bear right into the parking lot.

Clues

Ayup, it's 422 feet higha
To the Crystal Cascade up yonda
Lil o'er a mile from the parkin' lot heya
But shucks, don't you worry,
Halfway up there, levels off in a hurry!
Well you start up these steps of wood
Followin' the white blazes if you could

Bloodroot
Photograph by Ted Levin

Bloodroot is an early blooming wild flower with delicate white petals. Bloodroot seeds are dispersed with the help of ants.

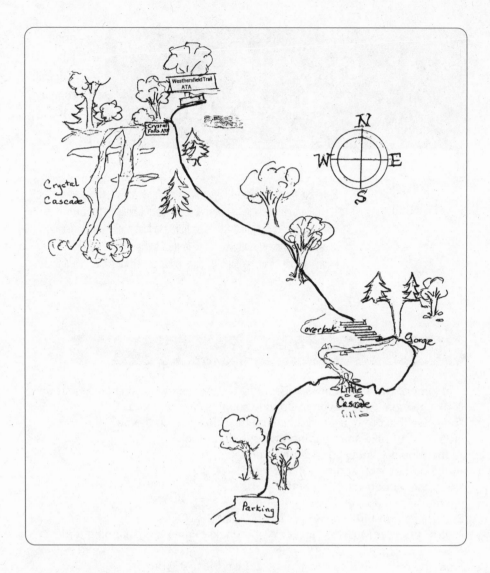

Cross the lil brook then uphill you'll scramble
Hope Lil Cascade's flowin' as o'er it you amble
Through gorge, up steps, why—there's a view
Near halfway there, rest'll be plain to you
Two ATA's (Ascutney Trail Association signs)
 Near Crystal at 1510 feet
'Neath one is a find that can't be beat

Created by Wendy Smith in 1999.

61

difficult

**Linny's Loop
Bicycle Quest**

2:00

bring:
bike
swimsuit
compass
pencil

natural
historical

Travel on Vermont Route 113 to the village of Post Mills. Then take Route 244 north along the west shore of Lake Fairlee to the Lake Fairlee access/boat ramp (.8 miles from the foot of the Lake). Your Quest begins there! You may want to take a dip at Treasure Island when you are done, be sure to bring some money for the entrance fee!

Clues

Welcome to our lake! Fifty-six feet at its deepest point—and six miles around.
Looking carefully, its seven in-flowing sources can be found.
Today we'll explore just two—leaving the other five up to you.
Hop on your bike and head northwest (left) to look
At the tributary known as Middle Brook.
At the bridge, stop and take in the view
Of all the nutrients flowing under you.
Nutrients, perhaps, that you cannot quite see …
But what about birds, beaver or otter? What do YOU see?
Eagles? Osprey? Muskrat lodges? Wood ducks? Painted or snapping turtles?

From the bridge find the white arrow. Take the first word
And fill it in the space labeled #1. That is how this Quest is done!

After a right turn on Middle Brook, to your left is a camp
And along the banks of the brook a willow alder swamp.
Now take a ride in style … for at least another mile.

Next to 1003 is something with many, many windows.
Fill that word in space #2, for that word is your next clue!

One side of this fine structure is marked clearly with two Xs.
The number of windows on this side goes in space #3. Really!

You'll pass a lake on your left and then the three silos of Stever's Dairy,
Still milking and shipping milk—which makes our hearts merry.

There is a breed of cow named upon their sweet sign.
Fill it in space #4 and you're doing just fine.

Three miles in, watch out for the griffin!
Upon a lawn on the right you may see him a-sittin.

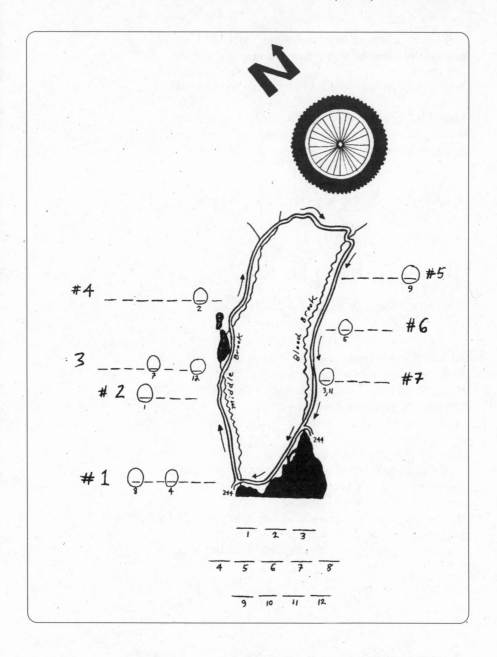

One part eagle, one part lion; lots of presence but hardly flying.
Straight on lies a church marking West Fairlee Center
Bear Notch Road turns left but do not enter.
Stay on the main road right and straight—
For Blood Brook Road is the name of your fate.
Turn up to the right when this road comes in sight.
The climb may be steep, but try and stay on your seat …
It's only a half-mile climb. Breathe, relax, take your time.
The reward comes as a long downhill without a clue …
For a little while the entertainment's all up to you!

There's a peaceful resting place under some trees,
And the top of its fence is marked clearly with these.
Mark this symbol as word #5—then off you drive!

You'll pass a one-room school house from 1871
Record the name of its number and clue #6 is done.

Take a right on Marsh Hill to see a neat old saw mill.

Lichen has covered the rocks in its cellar
Turning them to a quite curious color.
The seventh word names the color you've learned.

Lichen has covered the rocks
in its cellar
Turning them quite
a curious color.

Back to the main road and coast down to the lake
And at the stop sign a right turn you must take.
Here, Blood Brook flows in through a culvert
Offering the lake rich freight for dessert:
Rock flour, pulverized leaves, soil, and even pieces of trees.

Alas, the time has come to compute and to spell …
And if you've collected all the right words you can tell
The place the Linny Loop Treasure Box will dwell.

Use the map. Missing two clues? Aye, use your eyes! What bad puns!
Then bike .3 miles until you see
The small triangle where the treasure must be!

Created by Steve Glazer and Ted Levin in 1999.

62 :45

The Energy Quest at Boston Lot

moderate

bring:
field guide
compass

natural

Head north on Rt. 10 from West Lebanon, NH towards Hanover. After passing the Wilder Dam, turn right into the Wilder Dam Picnic Area parking lot. Your Energy Quest begins at the top of the stairs.

NOTE: For more Lebanon Quests visit our online Quests page at: www.vitalcommunities.org

Clues

Walk to the top of the stairs and turn around.
Look for the types of energy that abound.
The dam makes electricity that runs through the wires.
There is even kinetic energy in the car tires.

Olcott Falls was an obstacle the settlers found
200+ miles north of the Long Island Sound.
The 1st dam here was built for a saw and gristmill.
The Wilder Dam, erected in 1950, stands here still.

Charcoal, charred tree trunks,
    hollowed within,
            Open undergrowth,
ponder ... how did this begin?

Follow the white pines south along a line
As you walk, look for woodpecker holes (there are at least 9).
Now you're looking for a 15' circumference white pine.
Hanging on it is a "No Camping" sign.

Don't be fooled by my copycat friend,
Head towards the brown gate where a large branch bends.
Towering up to 200' feet tall, pine was the "Monarch of the trees."
With clusters of 5 needles, like solar panels function these.

The old King of England claimed the pines for his ships masts
Upon which sails harnessed wind to traverse the oceans vast.
Step over the non-native rock and head east—uphill—from the gate.
And your next clue? Just keep your eyes open, wait.

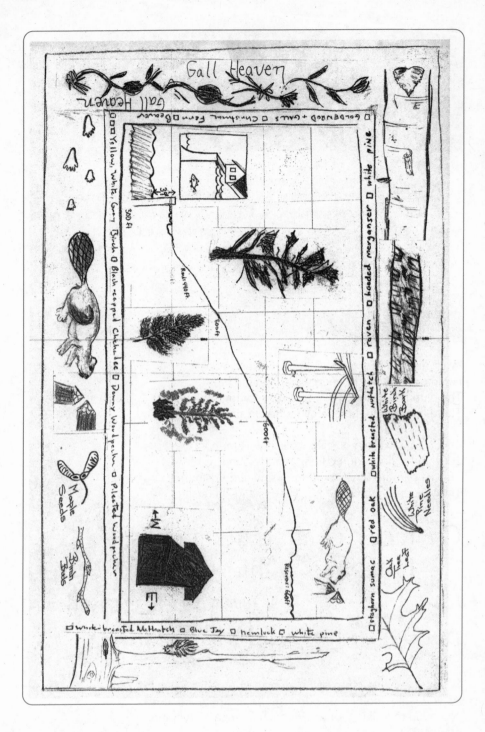

Scan for a tree with an old fence scar.
Opposite can you find the embedded metal bar?
Woodpecker holes and witches broom,
Rusty barbed wire—you should see these all soon.

Continue up the hill and around the bend
Yellow and white birches left, a water bar to transcend.
The water bar re-directs the downhill flow.
20 steps forwards, then to the right, we must go.

Step off the trail to visit the mossy log
Which is also known to block, slow and clog.
A fallen pine crossing the stream
Will provide energy as a nursery tree.

Hemlock seeds take root in the moss & lichen,
Find food and energy for which they have a likin!
We also find an abundance of ferns—
Once cut, twice cut, and thrice cut by turns.

Fruit dots and spore cases for propagation,
3 million years ago food for dinosaur invigoration!
Back on and up the path, stop at water bar two.
Evidence of fire waits to the left of you.

Charcoal, charred tree trunks, hollowed within,
Open undergrowth, ponder … how did this begin?
Head toward the power lines, to the crushed blue stone.
Onward and upward this Quest does roam.

Stop under the power lines if you like,
And eat a snack to power the rest of your hike.
Two kinds of energy are now overhead,
On sunny days you'll feel rays, warm & toasty like your bed.

The 2nd kind pulses through power lines, harnessed by man,
And goes to power your toaster, your fridge, and your fan.
From here, continue uphill through the gate
To the top of the hill where a map will await.

To the left see a field … an aspen grove you will sight
But you need to keep on the beaten path to the right.
Take 50 steps more to a hollow white pine,
Then look for 6 trunks that are hidden behind.

You may only see four, but believe us, there's more,
In fact one of the trunks lies down on the floor!
Find a rock den, where in winter a bear might reside …
For that's where your Valley Quest box does hide!

Please sign in, stamp in, and re-hide the box for the next visitor.
We also encourage you to explore the trails around the reservoir.

Created during a Valley Quest teacher workshop in 2004, with support from the Wellborn
Ecology Fund of the New Hampshire Charitiable Foundation / Upper Valley region.

63

:45

The Junction Quest

easy

bring:
pencil
compass

Take Exit 11 off I-91 and travel north on Route 5 down the hill toward the village of White River Junction. Continue straight through the second set of lights. Route 5 turns left, but you should continue straight on North Main Street to the stop sign. Continue for one block and turn left over the tracks. You will then follow the "Welcome Center" signs into the parking lot for the Court House and the Train Station.

historical
architectural

Overview

The Hotel Coolidge has been the center of hospitality in White River Junction since 1849, when railroading began. Formerly called The Junction House, owner Nathaniel "Than" Wheeler renamed his hotel when Calvin Coolidge became President of the United States in 1923, in honor of his good friend and patron John Coolidge of Plymouth, Vermont, the president's father. For generations it has been important place to stay, eat, greet and meet.

Clues

Life in White River has changed its ways,
since the railroad had its glory days.
With a short walk around the town,
there's lots of history to be found.

My wheels are not in motion
though I'm still a sight to see
Find 494 near the center of town
and start your Quest with me.

With the tracks on your left
follow the path to the RR crossing.
Turn right toward the district Court
and keep on walking.

Go left past two new buildings
the first houses RSG.
The second even newer building
is just as modern as can be.

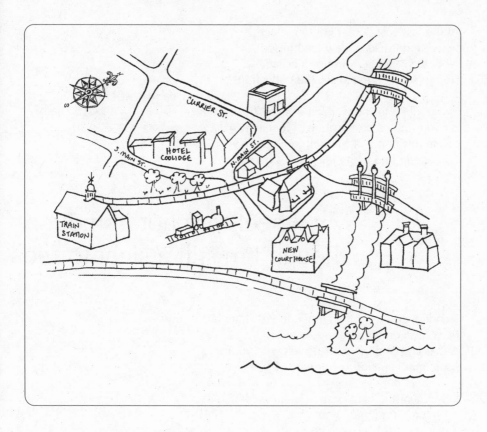

Then turn north across Ralph Lehman bridge
that spans our Class "B" water
Cleaner today and flowing free.
for fisherman, swimmers, and otters.

Follow the river east past a war monument
and on to a performance site.
(Bands sometimes play here at night.)
Then continue on to a scenic point
where in 1704 the Iroquois did alight.

Enjoy the confluence, take in the view,
Then head back to the west from here
Cross grass onto pavement
to a garden nicely planted; 1991 was the year.

Travel south along a road,
there's no need to swim,
count the ornate light posts
on your left as you see them.

Remember the number,
you'll need it soon,
to find the treasure
at the end of this Quest.

At the last post, look right to a place
where red trucks once were housed ...
Now the Main St. Museum's home,
stop in sometime and see the collection!

Slip under a trestle walking straight 'til you see
on your right a cornerstone of nineteen sixty.
Inside this home of Ma Bell for many a year
you would find many telephones here.

My wheels are not in motion though I'm still a sight to see

Heading east from the corner, travel along artist's row,
our Quest drawing soon to a close
At the end of the block turn left with your toes,
some mathematics to you we pose:

Remember the light posts you counted before,
subtract 6 from the number you got.
The answer this leaves equals the doors you must pass
before reaching our final Quest spot.

Inside this place there's a desk lit by lamps
and someone seated behind.
This is the person to ask for the box
that you've worked so hard to find!

Created by Linny Levin, Sue Kirincich and Marty Layman-Mendonca in 1999. Revised by
Laura Dintino in Marty's honor in 2007.

"9/16/07 Perfect day for hiking!
We brought apples + cookies + tea."

64 American Precision Museum Quest: Windsor in the 1860s

:45

easy

bring:
pencil
compass

Windsor is located on Rte. 5, between exits 8 and 9 off Interstate 91. American Precision Museum is located on Rte 5 (Main St.), at the south end of Windsor Village, just south of the stoplight at the intersection of Main and Union/Bridge streets.

NOTE: For more Windsor Quests visit our online Quests page at: www.vitalcommunities.org

architectural
historical

Overview

The American Precision Museum preserves the heritage of the mechanical arts, celebrates the ingenuity of our mechanical forebears and explores the effects of their work on our everyday lives. Housed in the 1846 Robbins and Lawrence Armory, a National Historic Landmark, the museum holds the largest collection of historically significant machine tools in the nation. Open daily 10-5 Memorial Day weekend through October. Admission is charged, special rates for families and school programs. www.americanprecision.org. If you enjoy this Quest, you may want to try the Machine Tool Quest located inside the Museum.

Clues

With Eighteen Forty-Six behind
Down a gravel path, water you'll find.

> Mill Brook dammed up power from streams,
> Here, generations of artisans made machines!
> Now look at the 1870 trade card below.
> What was made here? This card will show.

Back up the hill, then left up the drive
Cross the bridge—do not cross Route 5!
At the 3rd green metal plate, look right:
The old stone foundation is in your sight.

Note: This photo was
taken looking upstream.

Atop that stone wall a Grist Mill was found,
This is the place where the grain was ground.
And across the brook a foundry once stood
Where they melted iron in this neighborhood.

Continue to Union St. Cross it at the light
Walk to four trees ahead on your right.

100 years after the
peak of production
Ed Battison saved this building
from destruction.

Turn and see a house with two doors
Inside Kendall's ghosts float o'er the floors.

Nicanor Kendall, an inventor was he,
Designing guns & building and industry.
With Lawrence (as foreman) and Robbins' funds
They won a bid to make 10,000 guns.

Back to the corner—to "Slow Children" sign
And the 2nd of 9 doors in a very long line.

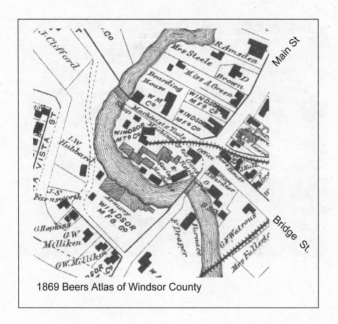

1869 Beers Atlas of Windsor County

In the 1860's these apartments weren't here—
There were many small shops as the 1869 map makes clear.
Use the map: follow the track to where it stops.
What did they load & unload at the shops?

Go west until you find 17 on a door
Where the "Brick Block" ends, you'll find the thrift store.
> *Maps from the 19th century show*
> *That this is where the workers would go*
> *To sleep and also get a meal …*
> *At a boarding house, that was the deal!*

Cross the street at the stripes; cross Mill Brook too.
A single tall chimney will come into view.

Head "One Way" past a low stone wall
The Armory bell tower and its golden gun call.

Pass steel girders; hear a humming sub-station
The Dry Cleaner is your next destination.

> *In 1860, this was the South School*
> *Children were here while their fathers made tools.*
> *As a child, Ed Battison studied here.*
> *Who is he? The answer is near.*

Continue on Maple Street to the stop sign.
Down a slope, apple trees you'll find.

Sit in the shade, take in the view;
The last of the story we'll tell you.

American Precision Museum Display
Photograph courtesy of Valley News

The museum's extensive gun collection traces the history of firearm design and construction in the Connecticut Valley, beginning with custom guns made by Nicanor Kendall.

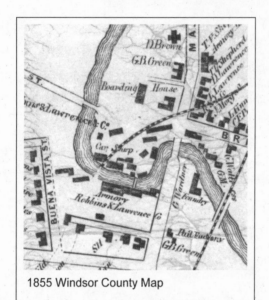

1855 Windsor County Map

The bell would ring for the workers to know
It was time for a shift to come and go.
100 years after the peak of production
Battison saved this building from destruction.

Find the treasure box on a young apple tree,
And you have solved this industrial mystery.

This museum has many Windsor stories to tell
Find them in the Museum beneath the bell.

Created during a Valley Quest workshop in 2007.

65 Quest for the Kestrel

:30

easy

Exploring an Old Field

bring:
compass
binoculars
field guide

From either Exit 8 or 9 off I-91, take Route 5 south or north to downtown Windsor. Turn west on State Street. Bear right at the fork, and then turn right onto County Road. After 2.6 miles, turn left on Weeden Hill. Then, after 0.1 mile, take your first left onto Marton Rd. After 0.7 mile, park in the pull-off by the low shed on the left.

natural
vista

Overview

Old fields include a mixture of annual, biennial and perennial herbaceous plants, along with grasses, shrubs and young trees. Old fields undergo a process known as succession. Any open field fills in, over time, with a succession of species. First to come are the "pioneer" species, herbaceous weeds like asters and goldenrod. Later, trees seed in, and eventually, a field—if left untended—will become a young forest. First to come are the sun-loving trees, like white pine and pin cherry. While this field is still open, look to the surrounding ridges: much of this land is returning to forest.

Clues

Look up, and around—
There is so much sky!
And so many habitats, too.

To the north there is field corn.
To the south, hay fields.
Floating up in the hills, a tree plantation.

The ridge lines march east: green, gray, blue,
Across the Connecticut River Valley to Cornish.
Close in, the land folds into an old field.

What lives here?

American Kestrel
Photograph by Ted Levin

This small falcon thrives in open fields. Abundant seed means insects, amphibians, birds, small mammals and reptiles: all food for the Kestrel.

Look. Wait.
Listen. Learn.

Find the wires, then follow the lane running east.
A sign says "No trespassing,"
But that's only for the cars.

Stop and sit awhile. Take in the field: goldenrod,
Wild parsnip, honeysuckle, white and red clover, milkweed,
Red osier dogwood, New England aster, Queen Anne's lace.

Can you find the boundaries of the old field?
Where the land is plowed or cut back year after year?
But in the old field, see young trees seeding in: willow, pine, and aspen.

This field is a community, ripe with seed,
And with insects, too—both are food for other species.
Who feeds on these two? Look: are they in your view?

Continue east on the road, toward the crab apples.
Leisurely, watching for movement, and listening for birds.
Who is working the fields, the wires, the trees?

Flitting in the thickets,
Song sparrows you might find, singing their bubbly
"Madge, madge, please put on the teakettle."

If you are lucky,
You may see an indigo bunting, from a shrub or treetop, singing
"Sweet, sweet, chew, chew, sweet, sweet."

A yellow warbler,
Lurking in a willow or shrub thicket calling out:
"Sweet, sweet, sweeter than sweet."

Field sparrows, common yellow throats,
Bluebirds, and who else do you see?
So many birds are waiting here for you.

Why all of these species?
It's all about habitat:
About cover, food and water.

An open field is an invitation for grasses and herbs. This richness and diversity invites insects and birds. All this humming in a field ... and the Kestrel is revealed.

Keep on following the wires east.
Soon you'll spy wooden boxes—
Houses for bluebirds and tree swallows on the fence posts.

Bluebirds nest in cavities.
Count all of the boxes that you see,
They are both above and below the field.

Higher up on a pole,
Find a much larger wooden box:
This one is for the American kestrel.

A jay-sized and open-field falcon,
It has two black stripes on a white face ... beautiful markings,
With curved beak and narrow, pointy wings.

Look for them perched on the wires,
Resting, hunting, watching for insects and small mammals.
The American kestrel's song, a rowdy and rich "killy killy killy."

An open field is an invitation for grasses and herbs.
This richness and diversity invites the insects and birds.
All this life humming in a field ... and then the kestrel is revealed.

On the southern hillside, a spring house nestled.
Now turn back, retracing your steps to the west,
Toward forest growing back—after fields put to rest.

Crickets and cicadas ringing call
Summer glories turn to crisp fall.
At Marton Road, left is the way.
An old utility pole covered with creeper today.

Another Kestrel house sits on this pole.
And at its base, you reach your field goal.

Open up the box: a notebook.
Patiently linger: see what you see,
Please record your discoveries faithfully.

The Kestrel Quest Species Check List

What did YOU see?

- [ ] Goldenrod
- [ ] Honeysuckle
- [ ] White Clover
- [ ] New England Aster
- [ ] Song Sparrow
- [ ] Yellow Warbler
- [ ] Common Yellowthroat
- [ ] American Kestrel
- [ ] Bull Thistle
- [ ] Milkweed
- [ ] _____

- [ ] Wild Parsnip
- [ ] Red Clover
- [ ] Red Osier Dogwood
- [ ] Queen Anne's Lace
- [ ] Indigo Bunting
- [ ] Field Sparrow
- [ ] Eastern Bluebird
- [ ] Common Dandelion
- [ ] Common Burdock
- [ ] _____
- [ ] _____

Created by Michael Quinn, Bill Shepard, and Steve Glazer in 2003. The Quest for the Kestrel and the Wellborn Ecology Fund Natural Communities Quest Series as a whole were made possible by a generous grant from the Wellborn Ecology Fund of the New Hampshire Charitable Foundation/Upper Valley region. www.nhcf.org

"This is what grandchildren are for ... everything is new."
— Grandfather (Bubba)

— Quest sign-in book

66 **:30** bring:
easy Windsor pencil
Architecture Quest

historical
architectural

From either Exit 8 or 9 off I-91, take Route 5 south or north to downtown Windsor. This Quest begins at Windsor House, across the street
from the Post Office in downtown Windsor. Note: This Quest can be
completed at any time, but is best done Monday – Friday before
5:45pm or on Saturdays before 3pm.

Clues

Architectural terms are noted in bold.

1. Look for three steps in between **columns** six,
    Then turn 'round to face a **façade** made of bricks.

2. In an age of cell phones and instant message e-mail,
    Let's reflect on our Post Offices and the U.S. mail.
    The Windsor Post Office we think is rather grand—
    Perhaps the prettiest in the Upper Valley land.

3. This **Italianate** structure was inspired by a Venetian palace c.1850–1900,
    With **brackets** evenly spaced along its upper **valance.**
    Look at the place where the roof meets the wall ...
    Then count the front brackets—there are _____ in all.

The patriotic décor features eagles
to spare; You will find them inside
& out by giving a good stare

4. Above the low **hip roof** are chimneys galore.
    We've a brick and cast iron monument to explore.
    Cast iron? What do you mean?
    Carefully cross the street to learn more about this scene.

5. Stand in front of the Post Office:
    Ami B. Young, born in West Lebanon, New Hampshire,
    Served as Architect for the Treasury as America expanded her empire.
    Post offices and customs houses supported commerce and trade,
    Ami made it beautiful, fire-proof and difficult to invade.

The Windsor House
Photograph courtesy of
Valley News

Built in 1836, this
building served as a
hotel for 150 years.
The threatened demoli-
tion of Windsor House
has reawakened civic
awareness in the re-use
potential of Windsor's
Main Street buildings.

6. The patriotic **décor** features eagles to spare;
   You will find them inside and out by giving a good stare.
   What you think might be stone may be a trick of the eye.
   Cast iron abounds—from granite **foundation** to the sky.

7. Near the front door, rummage in your pocket for change.
   Tap on what seems like **stucco**—sounds kind of strange!
   This metallic ping lets you know
   That what appears as stone is **faux.**

8. Fancy grill-work arches atop the front door.
   For alternative access use side **ramp** with sloping floor.
   Postal workers load & unload letters on docks in the rear.
   Customers have been served here for nearly 150 years!

9. How can we complain about the high cost of mail?
   How far can a person drive for not many cents…as far as a snail!
   Just think of the pleasure that can be bought and sent:
   Holidays, birthdays, Valentines, for just a few cents spent.

10. Inside the post office lobby small eaglets abound.
    Look to their hearts to find locks that are round.
    Count the eagles … How may do you see?
    They count up to the number ____.

11. Now out through the door that opens onto MAIN,
    And turn left on your Quest trail once again.
    Pass a fire hydrant and a low-down grate.
    Look up to see "Tuxbury Block" from 1898.

12. Cross over Depot to a soldier of late.
    Then turn right or "up" the street called STATE.

13. March uphill to a Church called St. Paul's,
    Passing renovated brick buildings—one used to have crumbling walls.

14. St. Paul's, built by Alexander Paris, was completed in 1822.
This building has distinctive architectural elements, too.
This brick church tells a story in its blocks of fired stone,
Combining stylistic elements from both Greece and Rome.

15. Large white columns are topped with curling **capitals,**
And support an arched window in a triangular gable.

16. Keep onward and upward to the Windsor Library—
Truly a temple of learning as you shall soon see.
Libraries of the 20th Century were built to stand
Looking old and stoic, massive and grand.

17. This building too, is built in a particular style—
One that is referred to as the **Georgian Revival.**
Here, classical details were used stylistically:
Look at the **columns** here, so thick and portly.
This building's architectural intent
Is to convey the subject's importance.

18. Inside, the Allyn Cox mural recalls ancient Greece & Rome,
And encourages readers to enjoy arts, prose & poems.
Behind this fine building find a shady Hemlock tree,
And treasure box quite near? The end of this Quest mystery!

GLOSSARY:

Column: a kind of supporting pillar consisting of shaft, base and capital.
Façade: the face of a building.
Italianate: having an Italian form or appearance.
Brackets: an overhanging member projecting from a wall or other body to
support weight falling outside the wall.
Valance: a decorative framework to conceal curtain fixtures at the top of
a window casing.
Hip roof: a roof with sloping ends and sides.
Décor: that which serves to decorate.
Foundation: a body, stock or ground material upon which anything is
built up.
Stucco: an exterior finish for masonry or frame walls, usually composed of
cement, sand, and hydrated lime mixed with water and laid on wet.
Faux: fake.
Ramp: a short bend, slope or curve in the vertical plane.
Capital: the upper most member of a column, crowning the shaft and taking
the weight of the entablature.
Arched: made with a curve.
Gable: the vertical triangular portion of the end of a building.
Georgian Revival: Colonial style after the reigns of the three King Georges
from 1714 to 1820.

Created by Judy Hayward and Steve Glazer in 2002.

67 The Forest Quest

2:00

at Marsh Billings Rockefeller National Historic Park

moderate

bring:
binoculars
compass
field guide
pencil

natural

Take Route 4 to Woodstock and then Route 12 north from Woodstock. Turn left onto Propser Road (2.7 miles beyond Billings Farm). Take Prosper Road for 0.7 miles to the trailhead parking lot on your left.

NOTE: For more Woodstock Quests visit our online Quests page at: www.vitalcommunities.org

Clues

Check the box when you have found the item.

1. **Make your way up the path to where a map stands.**   ☐ trail head
   Here you must tell me where we are, do your best!
   To learn the story of this land you must solve
   The mysteries of this Forest Valley Quest.

2. **Go right after the gate. Off the path in the woods: stone walls.**   ☐ stone wall
   But why these stone walls, inside some trees to keep?
   STONE WALLS are your clues to a time long ago
   When fences enclosed pastures for all the grazing sheep.

3. **Over a bridge then 80 steps to where the pines stretch tall.**
   Long cones and bundles of 5 needles the forest floor betrays.
   These clues confirm that our canopy is WHITE PINE.
   Below the plants of the understory await sun's shine.

   ☐ 5-needle bundle
   ☐ long cones

Westward Ho! And the farmers go leaving behind exhausted land

4. **Growing in dappled light, SUGAR MAPLES make their way.**
   Pine, on the other hand, requires a full day's sun.   ☐ sugar maple
   These white pine trees were planted in the 1930s,
   By the Billings family, once the farming was done.

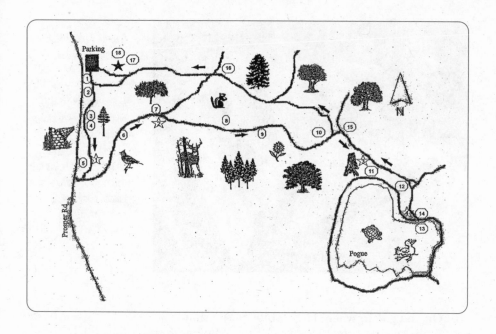

5. **Ahead looking right, hidden in the shrubs … an old rusted car.**
   Further up the path: concrete, piled rocks, a retaining wall.
   These things are all remnants of an old Vermont Farm.
   Before the forest rose? A working farm here with barns standing tall.

   ❒ rusted car
   ❒ old wall

   Westward Ho! And the farmers go, leaving behind exhausted land.
   Axes and sheep erode the land, leaving poor soil to plant.
   By the 1860s, fish, wildlife, trees and the watershed are in trouble.
   "The earth is becoming an unfit home for its inhabitants,"
   wrote George Perkins Marsh in 1864.

6. **Left turn on the carriage road and into a unique forest.**
   Frederick Billings and his family led the way on this land,
   Teaching farmers to replant the trees their fathers cut.
   On we go to where a tree with four white trunks stands.   ❒ white birch

7. **At the second fork you will find a rock**   ❒ red bark
   And two different kinds of pine left and right.   ❒ "egg" cones
   Plates of reddish bark, egg-shaped cones, paired needles …
   Know these and you'll know a RED PINE is in sight.   ❒ paired
                                                                  needles

8. **Keep on! In a while, a big tree on your left.**   ❒ white ash
   Does its bark remind you of cantaloupe skin?   ❒ ash seed
   It is a WHITE ASH, find the small seeds if you can
   After passing at least 5 ash trees, your next clue comes in.

9. **Patience … find smooth gray-barked trees covered with sores.**
   Beech scale disease, a fungus, is followed by insects.
   Sick beech trees, circled by young ones, show their hope.
   The trees sprout new trees from their roots … trying to cope.

   ❒ beech tree
   ❒ scale disease
   ❒ beech seed

George Perkins Marsh
Photograph by Jon Gilbert Fox

Marsh was considered one of our earliest environmentalists. His book *Man and Nature* was one of the first books to document the effects of human actions on the environment.

10. **On you go! To where large white quartz shines.**
At the second curve, a rock outcrop, red pines in rows.
Make a stop and find a young pine tree: can you tell its age?
Each year these pines send forth a new "limb whorl" to grow.
❏ Count the "whorls" to age your tree: _____

11. **At the T, to the right and down hill you will go**
As you walk please enjoy all this forest has to show.
You might just spy some NORWAY SPRUCE here.
Their cones look different, too … look and have no fear.

12. **Onward to the next fork and the giant HEMLOCK.**   ❏ hemlock tree
Over 200 years old, and still growing tall!   ❏ hemlock cone
Hold a tiny cone, lean on the trunk, and look up.
Amazing that something so big started out so small?

13. **Stay right, curving around until water is found.**   ❏ The Pogue
You've made it to the Pogue, the farthest point on this journey.
Sit, reflect, say a small thanks to Billings' granddaughter,
Mary Rockefeller, and husband Laurence … this park made at
their behest.

14. **What's a Pogue? This fourteen-acre pond was a wetland,**
Until its waters were dammed to make this special place.
Quietly walk along the pond and you might see
Painted turtles sunbathing … then OOPS, gone without a trace.
❏ painted turtle

15. **Now turn around and head back from whence you came.**   ❏ the sign
LONG reverse: back to hemlock; up hill stopping at the sign.
This one has eleven letters. Turning left is right!
Soon find a small trail to the right. Take it, you'll do fine.

16. **Down hill, stay to the middle where three trails diverge.**   ❏ bird song
Listen and look closely to observe who lives here:
Birdsong, chatter, rustling, color, leaves stir.
Quiet stillness reveals what in movement disappears.

17. **On you go! A small bridge, and then a fork.**
    Keep right looking for an ancient sugar maple, an 'ol pasture tree.
    One of its branches has broken off and left a big hole.
    Hidden there? The treasure box—and end to your mystery.

18. **Congratulations on completing your Quest!**
    Please write where you are from and your name,
    The date and some comments if you wish.
    Then return the box so others may do the same.

Created by Steve Glazer in 2002, as part of the Forest for Every Classroom program.

"1-1-05
One New Year's Day, 2005
We took a walk to feel alive.
Through slush and ice we came this way
A 'No Parking' sign did not deter our stay.
Seven of us, and a dog named Sofie too.
All looking for something to do.
This ghost town has us questions pose,
Like where did all those poor souls go?
And why and how and when?
And could it all begin again?
We would ponder more here in the snow,
But it is cold and time to go!"

— Quest sign-in book

68 :45

History Mystery
Barrel Quest

easy

historical

Take Route 4 to Woodstock. This Quest begins at the center of the Woodstock Village Green.

Clues

1. In the center on town, on the green
    There was once a chicken coop that
    Now delivers information in the booth.

    Look for the plaque with a coin on top
    Put your back to this, it will be your first stop.

    Peel your eyes now, for just up ahead
    Is a bridge that is covered, its color is red.

2. Go north over the bridge that was built many times,
    Look left toward the brick house that was built mighty fine,
    General Washburn lived here for a very long time.

3. Turn right at the stop sign,
    You're doing just fine,
    Go 'til you reach the place with lots of stones,
    Underneath these will be a whole bunch of bones.

    In the middle of these is a building marked 1865,
    When some of these people were still alive.
    Walk straight to the back where the Billings are dead,
    Their most famous family member's name was Fred.

4. Facing the street with the Billings behind,
    Go left to the trail we want you to find.
    To the left you'd go up, but turn right with your feet,
    It is time that you head out toward the street.
    When you come to the wall be careful, don't fall,
    Don't go back the way you came, 'cause that's too much the same.
    Instead turn left and go 'round the bend,
    Walk some more 'til the sidewalk does end.
    Beware of the cars as you cross the street.
    And on the other side another walk you will meet.

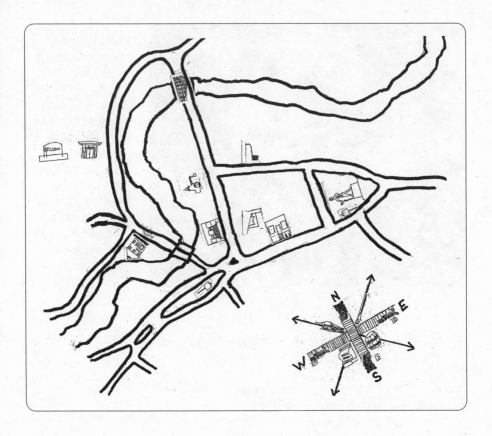

Turn left up the hill and continue along,
If you can see a bridge you haven't gone wrong.

Below you the river mighty and fast,
Head over the bridge and you won't be last.
Walk down the block to a white tower,
Look underneath you will find the right hour.

5. Now cross the street, of course with your feet.
    Head to the east, it's not time to cease.
    On your left you will pass a white house with an arch in the gate,
    This is a common architectural trait.

6. Continue on 'til the end of the road,
    On the right are some weapons they never will load.
    Make a U-turn and continue toward town,
    Whatever you do, keep your eyes off the ground.

7. Pass the old house with the tarnished bricks,
    Look up and see one of our favorite picks.
    This is a sign that looks like an open book,
    It's about a Morgan horse that had a special look.
    Continue along and head for the stores.

8. On the right, 60 minutes it takes,
    Keep on going for goodness sakes.

Gillingham's Store
Photograph courtesy of
Valley News

When F.H. Gillingham
opened his business five
generations ago, he
stocked his store with
every necessity imagin-
ble. More than 100
years later, the store is
still owned and operat-
ed by his family. They
offer everything from
caviar to cow manure!

9. You'll reach the corner where you should turn right,
    The Mortar and Pestle will be in your sight.

10. Go across the street to another store,
    Now you're at the end of our tour.
    Go tiny steps right, an arch is to the west,
    Go inside to finish this Valley Quest!!!

Created by Mr. Souter's 4th grade class at Woodstock Elementary School in 2003.

69 Mount Tom Quest

1:30

difficult

bring: compass

natural vista

Take Route 4 into Woodstock. From the northwest side of the Woodstock Green, cross the covered bridge and follow Mountain Avenue around to the park on the right. Take any of the paved paths to the trail going up Mount Tom. Follow the switch-back trail (the Faulkner Trail) up the front face of Mount Tom. Remember to switch back and avoid the cut throughs—they cause erosion!

Clues

The Quest begins when you get to the top! Up, up, up you go!

When you reach the final rise,
Turn around and open your eyes.

Take a rest and pull up your sock,
The town below is our Woodstock.

If you do not wish to fail,
Head towards Precipice Trail.
(Sometimes the sign is down – but it is the trail around the top.)

Don't head down this trail but stay up top,
With each step you are closer to the final stop.

Continue along the path but not too far,
Look up to see our Cross and Star.

When you reach the final rise, Turn around and open your eyes.

Keep on walking, look to your right and left for the rock wall.
Mt. Tom is basically flat up here so you will not fall.

The path will soon come to a T,
Please stay to the left and have a see.

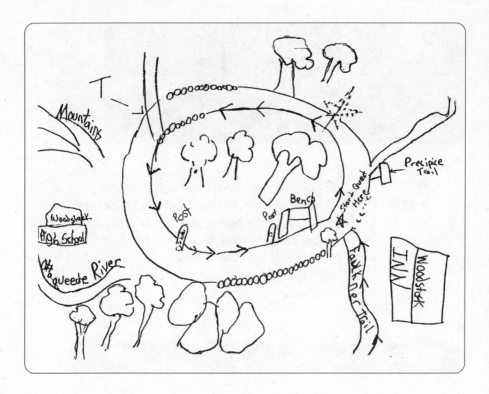

You will now be looking out to the west,
Killington is the mountain whose height is the best.

Look down and see the Ottauquechee River, which is cool,
Along Route 4 you can see the Woodstock High School.

As you walk, notice on your left is a post,
With faces that may remind you of a ghost.

As you walk further, the rock wall will be on your right,
And the town of Woodstock should come into your sight.

The big white building is the Woodstock Inn,
The Quest is near complete and you shall win.

The second ghost post will be behind you,
Find the Inn and point to it, too.

Follow that line to the edge of the wall,
Take care, good luck, and do not fall.

Find the treasure under rocks and leaves,
then be sure to re-hide it, if you please.

Created by Steve Pruyne and Jamie MacDonald in 1997.

70 Room with a View Quest

1:00

bring:
compass
binoculars
field guide

difficult | *A Hike Up Mount Peg*

natural
vista

Take Exit 1 from I-89 and follow Route 4 west for about 10 miles to the village of Woodstock and the Green. This Quest starts at the Woodstock Green.

Clues

Go south between twisting trees, look ahead way up high,
go to the eagle high in the sky.

Turn east to white birches, then south again.
Lilacs will accompany you to the end of the bend.

Left, over the river, follow the curve of the white picket fence,
your destination is immense.

At the end of this road stands a lined pole, 73 - 17.
Turn left up the road here, it's more than it seems.

Seven cedars stand at the gate
through which lies your final fate.

Hike up over roots on trail well worn to junction sign.
The forked white pine shows the way to go.

cross clearing to the right
and climb the sky

A narrowing path loops around fallen trees,
the trail bends 'round rocks pointing skyward among the leaves.

At knobby beech tree with sign, take a right
to trails that form a triangle within your sight.

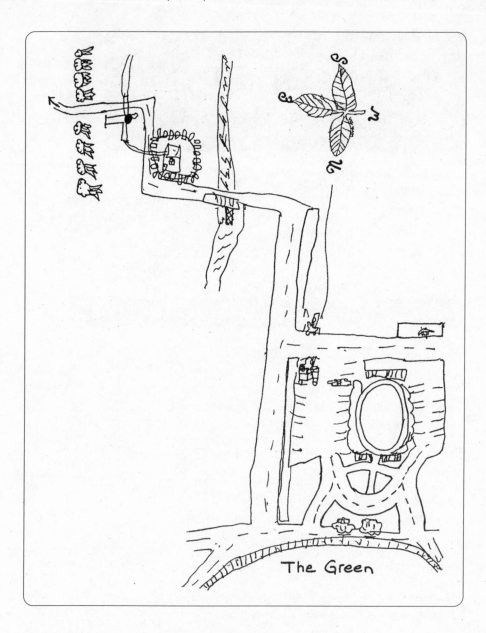

The Green

Your path takes you up between hemlock and ironwood.
Then right behind the big white pine

Go along to a left place to enjoy lunch or brunch,
then take a right toward the T. S. sign—follow your hunch.

Through red pine plantation and under wires, a red blaze shows the way.
Keep on through, then cross clearing to the right and climb to the sky to rest
your weary bones away.

Turn opposite the curved log seat and head up the wooded trail,
Find blazes on ironwood and oak, and you will not fail.

Between them lies a maple—with a home in its trunk.
You will find the secret box if you root around like a skunk.

To return, follow signs to Golf Avenue.

Created by Ms. Balenhorst's 4th grade at Woodstock Elementary School in 1999.

Trillium
Photograph by Ted Levin

This wildflower is all about threes: three leaves, three petals, three sepals. Also called stinking Benjamin for its lovely aroma!

Quest Resources

Questing: A Guide to Creating Community Treasure Hunts
This book explains how individuals and organizations can create and maintain Quest programs to foster place-based education, stewardship and fun. It offers inspiration and practical advice for parents, teachers, community group leaders, and others interested in learning about where they live. The book presents a rationale for place-based education; and clear goals, processes and outcomes that can be achieved in any community. $17.95

The Cemetery Quest
This standards-based curriculum unit is a series of eight lessons in which students: choose a community cemetery; inventory and photograph the headstones; collect and record headstone data; process it using Excel spreadsheets; "adopt" key families; and study them using primary and secondary sources. As a final project, the class creates a Quest which shares community history via a cemetery walking tour. Grades 4–8. $15.

The Village Quest
This standards-based unit is a series of nine lessons. Students use historical maps, field trips, primary and secondary resources, and interviews with community elders to create a Quest capturing "hidden stories" of their town. Grades 4 - 8. $15

The Watershed Quest
Valley Quest created this standards-based unit for KQED San Francisco, to accompany the *Jean-Michel Cousteau's Ocean Adventures* PBS series. The unit includes 10 lessons focused on the study of a local watershed, and culminate with the creation of a watershed Quest. Grades 5–8. Available on line at: www.pbs.org/kqed/oceanadventures/educators/watershed/

The Civil War Quest
Created with support from *The Flow of History,* this unit offers students, teachers and community members the opportunity to connect local history with the larger, American experience. Students visit a cemetery, adopt specific soldiers buried there, and then use primary and secondary sources to understand the larger contexts that influenced these individuals' lives. Grades 6–9. Available on line at: www.vitalcommunities.org/ValleyQuest/cwquest/overview.htm

The resources listed above are available from Vital Communities.

Upper Valley Resources

Field Guide to New England Barns and Farm Buildings
Published by the University Press of New England in 1997.
The barns of Vermont and New Hampshire are endangered species. Thomas Durant Visser's field guide documents a wide variety of agricultural buildings, interpreting their design properties and functional strategies.

New England Wildlife: Habitats, Natural History, and Distribution
Published in 2001 by the University Press of New England.
This book by Richard DeGraaf and Mariko Yamasaki presents the natural histories of 338 terrestrial and aquatic species. A fabulous reference tool!

The Outside Story
Published by Northern Woodlands in 2007.
Edited by Chuck Wooster, this volume collects dozens of essays on the natural history of the Upper Valley. Supported by the Wellborn Ecology Fund of the New Hampshire Charitable Foundation, the book is organized by season, and includes some of our finest writers.

Proud to Live Here
Published by Connecticut River Joint Commissions in 2003.
Richard Ewald and Adair D. Mulligan's wonderful book looks at our region's history and development. Chapters include geography, natural communities, Native American history, Euro-American settlement, agriculture, industry, architecture, civic life, and recreation.

Reading the Forested Landscape
Published by The Countryman Press in 1997.
Author Tom Wessels teaches us how to see through the forest to the pieces, patterns and processes that are at play. Written like a mystery book, you will learn to see many clues to landscape history. You'll never look at a forest the same way again!

Sightseeking: Clues to the Landscape History of New England
Published by the University of New Hampshire Press in 2003.
Christopher Lenney teaches us about boundaries, roads, placenames, villages, dwellings, materials and more. A curious and thoughtful book.

Valley Food & Farm Guide
Published annually by Vital Communities.
Use this handy guide to find farms, farm stands, farmer's markets, restaurants and stores near you. Celebrate all that is fresh and local in the Upper Valley region.

Wetland, Woodland, Wildland
Published by The Nature Conservancy and the Vermont Department of Fish and Wildlife in 2000.
Elizabeth Thompson and Eric Sorenson help us understand the wonderful array of the state's natural communities; and that all organisms live within distinct contexts which take into consideration geology, climate and landscape history.

Find these at your favorite local book store.

Other Quest Programs

Communities across the country are beginning to replicate the award-winning Valley Quest program for their regions. As your path brings you across New England and the United States look for Quests. There's treasure out there!

Keene Quests
The city of Keene began creating Quests in 2003. There are presently ten Quests in Keene, eight of which are published in Keene Quests, available from the Horatio Colony Museum. For more info:
www.horatiocolonymuseum.org/

KQED San Francisco's Ed Treks
KQED contracted Valley Quest to help them create a Bay area Quest program. There are Ed Treks at locations in the Golden Gate Recreational Area; and curriculum materials too.
www.pbs.org/kqed/oceanadventures/educators/watershed/

Quest Martha's Vineyard
QMV fosters a sense of community and partnership through the creation and sharing of treasure hunts that celebrate the island's special places. There are more than a dozen Quests published. For more information visit:
www.questmv.org/

Ski Vermont's Nordic Quests
Ski Vermont and Cabot Creamery have teamed up to sponsor a winter Nordic Quest program. The fourteen Quests are fun, encourage winter exercise and will help you discover new corners of the state.
www.skivermont.com/kidzone/nordic.php

Oregon Coast Quests
Oregon Sea Grant teamed up with Lincoln County 4H, Oregon State Parks and the Oregon Coast History Center, and others, to create a first booklet of eight Quests in the northwest.
www.seagrant.oregonstate.edu/freechoice/OregonCoastQuests.html

Orleans County Quests

The Orleans County Historical Society, with support from the Vermont Humanities Council, sponsored a Valley Quest workshop in 2006. Participants have created 18 Quests, published as a book in 2008.
www.oldstonehousemuseum.org/

South Shore Quests

South Shore Quests, centered in Hingham, Massachusetts and adopted by the Weir River Watershed Association in 2004, maintains a program of twenty Quests. They publish new Quest books annually.
www.geocities.com/ddthures/southshorequests

The Trustees of Reservations

The Trustees of Reservations preserves, for public use and enjoyment, properties of exceptional scenic, historic, and ecological value in Massachusetts. They publish and maintain more than a dozen Quests across Massachusetts.
www.thetrustees.org/.

Contact us if you'd like to help in developing a Quest program to serve your community and region.

How to Make a Quest

We invite you to create your own Quest. You may create a Quest in your backyard for your friends and family, or you can create a Quest as an offering to the greater community. We hope you will choose to do the latter, and submit a copy of it to us for possible posting to the Valley Quest web site! Here's how to do it:

A   Pick a spot that is a special place for you—perhaps a unique natural or cultural feature of your town.

B   Find out who owns or manages this property and request permission to make a Quest there.

C   Make a few trips to the site to uncover its details, and begin to think about the best approaches to making a Quest on the site.

D   Find people in your community who can teach you more about your site—community elders, members of your town historical society, conservation commission members, naturalists. Invite them to walk the land with you.

E   Take good notes!

F   Decide on your best Quest strategy: a detailed map Quest; a map-less Quest; a jumble Quest (collecting words); a numerical Quest; or some combination of these. Use your imagination and creativity! It's up to you!

G   Draw rough maps of your site. Also sketch or note the unique features that would make good clues.

H   Make a rough draft of your Quest Map and riddles or accompanying text.

I   Test your Quest with as many different people as can; and make appropriate changes.

J   Create a written description of what makes the site special. This should come from your research and should only be a few paragraphs long— small enough to be laminated and placed in your Quest Box. Depending on the site, possible things to write about include: the historical significance of the site; a true story about something that once happened there; trees to look for, special rocks, etc.; why people in your town love this site so much; fun or interesting things to do; amazing-but-true trivia facts.

K   Draw final Quest Map

L   Design a logo for your stamp and then carve it. Stamp making instructions can be found at www.vitalcommunities.org.

M   Get a waterproof box to use as your Quest treasure box. Laminate the introduction to the site and place it in the box. Label the outside of the box with a laminated copy of the Valley Quest label. Place in the box a log book; a pencil/pen; the carved stamp; an ink pad; and a pencil sharpener. Instructions for making log books can be found on the Valley Quest website.

N   Hide the box. Put it in a place where only those who are looking for it will find it!

O   Be sure you have permission and someone willing and able to monitor and maintain the box. Supply Valley Quest staff with names and contact information.

P   Fill out the Valley Quest Submission Form and send it in so that your Quest can be included in the Valley Quest program! If possible, please send your map and clues as electronic files.

New Quest Submission Form

Thank you so much for taking the time, energy and creativity to create a Valley Quest Treasure Hunt! We appreciate your persistence, as well as your offering of generosity towards our community. For Quests offer a unique way to share special places and special stories with those we may never meet, may never know.

In order to make sure everything is complete—and also insure that your Quest is posted to the Valley Quest web site—we ask you to please take a moment to review the following checklist, answer a few questions, and return this form to:

> Valley Quest Coordinator
> Vital Communities
> 104 Railroad Row
> White River Junction, VT 05001

Please call if you have any questions (802)291-9100 or email Laura@vitalcommunities.org.

Checklist

___Original Map Art, mail us the original so we can scan it.

___Clues (that have been tested—to make sure they work! On disk please, or by email attachment)

___Compass Rose, indicating North (if necessary)

___Precise directions to the Quest's starting point:

___Landowner permission (if required):

    Name _____ Phone _____

___Estimation of time required to complete Quest (round trip): _____

___Degree of difficulty: ___Easy ___Moderate ___Difficult

___Special features: ___ Architectural ___Historical ___Natural ___Vista

    (check all that apply)

___Walking conditions: ___Indoor ___Pavement ___Trail Other_____

___Optional Gear: ___Canoe ___Compass ___Bike ___Binoculars

    Other_____

___Season ___April–November ___Year-round (please check one)

___Treasure Box complete: ___Box ___ Stamp ___Stamp Pad ___Sign in book

    Other_____

___Treasure Box Placed out there! ___Yes ___No

___Quest Box Monitor:

    Name_____ Address_____

    Phone_____ Email_____

___"Cheater's directions"—i.e. the exact location of box for prompt monitoring—or helping frustrated callers find their treasure

___ Brief description of the Quest

___ Name of the individuals or group that created the Quest

___ Name of your Quest

Acknowledgments

The publication of this book would not have been possible without generous support from The Bay & Paul Foundations, the Wellborn Ecology Fund of the New Hampshire Charitable Foundation/Upper Valley region, Davis Weinstock, and the Robins Foundation.

In addition, the work contained in this book—undertaken over a dozen years—would not have been created without generous supported from: The Anne Slade Frey Charitable Trust, the Byrne Foundation, the Connecticut River Joint Commissions, The Flow of History project, A Forest For Every Classroom, The A. D. Henderson Foundation, the Hixon Foundation for Religion and Education, the Kitchel-Mclaughlin Family Fund, Lyme Foundation, Ellis L. Phillips Foundation, The Spirit in Community Fund, the Upper Valley Community Foundation, the Walker Fund of New Hampshire Charitable Foundation—and hundreds of individuals, families and businesses.

There would be no Quests without the hard work, good fun & contributions of students, teachers, school staff and community members from 50 towns across our two states. Thank you, to each and every one of you: Debbie Hinman; 4th and 5th grade students at the Acworth School; Tracy Hanson and Acworth's Silsby Library; Lynn Talamini; Hiram Allen; the Barnet School 4th graders; Mary Grove; 7th and 8th grade students at the Compass School; Pat & Alan Fowler of Village Square Booksellers; Nancy Jones and the Bradford Conservation Commission; Heather Trillium Toulmin; students at Oxbow High School; the VINS/Orton Community Mapping Program; Maeghan & Norm Paulhus; Victoria Sargent and Charlestown's Cemetery Department; Patty Collins; 5th grade students at Chelsea Elementary; the Chelsea Historical Society; Will Gilman of Will's Store; Georgette Thomas; the Hugging Bear Bed & Breakfast; Gregory Schwarz at Saint-Gaudens National Historic Site; Ros Seidel and her 3rd, 4th and Valley Quest Exploratory classes at Cornish Elementary; Hannah Schad; Bernice Johnson; Nancy Wrightman; Reigh Sweetser; Teenie Rock; George Hamlin; Stuart Hodgeman and the Cornish Select Board; Gabe Zoerheide and the Cornish Conservation Commission; the Kearsarge Region HomeSchoolers; Ted Levin; Simon Brooks; Deborah Stanley and the Ausbon Sargent Land Preservation Trust; the Elkins Fish & Game Club; Les Norman and the New London Conservation Commission; NH Fish & Game; National Fish & Wildlife Foundation; Ducks Unlimited; the home schooling family of Dale Shields, John Auble, and their kids Cecilia, Nathan and Devin; the Northern Rail Trail; NH Bureau of Trails; Hannah Lindner-Finlay; Rachel Lynch; Jeannie Kornfeld; Joanne Needham; Andy Johnson; Adair Mulligan; Mary Ellen Burritt's Girl Scout troop; Julie Orrok Slack and the Enfield Shaker Museum; Marjorie Rose & Betsy Davis' Hanover Brownie troop; Mitsu Chobanian's Girl scout troop; Linny Levin's 5th and 6th grade at Fairlee Elementary; Georgette Ludwig, Fairlee Town Clerk; Jack Henderson; Joyce Berube's Girl Scout troop; Harold Sargent; Allen Avery & the Lake Morey Inn; Margo Ghia and Grafton Nature Museum; Cathy MacDonald &

Pam Graham's Girl Scout troop; Molly Donovan & the Hanover Conservation Council; Ginger Wallis; Jay Davis; Jess Berna; Maia Tatinclaux; Anna Lotko; Anna Brown; the town of Hanover; JT Horn & the Appalachian Trail Conservancy; Hohn J. Serfass, District Ranger with the US Forest Service; Mary Bouchard's students at Hartford High School; Pat Stark & the Hartford Historical Society; Fred Bradley; Linda Conrad; Alex Johnson; Julie Jasmine; Rick Clavelle; Tad Nunez and Hartford's Department of Parks & Recreation; Jen Boeri-Boyce and her students at Hartford Middle School; Valley Quest 2005 workshop participants; Julie B. Barnes; Sarah Rooker and The Flow of History Project; Pat Zacharski; Bill Sweet and the Jericho Community Club; Michael Quinn and his students at Hartford Middle School; Sally Clement; Alex Good; Miss Bachelder's 3rd grade students at Hartland Elementary School; Allianora Rosse; Edith Celley; Al Stevens; Glen English, Haverhill Town Manager; the Wellborn Ecology Fund, NH Fish & Wildlife, NH Division of Parks & Recreation; Bill Gegas, Department of Resources and Economic Development; Mrs. Field & the Wheelock School 3rd grade; Antioch New England Institute; Paul Bocko; Anita Carroll-Weldon and the Horatio Colony House Museum; Marci Birkes and Stonewall Farm; Nicole Cormen and the Lebanon Conservation Commission; Gregg Mandsager, Lebanon City Manager; Kimmy Lavoie and Girl Scout Troop 2162; the Littleton Community House; Georgia Brehm; the Black River Academy Museum; Bill Shepard and the Connecticut River Birding Trail; Lee Larson; Matt Stevens and the Lyme Conservation Commission; Hellen Darion; Lynn Bischoff's 4th grade; David Kotz; Mark Valence; Crossroads Academy's 5th grade; Don Metz; Jeannie McIntyre; Peter Helm; Upper Valley Land Trust; Steven Dayno's 4th grade at the Lyme School; the Lyme Historians; Carol Langstaff; Mike and Jean Smith; Vivian Gregory Piper; Mrs. Pullen's 4th grade class at the Plainfield School; Meredith Bird Miller; Ralph & Mary Lou Spafford; Van Webb; Maggie Stier; Loa Winter; Karen Zurheide; Mary Kronenwetter; The Fells; Selenda Girardin; Annette Lorraine; 7th and 8th grade students at the South Congregational Church Faith and Nature Camp; Carrie McDonnell; Marguerite Ames and her 5th and 6th grade classes at Marion Cross School; Bill Aldrich and the Norwich Historical Society; Anne Silberfarb; the Norwich Women's Club; Nick Krembs and the Norwich Conservation Commission; Bill Ballard; Amy Vanderkooi and the Montshire Museum of Science; Sue Kling's 2nd grade class; the Orford Select Board; the Cross Rivendell Trail; Betsy Rybeck Lynd's 2nd grade class; Jane and John Taylor; Hugh McGraw and Kimball Union Academy; Julia Purdy; Brenda Greika; Bill Jenney; John Dumville; the Vermont Division for Historic Preservation; Amelia Good; Gayle Ottman and the Hartford Chamber of Commerce; Quechee Gorge State Park; Rick White and the VT Department of Forests, Parks & Recreation; the VINS Education Staff; Jinny Cleland; Jenn Colby; the White River Partnership; Randolph Area Family Farms (RAFF); Philip Major's class at Kearsarge Regional Elementary School; Jan Kidder and Twin Lakes Village; Susan Dreyer and students in the CHOICES program; Cheryl Cox; Russell Moore and the Springfield Town Library; Marita Johnson; Mike Frank; Gary Pelton; the US Army Corps of Engineers, Union Village Dam and North Springfield Lake; "Family Nights" participants at the Morrill Library; Stefanie Johnston and the Strafford Historical Society; Silas St. James; the Stafford Select Board; Kathleen Stowell and the Lake Sunapee Protective Association; Inge Trebitz; Terry Osborne;

Noel Perrin..."no bad legacy to leave" indeed; Joe Deffner's 7th grade students at Thetford Academy; Charles Latham and the Thetford Historical Society; Barbara Griffin's 2nd and 3rd grade class; Nick Brunette and Green Crow; Ginny Barlow; Kathy Hooke; Naomi LaBarr and the Vershire Select Board; Ruth Smith; Krista Katz and the Mount Kearsarge Indian Museum; Wendy Smith; Rick White, Forester, VT Department of Forests, Parks & Recreation; Ann and Scott O'Hearn; the City of Lebanon; Kenneth Alton and Trans Canada; Sue Kirincich; David Briggs and the Hotel Coolidge; Ann Lawless and the American Precision Museum; Karen Hull's 4th grade; Andy Boyce; Leslie Baker and the VT Department of Buildings & General Services; Judy Hayward and Historic Windsor; Amy McMullen and the Windsor Public Library; John Souter and many students at Woodstock Elementary School; Pat Davenport; Frank and Jireh Billings; F.H. Gillingham & Sons General Store; Chris Lloyd; Alison Clarkson and the Billings Park Commission; Jill Holran's 3rd Grade; Delia Clark; Tim McGuire and the staff of Marsh Billings Rockefeller National Historic Park.

We appreciate the support and dedication of our Valley Quest box monitors: Robin Model-Lornitzo, Anne Silberfarb, Sarah Woodhead, Pat Fowler and staff of Village Square Booksellers, Natalie and Jireh Billings, Meredith Bird-Miller, William Blaiklock and family, Brad Whitaker, Irene Mann, Janet Mondlak, Holly Braswell and family, Jen Brown, Jane Willard, Julie Jasmin, Will's Store, Jinny Hardy Cleland, Janet and Peter Pollock, the Fischer Family, Gloria Montague, Steve Dayno, Kimmy Lavoie, Sara Doolan, Kate Duesterberg, John Dumville, Joan Ecker, Carol Edwards, Susan Phipps and family, Sheryl Stotland, Judith Flint, Norm and Maeghan Paulhus, Kate Schall, Becky French, the Taylor family, Margo Ghia, the LaCrosse family, Selenda Girardin, Linda Machalaba, Alicia Simino and family, David Kotz, Pat Zacharski, Marita Johnson, Sarah Johnson, Nancy Jones, Michael Quinn, Nancy Serrell, Denise Reitsma, Judy Stone, Ann and Scott O'Hearn, Betsy Luce, Amy McMullen, Mike Mehegan, Bill Shepard, Amy Vanderkooi, George and Nancy Smith, Alex Good, Barbara Rhoad, Carol Williams-Suich, Dale Shields and family, Marci Birkes, Shiela Swett, Inge Trebitz, Georgette Thomas, Nancy Thornton and family, Pat Stark, Susan Brown, Keegan Monahan, Kendra Mitchell, Sue Reed, Kate Brown, Ellen Henderson, Paul Doiron and family, Jackie Jameson, the Seely Family, Mary Kern, Mary Kronenberg, Veronica Thurston, Heather Toulmin, Ingrid Svensborn and family, Lois and Ted Frazer, Sue Major, Aprille Reed, the Springfield Library, Alma Beals, Ellen Henderson, Kelly Stettner, Monique Cleland, Delia Clark, Anita Carroll-Weldon, Sally and Hunter Hall, Terri Clerico.

Special thanks to our Quest testers: Joanne Needham, Andy Johnson, Sandy Dion, Taylor Stedman, Mary Kay Brown, Evan Brown, Alex Good, Amelia Good, Tammy Ingham, Lisa Morse, Jane Taylor, Sean Taylor, Kyra Taylor, George Smith, Nancy Smith, Margo Ghia and family.

Many thanks to the Valley Quest Council: Arianna Alberghini, Dan Emanuele, Diana Wright, Mike Meller, Monique Cleland, Nancy Smith, Robin Model-Lornitzo, Sheryl Stotland, Anne Silberfarb, Simon Brooks Ted Levin. We appreciate your support.

Acknowledgments

The editors are grateful the encouragement and assistance of: Ros Seidel, Gary Barton, Sheila Moran, Joseph Deffner, Charles Latham, Jr., Deecie Denison, Becky French, Becky Bailey & Jim Schley, Georgette Wolf-Ludwig, Michael Quinn, Rob & Marie Hanson, Francis Dechame, Marguerite Ames, Kathy Hooke, Don Cooke, Steve Dayno, Carola Lea, Don Metz, Dorf Sears, Meredith Bird Miller, Ann Lawless, Judy Hayward, Sharon Francis, Adair Mulligan, Delia Clark & Tim Traver, David Sobel, Stacey Yap, Maggie Stier, Lizann Peyton, Sheila Hixon, Heather Trillium Toulmin, Pat Straughan, Megan Camp, Liz Soper, Lidie Robbins, Julia Payne, Julie B. Barnes, Susan Bonthron, Kelly Stettner, Sarah Rooker, Alan Berolzheimer, Lynne & Allen Whiting, Jen Boeri-Boyce & Andy Boyce, Suzan Bellincampi, Nancy Cole, Sandra Ryack-Bell, Stephanie Tuxill, John & Jane Taylor, Melanie Ingalls, Margaret Claudill-Slosberg & the VT Department of Health, Peter, Helen, Flo, Libby and Adrian from the Center for Whole Communities, Fred Bay, Kevin Peterson, Ellen Koenig, Margo Ghia, Amy McMullen, Betty Porter, Bill Shepard & Lelia Mellen, Steve Hoffman & Diana Wright, Beckley & Dave Showalter, Alex Jacacci & Maureen Burford, Greg Gundlach & Leslie Carleton, Annelise Orleck & Alexis Jetter, Lynn & Jay White Cloud, Robin Model-Lornitzo, and Simon & Sarah Brooks.

Laura and Steve express appreciation to our fellow staff members at Vital Communities: Len Cadwallader, Stephanie Carter, Cathee Clement, Debbie Diegoli, Anne Duncan Cooley, Stacey Glazer, Lisa Johnson, Deb Jones, Corb Moister, Fred Pond, Gabe Zoerheide, Melissa Zoerheide.

George & Nancy Smith: you are the BEST!

Ted Levin, Jon Gilbert Fox, and the staff of the Valley News: Thank you so much for your wonderful photos.

Thanks to Greg Gundlach and Pretech Color for digital imaging, Jeremy Lewis at Tele Atlas for map assistance, and Suzanne Church our book designer.

Laura would like to extend special thanks and love to her wonderful family, Jeff, Amelia and Alexander.

Steve sends a bow, a hug and a kiss to his partners on the long and winding Quest: Stacey, Kayla, and Emma Glazer.